EVANGELISM: THE FIRST BUSINESS OF THE CHURCH

The what, why, when, and how of parish evangelism by a seasoned pastor experienced in Church wide evangelism.

E. Dale Click

With a Foreword By
Wallace E. Fisher

CSS Publishing
Lima, Ohio

EVANGELISM: THE FIRST BUSINESS OF THE CHURCH

FIRST EDITION
Copyright © 1994 by
E. Dale Click

All rights reserved. No portion of this book may be reproduced or utilized in any form or by any means, electronic or mechanical including photocopying, without permission in writing from the publisher. Inquiries should be addressed to: CSS Publishing Company, 517 South Main Street, P.O. Box 4503, Lima, Ohio 45802-4503.

Library of Congress Catalog Card Number: 94-068890

ISBN 1-55673-958-3 PRINTED IN U.S.A.

TO

MY WIFE AND SONS
Martha Jane (Bunny) Gray Click
Barry Edward Click
Dean Raymond Click

ACKNOWLEDGMENTS

Readers of this manuscript were selected with sensitivity to region, to parish pastors of large and smaller congregations, to staff ministry, to administrators, and to respected church persons. Without their help and encouragement, this book would not have been undertaken or completed. They are, in alphabetical order:

Dennis A. Anderson, President, Trinity Lutheran Seminary (Columbus, Ohio); William E. Berg, former Augustana Lutheran Church's Director of Evangelism (Minneapolis, Minnesota); Barry E. Click, parish pastor (Prescott Valley, Arizona); Wallace E. Fisher, pastor-author (Pinehurst, North Carolina); Ross F. Hidy, a colleague in the Lutheran Evangelism Mission (Concord, California); T. A. Kantonen (deceased), my theology professor, Hamma Divinity School (Springfield, Ohio); Larry W. Matthews, parish pastor (Rockford, Illinois); Jerry H. Miller, former President of California Lutheran University (Thousand Oaks, California); Kenneth H. Sauer, Bishop, Southern Ohio Synod, Evangelical Lutheran Church in America (Columbus, Ohio); Jerry L. Schmalenberger, President, Pacific Lutheran Theological Seminary (Berkeley, California); Robert W. Stackel, a colleague in the Lutheran Evangelism Mission (Matthews, North Carolina); Clifton M. Weihe, a colleague in the Department of Evangelism, the former United Lutheran Church in America (Santa Maria, California); Lee Welker, a colleague in parish ministry (Carbondale, Illinois).

Lay persons in Ascension Lutheran Church (Thousand Oaks, California) read, tried, and applied many of the ideas in the book, namely: Lucille Gimmestad, Tim Hengst, Fritz Knauf, Paul Mueller, Ward and Therese Rineman, Robert Shoup, Dr. Kenneth and Jean Swanson, and Richard Webster.

My two mentors were Wallace Fisher and Robert Stackel. They stuck with me through six revisions. Dr. Fisher kept reminding me that there is a radical difference between the spoken word and the written word. He urged with fervor to "cut, cut, cut" and illustrated what could be done. His penetrating thoughts kept me re-writing and re-thinking. Dr. Stackel kept inserting question marks throughout the manuscript, challenging where needed. His keen insights theologically and theoretically aided me immeasurably. Both of these evangelism-minded friends are prolific writers with substance and distinctive styles. The book would never have gotten off the ground without them.

The cartoons in Chapter Eleven were drawn by my cousin, the late Richard Click, and myself.

My wife, Bunny, of a keen mind and editorial skills, plus an uncanny ability to find a book or resource material when I could not, was a great helper. Her encouragement and belief in the thrust of the book kept me going like a postage stamp, sticking to the manuscript until it got to its destination.

CONTENTS

FOREWORD 10

PREFACE 12

INTRODUCTION 14

PART I. THE CONTEXT FOR EVANGELISM

1. THE THEOLOGY OF EVANGELISM 19
   *Evolves from belief in God/Involves the Believer/
   Requires Solid Biblical Theology*

2. GOD'S PROMISES AND POWER 28
   Abraham/Moses/David/Prophets/Jesus/Apostolic Church

3. THE BIBLE IN EVANGELISM 42
   Endorsement of God's Revelation/Jesus' Method

4. PRAYER IN EVANGELISM 51
   Results/Direction/What Prayer Does

PART II. PREPARATION FOR EVANGELISM

5. THE PLACE OF PREACHING 61
   *Alone with God/Anointed and Sent/Time to Mature/Biblical/
   Relevant/Persuasive/Practice/Voice/Styles/Sound Systems*

6. THE SPIRIT RECYCLES EVANGELISTS 75
   *Know God Firsthand/Explain How Spirit Works/Illustrate/
   Dimensions of Apostolic Church*

7. THE TEAM SPIRIT: LAITY AND CLERGY 83
   *Role of Pastor—Reexamination/Exemplify/Write a Course/
   Role of Laity—Eighteen Ways*

8. EQUIPMENT FOR EVANGELISM 95
   *The Holy Spirit/Bible/Courses/Copiers, Computers,
   Telephones, Library*

PART III. OUTREACH EVANGELISM

9. WHERE TO BEGIN 103
   Focus/Task Force On First Business/Action

10. CREATE YOUR OWN THROUGH-THE-YEAR
    EVANGELISM PLAN 111
    *Mission Statement/Evangelism Outreach Committee
    Responsibilities/Enlist,Educate/Teach How To Invite/
    Possible Member List/Date Lists for Information Talks For
    Visitors/Schedule Work/Public Relations/Video/Bible Studies/
    Cost Proposals*

11. ENLISTING, TEACHING, RETOOLING
    EVANGELISTS 131
    *How to Enlist/Employment Agency/Teaching/Pointers/
    Retooling—Motivation/ Types of People*

12. THE INFORMATION TALKS FOR VISITORS 156
    *Sessions, Subjects/Outlines/Vocabulary for Christians/
    Mechanics/Tapes/Video*

13. ORIENTATION AND RECEPTION OF
    NEW MEMBERS 176
    *Sponsor Responsibilities/Agenda/Seven Components For
    New Member/Reception Service*

PART IV. INREACH EVANGELISM

14. NURTURING NEW MEMBERS 199
    Evangelism Inreach Committee Responsibilities/Bible Course

15. SUSTAINING AND STRENGTHENING
    ALL MEMBERS 207
    *Levels of Commitment—First Timers, Returnees,
    Inconsistent, Collapsed, Hearers and Doers/Factors in
    Sustaining/How Deepen Faith*

16. SOME CURES FOR THE SLOW LEAK 213
Tracking Habits/Communicate/Find Out When and Where Hurting/Admit Mistakes/Seek Solutions—Specifics/ Nationwide Transfer System

17. RHYTHM IN THE CONGREGATION'S LIFE 224
Rhythm Committee/Force Field Analysis/Calendar Day/ Know Constituency/Growth Groups

IN CONCLUSION 232

APPENDIX

#1 Forms That Help 233
Baptism/Individual Information For Church Files/Request for Letter of Transfer/Marriage/Funeral/Friendship Slip/Possible Member Data/ Report Form

#2 Letters That Help 251
First-Time Visitor/Invitation to Information Talks For Visitors/ To Those Who Attended Info/To Those Who Indicated Desire To Unite/To Those Who Became Members

#3 Tips 263
Sample Telephone Call on Possible Member/Ten Telephone Tips

#4 Program Ideas 267
Bring A Member Sunday/Bring A Friend Sunday/Evangelism Mission Week

NOTES 273

FURTHER READING 279

FOREWORD

Essentially, Christian evangelism is the sharing of the Good News so that persons in their freedom are persuaded, not manipulated, to say yes or no to Christ and his church. This sharing employs various emphases, forms and styles in different eras and places. Luther's style of evangelism was tied firmly to his incarnational theology. John Wesley developed a style marked by his views on revivalistic preaching and social conditions. William Temple declined to separate evangelism from social action. Dietrich Bonhoeffer merged evangelism with political action. The dean of evangelists, Paul, linked his experience of Christ on the Road to Damascus with a network of Roads to Jerusalem, Corinth, Thessalonica, Ephesus...and Rome.

Evangelism is prompted by Christ himself: Go into all the world and preach the Good News. Any congregation that neglects this command and/or reduces or adds to its Christocentric Trinitarian content saddens the gallant heart of Jesus. Dale Click knows that. His book underscores and demonstrates that the whole counsel of God and faithful witness to it are bound together inextricably.

Christian evangelism, personal and corporate, persuades many persons to accept Christ. It does not persuade others. It stirs some to wrath. That is so because Christian evangelism, inherent in the Word of God, cuts before it heals. It convicts one of sin and offers forgiveness and new life in Christ. Many churches today proclaim a crossless Christ to a world that is being crucified on a Christless cross. They cheapen Christ's promises by muting his demands. They obscure the Incarnation by ignoring or minimizing God's self-revelation in history. Christianity is particularistic and individual as well as universal and corporate (John 3:16). A church that does not share the whole Word of God in the world is unfaithful to its Lord. Dale Click knows that. His book underscores that reality and addresses it foursquare.

Evangelistic work is carried on primarily by the laity. That was true in the Early Church. Adolph Harnack, describing <u>that</u> church, wrote: "...the most numerous and successful missionaries of the Christian religion were not the regular teachers but the Christians themselves, by dint of their loyalty and courage." That is not true in many American congregations today. This book is a heartfelt, biblically-rooted, culturally alert call to all Christian congregations to learn and do biblical evangelism. The author understands that corporate worship is public witness. He understands the vital connection between the Damacus Road (Christian conversion) and the Jericho Road (Christian witness and service). He joins the theology of evangelism with a wealth of practical guidance for developing skills for Christian evangelism.

Dale Click has been an intentional and faithful Christ-bearer throughout his half century of Christian ministry. Architect of the United Lutheran Church in America's effective Lutheran Evangelism Mission in the mid-1950s, he has led evangelism missions throughout the United States, Canada, the Virgin Islands, Puerto Rico, and Argentina, and served a full-time ministry in three large congregations (California, Pennsylvania, and Ohio). In semi-retirement, he serves part-time on the pastoral staff of a two thousand member church, responsible for evangelism.

The message and the messenger are truly one in the person of Dale Click. His book, Christocentric to its core, is a rich contribution to Christian evangelism in America. It equips lay people and pastors to Go, tell the world what Christ has done, is doing now, will continue to do until God's end-time.

> Wallace E. Fisher
> Pinehurst, North Carolina

PREFACE

Here is a book that crystallizes a lifetime of experience and experiment in parish evangelism. It is a comprehensive treatment of the subject, and yet it picks up on the most helpful details. We need this book.

The author has spent his whole ordained ministry with evangelism as its heartbeat. He started out as pastor of a new congregation. As a young minister, he became a leader in evangelism in his denomination and the architect of a highly successful evangelism program of his church across the continent in the United States and Canada. Afterwards he has served as pastor of suburban and downtown churches, leading them in spiritual depth and membership growth. Even now he is a consultant to other churches in this field and is part-time on the staff of a large California church, guiding its whole evangelism ministry. Who could be more qualified to write on this first business of the church?

The book starts with the very basics, the theology of evangelism, which is an indication right off of the depth of its treatment. There is nothing superficial about its approach or casual about its concern. As for breadth, it is ecumenical in scope, suitable for use across all communities of Christ, because the principles and methods are so foundational. Ideas and approaches that have been tested for decades in the author's actual experience are spelled out in crystal-clear detail. The reader will discover that the author is a master of organization of material and logical sequence. He blends the theological with the practical in a happy balance. He also treats both outreach evangelism and inreach evangelism as a comprehensive whole. He wants evangelism to become "a way of life" for the Christian.

At a time when quite a few mainline Christian churches have been losing a large number of members, any possible strengthening of inreach and outreach evangelism is as needed as a drink of water on the Sahara Desert. And in an age that has been termed post-Christian, the church has a mandate to make more powerful its witnessing ministry.

This book will bring a world of motivation, encouragement and practical ideas to any congregation that wants to improve its witnessing skills. It will re-fire a pastor in this area of ministry and offer many specific ways to proceed. It is an essential tool for a congregation's Evangelism Committee or equivalent group, charged with the task of galvanizing the witness potential of the faith community. It would make an excellent textbook for a course in a theological seminary. It is valuable for an individual believer to reach a higher potential in personal witnessing and congregational involvement. Of course, to try to do at once all the things this book proposes would be self-defeating. It presents the ideal. Gradual steps over a period of time would be taken to achieve it. So it is a volume for the long run.

I have known E. Dale Click for forty years, have worked with him closely and respect him as an authority in this field.

Robert W. Stackel
Matthews, North Carolina

(Author's note: Dr. Stackel became a member of the Church Triumphant the morning of October 17, 1994, a prince of the church, a colleague, and a valued friend. He missed seeing the finished product by a few weeks.)

INTRODUCTION

"**Evangelism is not the only business of the church but it is the church's first business and what Jesus Christ made primary his church dare not make secondary. Evangelism is not an elective. It is a divine imperative...To evangelize is the greatest work in the world.**" [1]

The aim of this book is to help pastors and lay people plan and put into action through-the-year evangelism. Many parishes decline after a period of existence, some within several decades. Mainline church bodies fail to generate a continuing growth pattern. Christian churches have not persistently followed Jesus' command to go throughout the world and " ...make disciples."[2] The church raises money, promotes its programs, fosters social justice in the world, but lags despicably in doing person-to-person evangelism. Acted on, evangelism is the church's central business.

Both laity and clergy need to ask: "When did I introduce somebody to Jesus Christ?" Too many pastors, trapped into managing the church's institution, sidestep the urgent business of searching daily for the lost. The laity, scratching out a living and pursuing personal pleasures, fail to do the one thing the Christ commissioned them to do. Ask a dozen or so unchurched people why they do not belong to a church in the community and there will be some who reply: "Nobody ever invited me."

Retaining members is a commensurate concern. Churches lose thousands of people every year. And, regarding what hardly can be labeled evangelism, Christian churches play what I call beanbag evangelism — the tossing of members from one congregation to another, one denomination to another. There ought to be a church-wide law which prohibits congregations from counting transferees as accessions.

It isn't that the Christian churches do not love Christ; it is that the contemporary church has fallen into the false trap of relegating evangelism to Mr. and Mrs. Anonymous. Evangelism is the responsibility of every believer.

Where does the word evangelism appear in the organizational chart of national church bodies in the 1990's? Few have a Board, Department, or Division of Evangelism. It is difficult for me to locate evangelism in the organizational structure of my own denomination. It is tucked away as the second segment in the "Division for Congregational Life." That's characteristic of mainline Protestantism these days. Your church and mine are not in a natural growth mode, as in the Apostolic Church.

What percent of one's national church's program budget undergirds the work of evangelism? Most denominations funnel minimal resources into telling God's story.

It takes substantive money to evangelize. The centrum of the Christian faith is to reach people with the message of Christ. It appears, however, that the Christian churches of America are not aimed toward the lost. Boundless amounts of offerings to God are spent on preserving the institution.

Where in the structure of the individual congregation does the word evangelism appear? How many people are active evangelists? Is there a continuing education of members in understanding the multiphasics of evangelism? Is there an imbedded sense of responsibility in fulfilling Christ's command to make disciples all over the earth? Does the congregation's mission statement reflect response to the Word with enthusiasm and determination? Is there a volume of money set aside for evangelism?

Answers to these and related questions reveal how far Christian churches have strayed from their primary business. No business can thrive if it neglects its reason for existence; neither can the churches of Our Lord Jesus Christ.

This book describes the bedrock for evangelism, the preparation necessary to do evangelism responsibly, and demonstrates the dynamics for doing effective parish evangelism. It contends that evangelism is reaching out to people who have yet to believe, and, reaching in to sustain members in the Christian faith. Evangelism begins with God's revelation of who he is, what he has done through Christ, and what he continues to do through the lives of believers, by the power of the Holy Spirit. The Holy Spirit—God—made it possible for the church to be born and to reach around the world with the Good News. Evangelism is the heartbeat of the church. This book is a clarion call to the Christian churches of the world to make Christ's last command the Church's first business—EVANGELISM.

PART I

THE CONTEXT FOR EVANGELISM

CHAPTER ONE

THE THEOLOGY OF EVANGELISM

"Most evangelists are not very interested in theology; most theologians are not very interested in evangelism."[1]

A seminary student stated he was not a theologian. His professor commented, "If you are not a theologian, you have no business being in the ministry!"

In a sense, this observation is true for all Christians inasmuch as the word theology is the study of God's Word and reflection on his teaching. All Christians need to be grounded in biblically rooted beliefs. That is a life-long task.

If church people are reluctant to call themselves theologians, they are even less likely to call themselves evangelists! The word itself — evangelism— sparks negative feelings in many Christians. Television hucksters of Christianity, misusing their calling, selling themselves, and demeaning Christ's death on Calvary, have tarnished the word horribly.

The word evangelism is not to be ignored but understood. It is not to be scorned but used. It is not to be shunned but shared. Each Christian is called by the Holy Spirit to pass God's Word on to others. Evangelism is the privilege and responsibility of every believer.

Even business people use (or misuse) the word "Evangelist." Viktor Grabner has a business card which identifies him as "Evangelist" for Microsoft Corporation, Redmond, Washington. Another software evangelist, Jodi Slater, confessses she is not too enthusiastic about her title but it "...really describes what I do better than any other term." Guy Kawasaki, a former "evangelist" for Apple Computer, Inc. said "Religious evangelists are trying to change the world, and so are we." L. A. Winokur reported these examples, and cited a New York marketing consultant and trend watcher FAITH POPCORN who "...calls evangelism 'a sweet concept' and an approach that's 'quite correct and quite right' for the '90s."[2]

Evangelism is a "sweet concept" used in the biblical sense. In the first Christian centuries the writers of the four canonical Gospels were called "Evangelists." In Greek, an evangelist is "one who proclaims good news." The cognate verb "evangelize" and the Greek noun translated as "gospel" or "good news" resound in English as "evangel"— "messenger." Thus, an evangelist is a messenger of Christ. That is what Christians do. Evangelism is delivering the Good News that Jesus Christ has conquered evil and death, that believers participate in this eternal victory, and that God in Christ is with us now. Daniel T. Niles of Ceylon stated it clearly: "The call of the evangelist is not so much that (people) should engage in a battle with evil until evil is destroyed, as that they should share in God's victory over evil until evil is exposed. The Gospel is a call to a battle whose final victory is already won." [3]

Other definitions of evangelism are:
1) The World Council of Churches: Evangelism is "...making Christ known to people so that each is confronted with the necessity of a personal decision, Yes or No."
2) The National Council of Churches in the U.S.A.: "Evangelism is the presentation of the good news of God in Jesus Christ, so that people are brought, through the power of the Holy Spirit, to put their trust in God; accept Jesus Christ as their Savior from the guilt and power of sin; follow and serve Him as their Lord in the fellowship of the Church and in the vocations of the common life."
3) The Madras Foreign Missions Council: Evangelism is to "...present Jesus Christ to the world in the power of the Holy Spirit that people shall come to put their trust in God through Him, accept Him as their Savior and serve Him as their Lord in the fellowship of His Church."

Jesus' definition is best, "Go...and make disciples of all nations." The depth and breadth of evangelism are couched in all these definitions. John's gospel provides the finishing touch: "...that you may come to believe that Jesus is the Messiah, the Son of God, and that through believing you may have life in his name." [4]

Parish evangelism starts as members deliver this Good News, inviting non-believers and unchurched persons to "come and see," as Jesus gave his invitation long ago.[5] It is the responsibility of Christian churches today to invite people into the company of Christ. To be a Christian evangelist means to breathe in and out God's Spirit, just as God breathed life into us at the beginning. People who know how to revive a person from impending death by mouth-to-mouth resuscitation, illustrate the function of the Christian church—to breathe new life into people. This is the Holy Spirit (God) working through us "...like the rush of a violent wind."[6]

Theology and evangelism are inextricably intertwined. Evangelism without theology is proclamation without prescription; theology without evangelism is description without demonstration. Theology defines and describes the faith; evangelism communicates the faith. Evangelism puts theology into action. It is as St. Paul expressed it: "...for we cannot keep from speaking about what we have seen and heard." [7]

There are two premises: 1) Evangelism evolves from belief in God, and 2) Belief in God involves the believer in evangelism.

I. Evangelism evolves from belief in God.

Evangelism grounds itself in belief in the trinitarian God. Its basis is in the very nature of God. God was the first evangelist.

Since the world is God's and we are the creatures of his creation, it would seem plausible that human beings would respect him above all. The human situation, however, is that we are constantly endeavoring to displace God. Whenever or wherever that happens, a person is, as Martin Luther described "...bent upon himself (herself), seeking only his (her) own and loving himself (herself) above all, and not allowing God to be God." This inner bent results in alienation from God. There isn't anything worse.

The biblical story of Adam and Eve picture this condition. Human history records the results of it. Our own condition confirms it.

Under the circumstances of rebellion, we observe God's evangelism. He is a caring Father, seeking his own, sending a Noah, a Moses, an Isaiah, a Jeremiah, coming in person as Son, to deliver messages of freedom and love. God is never defensive, makes no compromises, yet does not sweep us away. He offers his children faith, help, hope, and love—continually reaching out to lead us.

So we discern God in this scenario—relentlessly reaching out to all people. He never abandons a single person, and endeavors to reclaim all of us. He does this because he is original love.

This is God's world; he is active in it. "But when the fullness of time had come...." [8] God came to live among us. Christianity is the only religion that has the Incarnation. "And the Word became flesh and lived among us...full of grace and truth." [9]

God is the pursuer. He leaves nothing to chance. He has stick-to-it-iveness. He wants every person on this planet to have an opportunity to know him. That is why God is the great evangelist. Chad Walsh understands this: "I suppose that if I persistently and consistently plead with God to stay away, He will at last say, 'Thy will, not Mine, be done.' But He is very hard to discourage; we cannot be sure whether this point of no return is ever reached in the present life. Before He gives up, He will have recourse to strong measures. If He cannot ravish you alive with beauty, He is not beyond catching you in a foxhole. He is the Father who knows no rest till the prodigal son falls at His feet and says 'Father'; he cares so little for statistics that He values one sheep more than ninety-nine." [10]

God came in Jesus Christ! God is not an observer; he is a participant. He conquers evil and death. "For we do not have a high priest who is unable to sympathize with our weaknesses, but we have one who in every respect has been tested as we are, yet without sin." [11] God, the great evangelist, establishes relationship with himself on the basis of forgiveness. What is just as astounding, God in Christ invites believers to be messengers of his love and forgiveness. This Jesus sends disciples to the corners of the earth in the work of reclamation. His Holy Spirit is provided, enabling believers to proclaim these truths.

This is the theological basis for evangelism. We are saved to be evangelists, agents of reconciliation in the world. It is not only the question of "...what should we do?" [12] but, "what do we do after being brought into a right relationship with God?" The answer is to be an evangelist.

II. Belief in God involves the believer in evangelism.

The work of our Lord Christ is meaningless to us until we appropriate it by faith. This faith is born of God. It is generated by the Holy Spirit. Faith cannot be earned or achieved. Faith is God's gift.

Emil Brunner states that "Faith in Jesus Christ is not an interpretation of the world, but it is participation in an event: in something which has happened, which is happening, and which is going to happen." [13] Thus, God chose the idea of the church as his instrument to reach out to people.

The church is the evangelistic body of Christ. God calls believers from within the church to go out and draw non-believers to Christ and his church. God sends his Spirit to help these believers. He empowers them to go out under the conviction that there is only one God, who has expressed himself as Father, Son, and Holy Spirit. Consequently, the church is the designated servant of the Savior. Converted, committed, convinced Christians make up the church. These believers understand that it is their God-given responsibility to help others know this Savior-God. They act upon the act of God.

The central command of Christ compels Christians to reach out to others. Motivated by Christ, they care for the lost. They see evangelism as their prime purpose in life. For a Christian to witness is as natural as breathing. When we tell the old, old story we are exercising the privilege of belief. The Christian sees that "...in Christ God was reconciling the world to himself, not counting their trespasses against them, and entrusting to us the message of reconciliation." [14]

Furthermore, Christ promises to be with us in carryng out his command to go into all the world. This was the last recorded promise of Christ. God never broke a promise or failed the faithful. Imagine! God entrusted you and me with this message of salvation! Believers evangelize.

God does not ask us to win anybody. Only He can do that. God doesn't even require us to rustle up a new group of members for His church. Only God can do that. Our responsibility is to plant God's seed. God will bring the increase. "...Neither the one who plants nor the one who waters is anything, but only God who gives the growth." [15] The doctrine of the priesthood of believers was recovered by the Reformers. It is biblical to the core. Both priest (pastor) and lay person have the same responsibility of witnessing to their Lord. The Reformation did not destroy the priesthood but in a sense destroyed the laity. We are all priests with the privilege of proclaiming the Word. Confessing to be a Christian and then refusing to participate in telling the story of God is a contradiction. Bishop Stephen Neill was right when he said, "A minister and a (layperson) are evangelists or they are not Christian." Or, as E. Stanley Jones related, "Christians who are not Christianizing are unChristian." That is plain and direct language!

We need to hear often the words of Our Lord in Matthew 7:18-20, "A good tree cannot bear bad fruit, nor can a bad tree bear good fruit. Every tree that does not bear good fruit is cut down and thrown into the fire. Thus you will know them by their fruits." We need to reflect on that awesome truth. We also need to act on it. God expects that. This saying of Jesus is pinpoint language which applies to a church which fails to reach out. "My Father is glorified by this, that you bear much fruit and become my disciples." [16] The whole church—all members of Jesus Christ— are to bear fruit because they are disciples.

A lay person in a Sunday Church School class directed to me this question, which was more of a statement than a question: "Don't you think," he asked, "that pastors are waking up to the fact that they cannot do all the church work alone and that they need lay people to help them?" Evidently, for the first time, in a lay visiting program, he saw the possibilities of personal witness. Perhaps for the first time he felt that he belonged and that God wanted him to be an evangelist.

Evangelism is the privilege of every Christian. It is not the responsibility of the few. We cannot transfer the duty of witnessing. In this witnessing, God empowers sinful people to do his work. Yes, we are sinners. We never reach the point where we do not need forgiveness. But at the same time we are saints—believers in God. The late T. A. Kantonen, my theological professor, reminded me just prior to his death in early 1993, that the words for lay person and saint are synonymous. "This is the highest honor—to be called a Kingdom person," he exclaimed.

III. Fruitful evangelism requires solid biblical theology.

There is need in every age for a theology grounded in scripture. The written word—the newspaper; the audible word—radio; the visual word—television; all are channels of information. But our world needs more than daily or hourly news—it needs the shared Good News in Jesus Christ, the Incarnate Word.

There is urgent need for solid biblical theology because Americans are experiencing a Babylonian Captivity in reverse, rubbing shoulders everyday with foreign religions which have infiltrated society along with the influx of people needing a home in a free land. Furthermore, wacky religions stalk our land. Our neighbors spout religion in some form or another. People are hungry for divine truth today, as in any age. Everyone has a philosophy of life, a fashionable "theology," a standard by which they live whether it be moral or amoral. The church member equipped to articulate the story of Christianity in these surroundings honors God and the church.

The Christian church— Roman Catholic. Orthodox, and Protestant— differing in various ways, has the same basic message—belief in God who has expressed himself as Father, Son, and Holy Spirit. So we have this truth, this theology which needs to be put into language understandable to people of any age. That is the task of evangelism.

From the point of view of the average person, however, it is the scientist who deals with reality. People enjoy products produced by science, such as equipment in the kitchen, the computer in the study, and the television set in the family room. Consequently, these realities residing in the home form a part of everyday life.

On the other hand, the Christian church may appear to people as abstract. An electric mixer has a handle but the knob of Christianity is not so easily grasped. Furthermore, pious, meaningless phrases encourage the belief that Christianity is abstract. The Church tends to make simple truth complex with the use of esoteric language. Jesus, in contrast, communicated in recognizable language. That's why crowds, as well as individuals, listened to him.

Jesus Christ is not abstact. Many who proclaim Christ in fuzzy terms are abstract. Christ was of the earth with descriptions of everyday occurrences which sparked excitement. He never waffled in answering questions. His parables rippled with the familiar and with the facts of life. He made God real. He broke into human life. He came to die and to live in us forever. What a story to tell to the nations!

Think about this: Our Lord was successful with the people in his parish, whether on the road or in a field or on the sea because of his ability to put profound truth in picturesque, plain terms. Simplicity is not shallowness. Jesus' Sermon on the Mount, for example, is profound. Not only was Christ able to help people understand the meaning of faith; his presence prompted people to act.

Evangelism is theology in action. People with clearheaded, reality-shaped concepts of God can relate how human beings can come to know him. They are motivated to do this by the knowledge that they are bought with the precious blood of Jesus Christ and that they are provided spiritual power beyond themselves.

Fruitful evangelism is impossible without biblically based theology. Theology and Evangelism go together, tied by the Spirit of God.

This trinitarian God, the main Evangelist, makes astounding promises to human beings, and provides people with the power to carry out his proclamations. Evangelism, rooted in the heart of God, demonstrates the way he does this through the lives of believers. The next chapter centers on the evangelism work of God.

CHAPTER TWO

GOD'S PROMISES AND POWER

"The biblical witnesses testify that God's Word confronts (people) in history, i.e., that the time-and-space-bound arena of history is where the Word of Yahweh meets (people) and where it is manifested in terms of the unfolding of his will." [1]

It is surprising that the word "problem" is seldom alluded to in the Bible. Assuredly, the patriarchs, prophets, and the apostles faced problems, but they were not preoccupied with problems. Interested primarily in the promises of God and the power that God provides, biblical people were able to experience God in life situations. When God's promises and power are kept in tandem, problems are solved.

Look at the Church in the beginning in contrast to the Church of today. The Apostolic Church people could have immersed themselves in problems. They could have spent their resources and energy on a list of secondary concerns:

1) Outnumbered;
2) No real estate;
3) No start-up money;
4) Dangerous life in an occupied country;
5) No experience;
6) Leaders not college or seminary graduates;
7) No people of renown in their congregation;
8) No bound Bible for people to read;

9) No equipment;
10) No Christian education curriculum materials.

The list goes on! The point is they focused on what they did have—the promises and power of God. For example, their first act was not to find a central site for a church building and to conduct a building fund campaign. The Apostolic Church began with evangelism, not stewardship. The scriptures attest that after the mass baptism on Pentecost (3,000 people) "They devoted themselves to the apostles' teaching and fellowship, to the breaking of bread and the prayers. Awe came upon everyone, because many wonders and signs were being done by the apostles." [2] Evangelism came first. "And day by day the Lord added to their number those who were being saved." [3] Note well that it was the Lord who did the adding. Therein is the promise and the power.

And, they kept growing in numbers and in spiritual depth, from 12 to 70 to 120 and 3,000. It is estimated that by the end of the first century there were 500,000 Christians; by the end of the second century 2,000,000 Christians; by the third century 5,000,000 believers in Christ. The whole Roman Empire was turned around. How? First a handful, then many took the promises of God seriously and relied on his power.

Can the Church today claim such achievements? Not in America! The Christian churches of America have immersed themselves not in their baptism but in issues. Many a church convention or an assembly of churches has had to squeeze the time agenda because of disputes, if not quarrels, over money or social issues. We love to tackle problems, so much so that we start there. We take ahold of the stick at the wrong end. We have difficulty discerning and yielding to God's power which dissolves problems. In brief, we tend to begin where we are instead of starting with God. It is wrong. We are not the possessors of power; we are the recipients of spiritual power.

One must ask if our churches are more interested in having enough money than in having converts? More concerned about issuing edicts or saving people? People will demonstrate on a pressing social issue before they will talk with a stranger about eternity.

The Church is in danger of derailing itself and running on

a different track from God. That is what happened between the testaments when it was difficult to discern who, if anybody, was speaking for the Lord. "The Church can never speak for the Lord if it speaks for social reform in general but has no precise word for the man with a broken heart or for the woman with a broken dream," admonished the late Methodist Bishop Gerald Kennedy.[4]

The Apostolic Church and the Early Church found their direction and strength in the promises of God and God's power! The entire biblical account rests on this premise. What God promises does not depend upon circumstance. His promises are unchangeable. They are true.

First, take a quick look at some of God's promises in the Old Testament.

I. THE PROMISE TO ABRAHAM.

There are promises which precede the calling of Abraham of the Chaldees (recorded in the twelfth chapter of Genesis), notably God's conversation with Adam and Eve, and with Noah. The lives of Adam and Eve deteriorated when they disregarded God's promise of demise if they misued the land of Eden. Noah's destiny changed by embracing God's promise of the flood, when everyone around him scoffed and ridiculed him for building an ark in his backyard. God put a rainbow in the sky to remind Noah of another promise— such a flood would not occur again.

The promise to Abraham is pivotal to the whole Old Testament record of God's communication with the people of Israel. "Now the Lord said to Abram, 'Go from your country and your kindred and your father's house to the land that I will show you. I will make of you a great nation, and I will bless you, and make your name great, so that you will be a blessing." [5]

Suppose Adam and Eve and their successors had taken God at his word? It would be a different world. Suppose Noah had not acted on the promise of God? Civilization could have been wiped out. If Abraham had ignored the word of the Lord, his people would have missed the land of promise.

How pivotal it is for us to act on the promises of God! It is dangerous to ignore God. God created us to be a blessing to others—the essence of evangelism. When our outlook becomes ingrown, like a painful toenail, it hobbles us; we miss being used by God's power in everyday life. We are born to use the power of God and thus be a blessing to others.

II. THE PROMISE TO MOSES.

Moses was born at a dangerous time. The Egyptians became fearful of the exploding population of their slaves and ordered all newborn Israelite male babies to be killed. In an attempt to save his life, Moses' mother set him afloat in a basket on the Nile. A daughter of the Pharoah found Moses as she walked along the river. She always wanted a child. She saved Moses and even assigned the mother of Moses (unknowingly) to care for the child. Moses grew up in the palace of the Pharaoh, received the best education, and was reared in grandeur. However, something gnawed at his heart. He couldn't stand the sight of slave mistreatment. One day he murdered an Egyptian for striking a slave. In order to save his own life, he fled to the mountainous valleys of Sinai and Horeb. There he met seven daughters of an Arab sheik and married one of them, Zipporah. This cultured man became a shepherd. From the marriage came a son. Years passed. One day Moses had an experience which changed his life. God talked to him and Moses listened. God wanted him to do something. The great God "I Am" appointed him deliverer of his people out of slavery. Moses tried to get out of the assignment (and all of us can relate to that) pointing out that he had an impediment of speech. God told him not to worry about that and to ask his brother, Aaron, for help. God told Moses he would supply him with words. Moses acted on the promises of God.

Moses told the elders of Israel and all the people of Israel what God had said to him and what God promised: "'The Lord, the God of your ancestors, the God of Abraham, of Isaac, and of Jacob, has appeared to me, saying, I have given heed to you and to what has been done to you in Egypt. I declare that I will bring you out of the misery of Egypt, to...a land flowing with milk and honey.'" [6] And God did! God took a murderer, a stammerer, a reluctant follower, and turned him into a leader. Such can happen when a person, any person, will act on the promises of God. Power then flows!

What if Moses did not go? The people would not have

been let go. Millions of lives were changed because one person listened and acted on the promises. That is evangelism. God can take any person willing to receive forgiveness and put promises and power into the human heart. God can take human limitations and change situations. What God has done for others, he is willing to do for us. God is not only the God of the past but of the present. When any person is willing to take God at his word, God will provide the power to meet any situation, be it a Pharoah or a Red Sea.

III. THE PROMISE TO DAVID.

There is a tendency to glamorize the lives of great personalities in the Bible. They are great, not because they were perfect and deserve adulation; they are great because they permitted God to work in and through their lives. Upon close investigation, each personality in the Bible displays both strengths and weaknesses. This should be encouraging to all of us. We get down on ourselves, especially after some weakness has taken over. It is the force of God's promises, understood and accepted, that marks a person "great," in the biblical sense of the word.

Such a person was David, second king of Israel who reigned from ca. 1,010 to 970 B. C. He rose from the rank of a shepherd. Talent is a gift from God. Everybody has talent. Some develop their talent more than others. And, it is evident some people have more talent than others. We envy such people, yet we need not do so. We need to develop the talent that is within us. God gave us far more talent than we are prone to realize.

When we speak of a person having charisma, we usually mean a personality that arouses enthusiasm and loyalty. Such a person appears to be aware of the presence and power of God, and acts on behalf of God. Such a person seems to sense an inborn gift and uses it.

There is much evidence that David possessed charismatic qualities. When King Saul was despondent and needed someone who could play the lyre and boost his spirits, one of the servants suggested David: "I have seen a son of Jesse the Bethlehemite who is skillful in playing, a man of valor, a warrior, prudent in speech, and a man of good presence; and the Lord is with him." [7] This is David: poet-musician; warrior; diplomat; organizer; believer. Yet, with all of those qualities, the sins of lust and murder set off a chain reaction of tragedy. David was guilty of ordering Bathsheba's husband into the front lines of battle so that he would be killed. Meanwhile, he seduced Bathsheba and after the death of her husband, took her as his wife. It took the prophet, Nathan, to show David where he was wrong.

There was tragedy when a son, Ammon, raped a virgin half-sister. Another son, Absalom, in revenge killed Ammon. In the end other sons engaged in treachery in an attempt to succeed to the throne of David. Fortuitously, one of David's sons, Solomon, became king and carried on where his father left off.

What kept David going during these tension-filled times? The promise of God. "And what more can David say to you? For you know your servant, O Lord God! Because of your promise, and according to your own heart, you have wrought all this greatness, so that your servant may know it. Therefore you are great, O Lord God; for there is no one like you, and there is no God besides you, according to all that we have heard with our ears." [8]

David listened to God and acted on God's promise to him. What if David had not listened? Israel could not have reached its potential.

Nations can be changed when only one person acts on the promises of God. That is why evangelism is important. Our work is world-wide. We cannot rest until we have reached every person on the face of the earth with the good news that God has defeated evil and death and invites us all to the resurrection life beginning now. Evangelism is in the resurrection business.

IV. THE PROMISE TO THE PROPHETS.

The prophets were the voice of God. They saw raw human behavior. They observed how easily people broke promises. They perceived clearly that God never went back on his promises. The psalmist comments: "Then they despised the pleasant land, having no faith in his promise. They grumbled in their tents, and did not obey the voice of the Lord...Then they attached themselves to the Baal of Peor, and ate sacrifices offered to the dead...." [9]

Israel's sin was not standing on the promises of God. They became discontent with God and content with their own conclusions about life. It took an Elijah, a Jeremiah or an Amos not only to tell it like it was but also to describe again who God is and that his promises are worth acting upon. Through the prophets Israel was able to see something of God. Willis J. Beecher insisted that the prophets formed the habit of "...looking upon Israel as the people of promise." [10] That was their covenant relationship.

That is the role of the Church today—to be the voice of God. We are the people of the promise. Getting ready for the next century, we are concocting "mission statements" as if we never knew what we were supposed to do in the first place, when all we had to do was make Matthew 28:19 our mission statement. Some of these mission statements skirt around that 28th chapter in fear that it is too confining. The language of these statements are often couched in a vocabulary only church people can understand. It is right to have a mission statement. It is wrong when our congregations conclude, after outlining a plan of action, that the job is done. The prophets of old did not work that way. Their mission statement included God working through them in giving the world important news. God's promise and their acting upon the promise gave them power to transform their world.

V. THE CONTINUING PROMISE OF GOD IN JESUS OF NAZARETH.

The Old Testament is the story of how God worked through the lives of people who embraced his promises and experienced his power. Jesus said "...apart from me you can do nothing." [11] It applies to both testaments. Placing God in the center of life makes the difference. It is so simple that we stumble over obvious truth.

Jesus is the best promise God ever made— the fulfillment of the ages. The Old Testament prepared us for his coming. The New Testament validated God's promise of a Savior. Of course, we didn't expect God to come in human form. God surprised us! We didn't imagine God breaking into the world as a child. He amazed us! We didn't anticipate God placing himself in dangerous surroundings. He shocked us!

This coming of Jesus is God incarnate. God's promise of a Savior illustrates the astounding depth and breadth of God's love for his creation. If we were God, we would not have done it that way. God took some chances, entrusting himself to a couple in love. Ah, the love of that Joseph! What man would have believed Mary when she told him how she became pregnant? And who would have believed some angel conveying to Joseph that that was the way it was! This couple in love demonstrate the utmost in belief. Usually young couples in love can hardly see anything but themselves, so wrapped up in love for one another. The love of Mary and Joseph goes deeper. It is pure unadulterated trust. Oh, if the world only believed in the promises of God—his power would flow over the banks of humankind.

Think of what it took for God to become a human being. Envisage the dimensions of God's love. Illustrate it something like this: Did you ever have a pet in your home, a pet that you dearly loved? As a youth, for me it was a pig! My uncle was one of the founders of the 4-H Club. My father's name, Raymond E. Click, is emblazoned on the Graham building in Springfield, Ohio, as a member of the first group of youth in what became the 4-H Club. Anyway, it was my 4-H Club assignment to raise a pig. I spent a lot of time with that pig, so much time that the pig became as obedient as a dog. I called that pig "Honey"! That pig might be out in a field and I could call "Honey, on-e-oney" and that pig would come, nestle down next to me, and I scratched the pig's tummy. When it came time for the county fair, all boys and girls displayed their 4-H Club projects; I didn't have to corral my pig like the other boys and girls. All I had to do was say "Come on, Honey" and my pig followed me. I received first prize for that pig and I still have the blue ribbon affirming that feat!

How much did I love that pig "Honey"? If I had God's power, would I love that pig enough to deliberately become a pig?! Incongruous thought, isn't it — a human being becoming a pig?

But, imagine what it would be like for a human being to become a pig. Envisage that you had the power to do this and now you are a pig, yet have all the knowledge and experience of being a human being. Visualize: you must walk on all fours, close to the ground; root around with your nose in the ground as a pig scrounges for food. Your vocabulary has been reduced to a grunt; no shower in the morning; no televison; no making love in a decent manner;

and, there is the distinct feeling you are being fed for the slaughter. As a pig, you are far more limited than a human being.

It would be a humiliating and humbling experience for a human being to become a pig. I wouldn't love a pig named "Honey" so much that I would willingly and knowingly become a pig, even if I had that kind of power to do this. But, God did! "...In Christ Jesus, who, though he was in the form of God, did not regard equality with God as something to be exploited, but emptied himself, taking the form of a slave, being born in human likeness. And being found in human form, he humbled himself and became obedient to the point of death—even death on a cross." [12]

God becoming a "slave" is far more humbling than for a human being becoming a pig. In Jesus, we see what God looks like—pure love!

Picture what it meant for God to become a human being. Omniscient and omnipotent with the world in his "hand," God deliberately and decisively becomes a human being. He made that decision long before Jesus was born. It wasn't a hurry-up plan. As the scriptures attest, "In the beginning was the Word, and the Word was with God, and the Word was God. He was in the beginning with God. All things came into being through him, and without him not one thing came into being." [13] This is the most declarative way the scriptures have of telling us that Jesus Christ is God. It is difficult to fathom. It takes faith. Those who have embraced this premise and have acted on the promises of God have found power in human life.

This Jesus was born like any other child except that he was born in a manger instead of a hospital or house. Mary carried him in her womb and traveled 90 miles by donkey just before giving birth, a dangerous thing to do. Joseph couldn't even find a decent place for the Savior to be born. What chances God took in being born as a human being. Furthermore, God permitted a scoundrel like Herod to threaten his human life. The family had to beat it out of town and out of the territory into a foreign land. Egypt had some doubtful memories in Joseph's background. Yet, Joseph acted on what he believed God told him in a dream. What if Joseph had not acted on the message (promise) of God?

The family finally returned to a familiar place, Nazareth. There Jesus grew from boyhood to manhood, matured in the family faith, learned Joseph's occupation, carpentry. With other brothers and sisters (Matthew 13:55-57), he experienced family life, suffered loss when the father died, and accepted family responsibilities. Mary needed him. Not until he was in his thirties could he launch out into a ministry to all human beings that was destined to lead to death. The family could care for themselves at this juncture. Now he gave himself to all families. This Jesus was surely human in every sense. Envision what it meant for God to come just like that—as a human being! Only God could think up that idea.

There is more. In Jesus' occupation as a messenger to humankind, he experienced adulation and rejection, two basic occurrences in human life. Jesus was praised. He was successful. Unusual events occurred. Water was changed into wine (John 2); people were healed (Luke 5); a man was raised from the dead (John 11); multitudes were fed in a mysterious way (Matthew 14); tough questions were answered (Mark 12). This is what was said of him, "...the crowds were astounded at his teaching, for he taught them as one having authority...." [14] There is affirmation.

Then the adulation changed to rejection, that awful feeling that results in a king-sized headache. The religious leaders (imagine that) suspected him of being a fraud and considered him a threat to their religious lifestyle and thinking. They were so captive to their own human history that they could not listen to new and different ideas. They decided that the only way this Jesus matter could be settled was to eliminate him. They plotted to kill him. And God himself, encased in a human body, let it happen. God is consistent. He made free will. Human beings exercised the power of their own freedom to do as they liked and they executed this Jesus in criminal fashion. God in Jesus let it occur, deliberately. Being God, he could have avoided the cross or could have come down from the cross, but that would be missing his mission. God came for this purpose. Christ gave himself as a propitiation for our sins— "...whom God put forward as a sacrifice of atonement by his blood...." [15] This Jesus—God—purposely died on the cross so that people could see the limitless love of God in a world of limited vision of who God is.

Actually, when you and I think of the life of Jesus, we see no struggle for security; only the struggle for identity. Nobody expected God to be like Jesus. We have difficulty handling that, too. It is because we never picture Jesus a participant or spectator at a Masters' Golf Tournament; going bowling or enjoying the theatre; reading Hamlet or the poems of Milton; being enraptured by Bach; telling a good joke; going to the grocery store or sitting down to watch television. We just never think of Jesus as being for real, anymore than those who lived in the first century. Jesus wanted to be human to human beings and to be God to human beings.

Jesus' life is one big surprise after another. God planned it that way. God kept his promise of sending a Savior. He was supposed to be born in a stable and not an inn; a carpenter and not some CEO of a corporation; tempted like any blood-red person. He was supposed to be a teacher and healer. He was supposed to be killed. He was supposed to rise from the dead, as every believer will.

We have a way of making Jesus into some kind of freak. Most paintings of Jesus do not picture the real Jesus. We have visualized Jesus as some sweet, inoffensive, afraid to confront anybody, never hurt a flea kind of guy. Why doesn't somebody picture him wringing his hands about what to do next, instead of hands folded in prayer? Neither we, nor our ancestors in Jerusalem, expected God to become a human being, bone of our bone, blood type of our blood type. We have put God in the sky instead of in a real Person on earth. We have made God unreal. We have a hard time believing that God's promise of a Savior is true.

There is a story of a young man who came to the philosopher, Socrates, with this request: "Show me how I can be enlightened?" "How badly do you want it?" Socrates asked. "More than anything in the world" the young man replied.

Socrates took the young man to the shore of a lake and they waded into the water until it was up to their necks. Then Socrates put his hand on the young man's head and pushed him under the water. The young man struggled desperately, but Socrates did not release him until he was about to drown.

When they returned to shore, Socrates asked the young man, "Son, when you were under the water, what did you want more than anything in the world?" "Air," he replied without hesitation. Socrates said, "When you want enlightenment as much as you wanted air, then you will get enlightened." [16]

What do you want more than anything else in the world? Health? Security? Happiness? Friends? Money? Travel? Love? When you and I want Christ as much as a drowning person wants air, then Jesus will come into our lives with promises and power.

*

The fourteenth chapter of John is a concise summary of Jesus' ministry and what he promises to followers. "I have said these things to you while I am still with you. But the Advocate, the Holy Spirit, whom the Father will send in my name, will teach you everything, and remind you of all that I have said to you." [17] There is the core promise to people in any century. The Holy Spirit will teach us everything. He will remind us of God's promises. He will help us carry out the Great Commission. In brief, God in Christ is around!

The Apostolic Church got the idea in a hurry. They latched onto the promises of God and thus experienced his power. It isn't that the Apostolic Church did everything right; they had their setbacks and arguments, but, they recognized and experienced the everlasting Presence. They went forward in faith because they were not backward about depending on God's power.

Jesus taught the disciples almost everything, but their memory apart from the Holy Spirit was not any better than ours. He said there would be reminders along the way (John 14:26). In this century and into the next, we need reminding to start with God's power instead of starting with problems—to begin with God and not ourselves. We need reminding that the promises of God are true for any age and that his power can flow through people when they remember who they are.

Roland Hayes, great American tenor, was invited to sing before the king in Buckingham Palace. His parents had been slaves. Born in a tiny cabin in Georgia, his father died when Roland was a boy, but he was brought up by a wonderful mother who taught him important principles of living. A music teacher heard Roland sing, and doors into the musical world began to open. Finally, the door of Buckingham Palace opened. Thrilled with the opportunity, he cabled his mother telling her about it. She cabled back a message with just four words: "Remember who you are." Roland said that was exactly what he needed at the height of his career—to remember who he was and where he had come from.

It is easy to forget who we are as we strive to be successful. We are God's chosen and we come from Pentecost.

Many church bodies in America are struggling and have confessed they need to get back to the basics, including my own church. The call to do so says that something happened to the Church along the way to the world. Did the Church forget its reason for existence? A reminder, indeed, we need.

The Apostolic Church and the Early Church stuck to the basics. They never forgot who they were. They grew rapidly and deeply in the faith. By the time of the Medieval Church, however, the recollection of the church's roots faded. How can you crown heads of state and own two-thirds of the land of Europe, without losing an inch of faith? The Church became enthralled with itself instead of with the scriptures. Our ancestors in the Medieval Church lost their way. They forgot who they were. Their kind of power ignored the promises of the Christ. Division occurred instead of multiplication.

There is reason to believe the Church of today has fallen into a corresponding trap. We approach problems of church membership decline, lack of funds, etc., without concentrating on God's promises and power. We juggle programs and worship formats hoping to latch onto a formula which will attract people to our edifices. We struggle to survive. We are afraid the church will die. Our goal seems to be church growth. That is not what evangelism is about. Evangelism is making disciples. Evangelism is using God's power. Evangelism is acting on God's promises. Evangelism is the result of God's action through the lives of believers. The end result may be church growth but not growth for the sake of growth; it is growth for the sake of Christ. Believers who remember who they are, stand on the promises and experience the power of God in their daily lives.

The evangelist begins with the promises of God. Willis Beecher expressed the feeling: "...the fulfilment in the person of Jesus is so marked as to be classed by itself. He is the representative person of the promise and its accomplishment." [18] It is this Jesus we proclaim.

CHAPTER THREE

THE BIBLE IN EVANGELISM

"The New Testament writers were not just writing history; they were writing for a verdict."

"Throughout its history the Christian Church has used the Bible as a main instrument of its evangelistic activity....The Bible has in fact been the cutting-edge of its advance."[1]

Christians tend to talk about the Bible more than to study the Bible and relay its message. As a consequence, our testimony can taste stale and mildewy.

Literalists wave the Bible in the air, as a patriot waves a flag. They cry, "Thus saith the Lord"! There is power in that approach. It is simple, direct, uncomplicated. But, it has distinct limitations.

An old phonograph record had an actor mimic a revivalist. Every time the revivalist wanted to prove something, he exclaimed "It's in the Book! It's in the Book!" Well, not everything is in the book. The horrendous problems of our day, including AIDS and the question of distributing condoms at our schools in order to protect our school children from the dangers of promiscuity, cannot be settled by just quoting the book. Life is not as simplistic as all that.

Luther's large catechism speaks relevantly here: "People must know Christ by faith before they can know the real meaning of the Word of God. They do not accept Christ because they have accepted the scriptures as their authority, but they accept the scriptures because they reveal to them the Christ whom they receive in faith."

Our faith does not hinge upon a book. People of Old Testament times did not have the Pentateuch until 400 B.C. It took until A.D. 98 at the Council of Jamnia for Jewish scholars to determine what became known to Christians as the Old Testament. Between about A.D. 50 and 125 the New Testament was written, and it took three more centuries before all 27 books were adopted as authoritative. For centuries, without books as we know them, God spoke and worked through the lives of people by oral tradition.

Our faith comes from the living Christ. The Bible is the endorsement of God's revelation. Those of this persuasion do not think less of the Bible than the literalists. We who appreciate textual and documentary criticism as a mode of understanding the Bible consider the Bible authoritative.

Yet, most churches throughout their history (except during the time of the Reformation, the era of colonialism, and early America) have not made extensive use of the Bible in evangelism. The Reformers sought to provide access to the Bible for all people. Luther sat high in the Wartburg Castle translating Greek and Hebrew into the language of his people because the book of Romans and Galatians had changed his life and set him on the road to what became the Reformation. Tyndale experienced the presence of God in his life by opening the scriptures, and it motivated him to make the first translation of the English Bible. "It was by reading the Bible that Justin, Tatian and Theophilus...became Christians. Justin's interests were, he tells us, wholly philosophic, and he attended the lectures of many of the best known philosophers of the time. He studied under a stoic, a pyhthagorean, and a platonist—in turn. But none of them satisfied him. At last an old man 'led him from Plato to the prophets, from metaphysics to the gospels.'" [2] It was an old man and the Bible that led Justin Martyr at the age of thirty to Christ.

That is what evangelism is about—reading and describing the story of God in Christ. When was the last time you introduced someone to Jesus Christ?

"How dare you ask me a question like that?" exploded an attendee at a conference on evangelism. "Why not?" I countered. "Well," she said, "Don't I go to church and Sunday School and the Women's meeting and tithe—yes, siree, I tithe—what else can be expected of a Christian?" I answered gently but firmly: "I can see by what you tell me you are an informed person. Then you are ready to go." "Go where?" she snapped. "Out and tell somebody about this wonderful faith you have." "Oh, I couldn't do that," she protested!

There is where Christianity ends for a greater percentage of Christians, and that is why there are not more Christians in the world. Furthermore, we are loathe to suspect that our own spiritual tempo is linked to the expression of our faith or the lack of it. Because we cannot possibly "do that" our faith goes flat.

Jesus' Method

The Bible was the method of our Lord in leading people to faith that he was the Messiah. Luke said that after the resurrection Jesus "...opened their minds to understand the scriptures." [3] It was not the first time that he opened the minds of the disciples to the scriptures.

Notice that after the resurrection, Jesus didn't take his disciples into downtown Jerusalem and show himself off, allowing the disciples to display him. Jesus didn't even bother to make visits on Caiphus or Pilate or the Pharisees and Sadducces and shout with glee, "Surprise!" Sometimes we wish he did so that the world could believe without second-guessing the disciples.

What did Jesus do? He simply appeared to his followers and began relating the story of the Bible. He didn't even take time to tell them what it was like to die and come alive again. Thus, the Bible is where to begin in leading a person to authentic faith.

Jesus, in his post-resurrection teaching of the disciples, began with Moses, the prophets, and the psalms. He wanted the disciples to see the scriptures as a whole and how God had been working through the lives of people from the beginning of time. He desired the disciples to understand the progressive revelation of God in history. In fact, when Jesus related to them the teachings of Moses, the prophets, and the psalms, this was a review for them.

For three years he had been telling them of biblical events. He didn't think repetition would hurt them. Then he reminded them that what happened to him between Good Friday (good because God brought people into a right relationship with him) and Easter (the resurrection from the dead) was what the scriptures recorded would occur to the Christ. He quoted the prophet Hosea so that Luke could write, "Thus it is written, that the Messiah is to suffer and to rise from the dead on the third day...."[4]

Jesus reviewed the scriptures with the disciples for forty days following the crucifixion and resurrection for the purpose of equipping them for evangelism. Jesus comprehended the monumental task facing the disciples in their future. He wanted to give them the best equipment—an understanding of the scriptures. If they had that background, Jesus knew they could plant the seed of faith, even when he was no longer visible. Because of this indoctrination the Church came into existence and thrived.

This was not an unusual procedure for Jesus—opening the minds of people to understand the scriptures. He did this by first opening his own mind to the scriptures. As a lad of twelve he added to his knowledge gleaned from the local rabbi by going to the temple in Jerusalem and "...sitting among the teachers, listening to them and asking them questions."[5] He further equipped himself through the "silent years" studying the scriptures, as any devout Jew would have done. By the time he was thirty years of age, he was ready to open the scriptures to others, including those in his hometown. He made final preparation by spending forty days on a backpacking trip in the wilderness, sifting through things for his impending ministry. His life was always soaking up the presence of the Father, whether on a mountain alone or when walking a dusty road in search of converts.

Jesus knew who he was. When he went back to Nazareth, he read from the book of Isaiah: "The Spirit of the Lord is upon me, because he has anointed me to bring good news to the poor. He has sent me to proclaim release to the captives and recovery of sight to the blind, to let the oppressed go free, to proclaim the year of the Lord's favor."[6] Then he said, "Today this scripture has been fulfilled in your hearing."[7] They drove him out of town! Opposition loomed its head from the beginning, even in his hometown. He never turned back. His goal was clear. Jesus kept evangelizing until his mission statement was finished.

We haven't described in detail how Christ led a non-believer to belief, through the use of scripture. There is a good example in John 4:5-30. Jesus stopped at Jacob's well while the disciples went into the city of Sychar for food supplies. A woman of Samaria came to the well for water. It was about noon. Jesus asked her for a drink of water.

That was the introduction. Jesus had a habit of seeking out people wherever and whoever they were, Jew or Gentile. Status in society didn't make any difference to him. He knew that a rich person, a poor person, beggar or thief on the cross needed God. That was his target—people. He was in the people business. He was continually mindful of their total need.

Imagine an all too common conversation, if we had been in Jesus' place, and how we might have approached the situation. Church person: "Nice day, isn't it?" Woman: "Sure is." Church person: "A little hot, though." Woman: "Yeah. That's why I came to get some water. Want some?" Church person: "That's a good idea. Thanks. You from Sychar?" Woman: "Yes." Church person: "What kind of town is it?" Woman: "Oh, I don't know. Not much happening there." Church person: "Well, I and my buddies won't be here long anyway. We're just passing through." Woman picks up her pail and as she starts to leave the well says, "See ya around. Have a good trip!" Church person: "Have a good day! So long."

Thankfully, that is not what happened! But it could have happened that way, if it had been one of us. We engage in trivial conversation, passing the time of day, without reminding ourselves what we are in existence for. Opportunities pass our way every day and if we are not alert, they slip away from us, and people who need God remain lost.

Now think through the steps of this conversation as it really occurred. Jesus did ask her for a drink of water. As he did so he asked himself the question why she came at noon to get the water when almost everybody went for water when it was cooler.

She must be some kind of outcast, he concluded. And, going through the mind of the woman was why Jesus spoke to her the way he did. She was taken by surprise that Jesus talked to her since Jews didn't have anything to do with Samaritans. So, Jesus sensed her need for something beyond herself and his need to do something more than just drink water at high noon while waiting for the disciples.

The woman was blunt and to the point: "How is it that you, a Jew, ask a drink of me, a woman of Samaria?" Jesus came back with an answer that was not mere conversation. By this time he had made up his mind to try to lead her from herself to recognizing who he was. He dropped a couple of words—"living water." She couldn't dismiss the expression from her mind. She wanted the kind of water that would quench her thirst forever.

After creating this interest, Jesus described what a human being is like—hiding from God and faking authentic existence. He knew that her life was mixed up, marrying one man after another and now living with a man without the "benefit of clergy." He wasn't afraid to confront her with her past. He could have detoured this matter but did not. He wanted to help her see where she had been in life and how she could change. Now, the woman became curious. The woman could have left the well in a huff! That was the risk Jesus took. Instead, she complimented him: "Sir, I see that you are a prophet." She had a little knowledge of scripture. Somebody had planted a scripture seed along the way. Even the Savior appreciated that and made use of it. She said, "I know that Messiah is coming (who is called Christ). When he comes, he will proclaim all things to us." It is then Jesus goes for commitment. "I am he, the one who is speaking to you."

The disciples return and are surprised that Jesus would talk to a person like that, especially a Samaritan woman. Note well the result of this conversation. The scripture states, "Then the woman left her water jar and went back to the city...." [8] The woman was so excited about the conversation with Jesus that she left her water jar! She became so caught up with meeting the Master that she forgot why she had gone to the well in the first place. She rushed back into town and told people about Jesus. She was no longer afraid of her past or present. She had to share this news about the Messiah, and the people who heard her story began to seek him out. "Many Samaritans from that city believed in him because of the woman's testimony...." [9]

What a beautiful conversation Jesus had with this woman at Jacob's well. Perception, progressive thought, persuasion, revelation, conversion! Our conversations with strangers can help lead people to Jesus.

Scripture was Jesus' evangelism tool. The disciples and the Apostolic Church used the same tool. Philip, traveling from Jerusalem to Gaza, heard a man (who turned out to be the treasurer of Ethiopia) reading from Isaiah. The man was hung up on a passage he could not understand. "Then Philip began to speak, and starting with this scripture, he proclaimed to him the good news about Jesus." [10] The result? A baptism!

It is not different in our day. We dare not give people just the leftovers from our personal philosophy. Any radio or TV talk show can give them that. The true witness of God gets food from the Bible. It is never stale bread.

At a time when congregations were sponsoring families from Asia, the congregation I was serving provided such a family with an apartment, furnished it, obtained jobs for the parents, and in a real sense gave them a headstart in America. One parishoner was heard to say, "We gave them everything they needed!" Not so. We needed to give that family a Bible in their own language, to nurture that family in understanding the Christian faith, to give that family Jesus Christ, and to prepare that family for baptism.

Too many Christians are content to do good works. We relish telling the unchurched what wonderful facilities our church has, what marvelous pastors we have, what tremendous programs we have, what a friendly group we are and how we care for one another, and how the lights are on at the church every night with exciting events. This is not entirely inappropriate. But what we need to do first is to tell them what a beautiful Savior-God we have! Our witnessing needs to get beyond the obvious and the mundane.

It is good to remember that Jesus didn't much use the temple as a tool to get people into the kingdom, although he went to the temple to pray. His approach was to help people know God. God isn't some idea that began with Moses on a mountain. "You have heard that it was said to those of ancient times...But I say to you...." [11] illustrates that Christ came to fulfill scripture. He didn't come to condemn. He came to reconstruct. He didn't come to lecture. He came to give life. He didn't come to tell people how to be successful. He came to tell them how to be saved.

Jesus actively sought out people. His parables of the lost sheep, coin, sons—are descriptions of how God sees the human situation and how he seeks out persons. He didn't say, "Well, now, if you people want to go to the temple, it is there right in the middle of town." No, he took the kingdom message to the people. He took his disciples on the road. He took with him the story of the Bible and its fulfillment in him. He spoke with authority because he knew the scriptures and its message for life.

"I can't do that" is a copout. If you are going to introduce somebody to Jesus Christ, how would you go about it? Certainly, you would begin with the Bible. You wouldn't end it there, however. Even John admitted, "...There are also many other things that Jesus did; if every one of them were written down I suppose the world itself could not contain the books that would be written." [12]

There are numerous signs which evidence God in human life that are not written in the Bible, which the world needs to hear. Tell them your story of meeting Jesus Christ! That is our responsibility as Christians. That is evangelism. Plant the seed. God will bring the increase. As Paul wrote, "I planted, Apollos watered, but God gave the growth." [13]

The place of the Bible in evangelism can be summarized:

1) The Bible gives us insights as to how God worked through the lives of biblical people;
2) The Bible cites examples of how biblical people approached non-believers;
3) The Bible illustrates the way the greatest evangelist in his-

tory, Jesus Christ, dealt with people in specifics, revealing his gentle yet forceful power of persuasion;

4) The Bible reveals how great personalities used the history of the Bible so that others might get a glimpse of God;

5) The Bible generates enthusiasm for kingdom work;

6) The Bible serves as a basis for evangelism;

7) The Bible reminds us that Jesus left the work of evangelism in the hands of the disciples and people as we are, and promised to be a present help in accomplishing his will;

8) The Bible demonstrates it is the honed tool of evangelism and the best tool we will ever have.

In brief, the Bible is the place to begin in preparing to be an evangelism person. Prayer is next.

CHAPTER FOUR

PRAYER IN EVANGELISM

"What no eye has seen, nor ear heard, nor the human heart conceived, what God has prepared for those who love him." [1]

The secular world is interested in results. Coaches in sports are keenly aware that their job is hinged to successful seasons. Business expects a profit, whether it be automobile manufacturing, housing, or oil. A grocery chain closed hundreds of stores in several states because they were not showing a profit. Wall Street is swayed by a slight increase or decrease in the gross national product. Results count.

The President of the United States of America, or the head of any nation, must show some results or be ousted from power. You can't run a business, let alone a nation, without positive results. From the grade card to the corporation chart, the idea is to produce positive results. Results count.

Why do we not talk more about results in religion? One reason is—the benefits of religion are not always visible. For example: What does it get you by going to church every Sunday, reading the Bible everyday, praying morning, noon, and night? We cannot always see the results of our religion. We look around and see non-going church people just as happy and often better off emotionally as well as financially. What does it get us, we ask? Where are the results of our religion? We can be so anxious for results that we send the wrong message.

A professor in a church I served shared a paper written by a young man in his first year English course. A paragraph or two will suffice to illustrate:

"I enjoy saying that I'm an atheist to see people's reactions. Mostly, they don't care, but sometimes a really religious person will argue that there is a God and that if I would come to this person's church, I could get in touch with Him. I always wonder how these people know God is a Him. My next door neighbor is very religious. He told me if I would come to his church just once, I would get a better understanding of God. His congregation just finished building a new church, and it cost a little over one million dollars to build. He worked for the church for a while doing some painting. The church made his check out to his wife so that he could continue drawing unemployment benefits. I don't want to learn about God from them! I told him I would come to his church if he would quit smoking cigarettes. He said he would try. Two weeks later he told me he couldn't do it. You know what I said? 'What's the matter, man, no faith?'"

The student concluded his paper by saying, "I guess we should quit building so many one million dollar churches and build some real churches in our hearts and in our souls. That way we will never have to repaint them."

That well-meaning religious neighbor turned the young man off instead of on. "I don't want to learn about God from them"—this neighbor and his wife who cheated on unemployment and could not break a habit. Who could blame the student for not wanting to learn about God from a person with two standards!

The question is: **What are people learning about God from us?**

The disciples searched for learning about God from Jesus. Scripture states that Jesus "...was praying in a certain place...." [2] The disciples heard Jesus pray, observed the results of prayer in his life, and asked that he teach them how to pray. They wanted prayer to be a part of their lives, as it was with Jesus. They wanted some results.

Some have been Christian for years yet when called upon to pray at the table or before a group at the church protest: "Oh, I couldn't do that! Somebody else can do that better. Why don't you ask the pastor? After all, that's what he's paid to do." And we can hear the first year English student ask, "What's the matter—no faith?"

We can't learn about God from people who do not pray.

Think about what prayer is not. Prayer is not like a coach giving a pep talk. In other words, prayer is not a matter of doing better in the second half of the game. Prayer is not like putting a million dollars into your personal account. In other words, prayer is not bargaining with God. Prayer is not like facing a parent for discipline. In other words, prayer is not a spanking.

Prayer is a personal relationship with God. It is talking to somebody you love talking with—God in Christ. It is learning from God. If you can talk, you can pray. The disciples might well have requested of Jesus, "Teach us to talk with God."

Prayer is listening to God. He has something to say to every person who will listen. If you can listen, you can pray. The disciples might well have requested of Jesus: "Teach us to listen."

Prayer is thinking God's thoughts after him. For example, how frequently we need to stop in our tracks and say to ourselves: "Where in the world am I headed?" Prayer is like getting off into the woods with time to think. The disciples might well have requested of Jesus, "Teach us to think." If you can think, you can pray.

If prayer is talking with somebody you want to talk to, if prayer is listening to someone you want to listen to, if prayer is thinking with God about things that matter, there are going to be some positive results. Here is a list of some:

1) Prompts plain, honest, straightforward talk with no strings attached;
2) Increases listening capacity;
3) Gets and helps keep our heads on straight;
4) Puts our priorities in order;
5) Keeps our emotions under control;
6) Reveals new paths;
7) Gives knowledge from God about life;
8) Tests decisions;
9) Reaches some stars without taking our feet off the ground;
10) Develops a sense of companionship with God.

Bishop Charles Henry Brent of the Protestant Episcopal

Church of America, wrote: "The most comfortable result of a life of prayer is the security which fellowship with God imparts. His kind and cheering counsels come darting into the soul like rays of light into a dark room. Good desires increase in multitude and vigor. Unlooked-for succor rushes in to support us in moments of trial. Life expands until its branches are aflame with the sunny blossoms of hope."

Bishop Brent concluded: "Probably the greatest result of the life of prayer is an unconscious but steady growth into the knowledge of the mind of God and into conformity with his will; for after all prayer is not so much the means whereby God's will is bent to man's desires as it is that whereby man's will is bent to God's desires." [3]

Prayer matters. Without it, nobody can learn anything from us about God. With prayer, we can learn something from God. Our prayer could very well be: "Lord, teach us to talk to you; to listen to you; and, to think with you." And God will "...speak to us through the earthquake, wind, and fire—this still small voice of calm!" The words of Frances R. Havergal in the hymn "Lord, speak to us, that we may speak" sounds the evangelism person's note. We dare not speak to others before we speak to God. Others cannot come to know God through us until God has gone through us. That is what prayer does. It is a fundamental premise of evangelism.

Ask: What has been the effect of my prayers? Is there a difference in attitude, a sharper outlook on life, a wider range of thought in decision-making, a quality of life that triggers in people the thought that that person has been with the Lord?

Ask: What has been the effect of not praying? If we can see no difference, it is likely we have been only talking to ourselves—which is to say, we really didn't believe anything was going to happen by praying anyway.

Prayer is crying out loud. It is sharing in silence. There is nothing too big or too small or in-between that cannot be shared with a real friend like Jesus. If you are a farmer, there is nothing wrong with praying for good weather for the crops. If you don't have a job and are worryng about putting bread on the table, there is nothing wrong with praying for a position that is worthy of your capabilities. If your business is bad, there is nothing wrong with praying for it to get better. If the world is in turmoil, there is nothing wrong with praying for peace. If you are ill with cancer, you can pray for the scientists to hurry up with a cure.

The true appraisal of an effective prayer is not that we get what we want but the effect prayer has on our lives. God doesn't have a toll free 800 number. Prayer is always going to cost something. There is no need to pray if you are afraid of the price. It will cost you to go in the direction of God. That's why the cross was unavoidable.

Thomas Merton writes: "In...prayer, one thinks and speaks not only with his mind and lips, but in a certain sense with his whole being. Prayer is then not just a formula of words, or a series of desires springing up in the heart—it is the orientation of our whole body, mind and spirit to God in silence, attention and adoration. All good meditative prayer is a conversion of our entire self to God." [4]

*

There is a great struggle going on among humankind. You sense it. This is not to think primarily of political situations or of calamaties caused by nature, although they assuredly affect our lives. The struggle for humankind is primarily the struggle for inner composure.

A live dog was found in a dark hole covered by branches. His little legs were tied and his mouth was gagged. His body was scorched to the bare skin in his struggle to get free. They had to put him to sleep to relieve him of his misery. What a terrible thing to do—to tie and gag a little dog and put him in a dark hole to die.

More and more people feel tied and gagged and left in a dark hole to live. Prayer is running "out of a dark house into the sunshine," exclaimed Luther.

The disciples struggled with life, as we do. Surely these men, chosen by our Lord to serve as his followers, knew how to pray. But, had the domineering political situation imposed by Rome strangled hope? Had the religious puppets in the land siphoned inspiration out of their hearts? Had the pains and woes of humankind sapped their spiritual energy? Had their own inadequacy to meet life's terms come to beat so forceably upon them that their own inner composure had dwindled? In effect, did the disciples feel tied and gagged and left in a hole to live?

Whatever it was, they had sense enough to ask Jesus to teach them how to pray. Jesus taught them many things while he walked the earth but likely not anything more important than prayer. After the Ascension, they must have thanked him over and over again for his last recorded words to them, "And remember, I am with you always, to the end of the age." [6]

Without continuing conversation with the risen and ascended Lord, the disciples could not have experienced the gift of the Holy Spirit at Pentecost. It was prayer in the upper room that shook them up, erasing concern for personal safety, and enabling them to face Jerusalem as their Lord did.

And, the Apostolic Church was able to gain momentum because "They devoted themselves to the apostles' teaching and fellowship, to the breaking of bread and the prayers" [7] We can rejoice that the disciples taught New Testament people how to pray, just as they were taught by Jesus.

People have tried to run out of the dark only to find more darkness in artificial stimulants. Inner composure comes from talking with God. Prayer is the entrance to a wholesome life. That's what the disciples must have seen in Christ as again and again he went apart to pray. They wanted to learn how to pray.

Before we attempt to lead someone else to Jesus Christ, it is imperative that we first get direction from God. Evangelism doesn't get done when the people of God just talk to themselves. We need to talk to God and we need to listen to the nature of his call to us. Our praying is not like walking through a cemetery in the middle of the night whistling "Dixie" just to be encouraged by our own sound. We are not engaged in some sideline pep talk so that when we go out and talk with people about God we are better able to do so because we have inspired ourselves. In prayer, we are talking to somebody with a name. God is personal. He is not impersonal like a box of puffed rice. He is there to talk to, a two-way conversation as real as when you talk on the telephone and somebody says, "Hello." In prayer, we must know to whom we are talking. I can sit in my dentist's chair and hear him talk about God as some "cosmic gent." But, you see my dentist doesn't know God yet. To him God might as well be in tie and tails, a respectable fellow who understands that we are too busy to talk to him and to understand him.

Prayer is talking and listening and comprehending the marching orders of God. Before we dare go out, we need to have something happen within us. That inner composure, that assurance that God calls us to share the Good News with people, is the result of prayer.

Here is what prayer does for evangelism:
+ God assures us of his presence and help in the telling of the News.
+ God reassures us that he has confidence in us to tell the Story since he left in our hands the awesome responsibility of telling the world the News.
+ God equips us with the gift of the Holy Spirit, after our conversation with him.
+ God invites us to think about people for whom he came to this earth to give life.
+ God sets the tone for our lives by giving us the privilege as well as the responsibility for telling people about Christ.
+ God gives the gift of conversation with him and with others.
+ God promises he will never fail the faithful who consult him.

There are mega churches with staff persons assigned to lead leaders and people in a life of prayer. They testify to the miracles that occur. They declare the mighty acts of God in leading them forward in faith. New insights, new adventures, new directions, new people are wrought by prayer. Prayer is not a gimmick. Prayer is God's way of tuning up our spiritual engines.

Warning: Do not try evangelism without talking with God first. Without prayer, we simply try to build up an institution. With prayer, God can extend his kingdom through us. Churches that neglect prayer stagnate and shrivel. Get the right advice, direction, and empowerment from the best Consultant in the business of evangelism—God himself!

PART II

PREPARATION FOR EVANGELISM

CHAPTER FIVE

THE PLACE OF PREACHING

"Only authentically biblical preaching can be really relevant; only vitally relevant preaching can be really biblical." [1]

Proclamation of God's Word belongs to the laity and clergy alike. But the ordained are called to preaching as a part of their full-time vocation. It is an evangelism responsibility. Any preacher worth salt is proprioceptive, sensing that among worshipers there will be seekers as well as finders, and that even among the faithful there will be those who need fresh confrontation with the claims of the living Lord. Authentic preaching can penetrate deeply into hearers' hearts. God depends upon preachers to pass on this transforming gospel, an awesome responsibility. Thus, preaching is an engagement in evangelism.

Jesus sets the example for preaching. Before he began, he spent many days in the wilderness, away from everybody, except from the Father and the ever-present Satan. He was strengthened by thwarting temptation, defeating the devil. The scriptures record, "Then Jesus, filled with the power of the Spirit, returned to Galilee, and a report about him spread through all the surrounding country." [2] The report was about his preaching. Jesus came out of the wilderness Spirit-filled and thus prepared to meet the demands and needs of the world.

When Jesus came to his hometown, Nazareth, he was invited to read from a scroll, the writing of Isaiah:

> "The Spirit of the Lord is upon me, because he has anointed me to bring good news to the poor.

> He has sent me to proclaim release to the captives
> and recovery of
> sight to the blind, to let the oppressed go free,
> to proclaim the year of the Lord's favor." [3]

Then he made a startling statement—"Today this scripture has been fulfilled in your hearing." [4] The reaction of his hearers? The townspeople tried to throw him off a cliff. They could not accept him or his message. Jesus came preaching and one of his first experiences was to be thrown out of town, literally!

I remember Roland Bainton, Quaker and world renowned Yale scholar on Luther, telling me in the privacy of my own home what his father told him: "Unless you have been thrown out of at least one congregation in your ministry, you haven't been much of a preacher!" In actuality, I have come pretty close! And, maybe some preacher reading this will take heart. Your Lord was rejected, too; not because of a bad sermon but because of proclaiming truth.

There are some essentials gleaned from Jesus, in preparation for preaching:

1) Set a time to be alone with God and the scriptures.

Preachers are familiar with the temptations of the devil! One is to wait too late in the week to prepare the Sunday message or speaking engagement. People can tell within two minutes whether the preacher is prepared or is talking from the dregs. There is no excuse for lack of preparation. It is sinful for a preacher to step into a pulpit without something burning from within. Jesus came preaching, after careful preparation.

Blessed is the preacher who can spend a few weeks away from the pulpit, away from the responsibilities of parish life, even away from family for a time, and concentrate on the Word, opening the heart and mind to the Spirit. An entire year of sermon planning can result. Wise is the congregation which insists their pastor(s) spends time apart in preparation for proclamation. Thoughtful is the congregation which provides time and funds for continuing pastoral education. The preacher needs to go back to seminary, hear others proclaim, and learn from homilists how they obtained their skills. Businesses send their administrators to seminars to expose them to new insights, to regenerate enthusiasm, and to prepare them for a higher level of performance. Smart is the parish which gives time for its pastor(s) to become drenched with the Spirit, and, to learn what is going on in the world of religion.

Furthermore, throughout the year, with week after week of consistent high level preaching expected, the pastor needs to get away from it all (including the telephone), to a kind of weekly "wilderness" experience, spending at least an entire day each week soaking up the scripture being planned to proclaim. Only emergencies need require the pastor's time. Mature messages come from a season of research and reflection. Any pastor too busy to set aside such a day each week (or some such plan) has not acknowledged the import of preaching.

Jesus did. That's why people, after hearing the Sermon on the Mount, remarked that he taught or preached "...as one having authority, and not as their scribes." [5] Evidently the scribes neglected to linger with God and did not ring true. The people sensed it. People are hungry and thirsty for the real thing, and know when they are listening to authentic preaching. They worship to catch more of the Spirit. The preacher can pass to them only what has been received from the Lord. That takes time alone with God and the Bible. There is no fast food place where God dishes out the Spirit on the spot. The Spirit comes when a person is open to Christ's promise to send the Spirit. There is no timetable. It just happens. That is what is meant by preparation. A person can rightfully step into a pulpit when prepared by God and only then. The ring of authority will reverberate from that pulpit when so prepared.

This means the proclaimer will spend time on more than the Book. God speaks in numerous ways, including through the secular world. Karl Barth once remarked, say some, that the preacher should have a Bible in one hand and the newspaper in the other. The late Joseph Sittler, theological professor at Chicago Lutheran Seminary, encouraged preachers to trot down to the newsstand, browse through the magazine rack, and find out what was going on. Read novels, poets, playwrights, book reviews, editorials. Go back over the classics. Keep up with the latest theological insights. In brief, one of the main responsibilities of a preacher is to be a reader. Take a speed reading course, if need be. Get into the habit of reading at least a book a week. The preacher needs to know what is going on with God as well as what is going on in God's world. (Television is not a substitute.) A reader never worries about having the right illustration at the right time.

Our Lord was a reader. He didn't have to fumble through Isaiah to find the right text for his inaugural sermon. He knew the exact place in the scroll.

Another characteristic of Jesus' preaching—he was an observer. He noted different occupations such as agriculture and fishing; knew about family life and how it is rearing two sons; appreciated the beauty of creation—the lilies in the fields, the birds of the air, the fig tree, landscapes; sensed power structures politically and religiously; and, he comprehended what it is like for people to be without right relationships. Jesus observed human beings in their habitat and spoke to their gut feelings. Jesus was no patsy who gave tidbits of advice on how to be happy and successful. Jesus didn't come as a psychologist; he came as a proclaimer of Good News which sets people free. We come to preaching by the way of Jesus—— "By this we may be sure that we are in him: whoever says 'I abide in him,' ought to walk just as he walked." [6]

That is the way of Kerygma—the apostolic proclamation of Our Lord. And that is why the Reformation principle of sola scriptura can be cherished. Luther thus observed, "To have scripture without the knowledge of Christ is to have no scripture, for scripture, rightly understood, contains nothing but Christ." We proclaim this same Jesus with authority.

2) Sense that you are anointed and sent.

Our Lord, in quoting the prophet Isaiah, mentioned two important words for the preacher—"anointed" and "sent."

Every clergy person can benefit by recalling words used on the occasion of ordination:

"According to apostolic usage you are now to be set apart to the office of the Word and Sacrament....Before Almighty God, to whom you must give account...I ask: Will you assume this office, believing that the Church's call is God's call to the ministry of Word and Sacrament?" The answer: "I will, and I ask God to help me." [7]

That was our anointment (whatever your Ordination Service stated), our return from the wilderness to do ministry, our recognition that we are set apart to proclaim the Good News. What a responsibility! And, privilege!

This is the frame of mind we need to take with us into the study and pulpit. In churches where a stole is worn, it symbolizes the responsibility of the pastor to proclaim the pure Word of God. Whether choosing to wear a stole or not, this is what the preacher is to do.

3) Give God's message to you time to mature.

The one day a week retreat (or whatever plan works for you), is primarily for research. It is more a day of accumulating information than it is a day of sermon writing. It is my habit to spend Tuesdays in research, often spending the entire day in the library, targeting material for a series of messages, spread over a span of weeks. Whatever text selected to proclaim, chosen weeks previously, I make sure I know the background of that scripture, as well as what it states. Wednesday through Friday mornings my study door is closed. The secretary is instructed to say to callers, "Pastor is studying; I would rather not disturb him. May I have him telephone you at noon." People are understanding. In emergency, she gives me a buzz. I labor to bring that scripture to light, using every commentary and resource available. My reading habits furnish illustrations and insights of others. Friday noon is the deadline for the message manuscript. In the afternoon, it is typed while I am at lunch and making hospital calls, ready to pick up before going home for dinner. (Copies are also produced for people to pick up after worship, in addition to tapes. We keep track of the number taken, clueing hearer interest.) I let the manuscript gel until Saturday evening, when I do my final practice session. Somehow, the time from Friday noon to Saturday evening, that message matures in my mind. Seldom do I go out Saturday night, and I go to bed early. I rise early on Sunday with time for prayer and practice, and a warm-up of the voice. I walk into that pulpit feeling I have given myself every chance to touch somebody's mind and heart, totally aware I am dependent upon God's blessing.

I am not trying to push my habits onto anybody. It is just one illustration of how it can be done.

While in seminary, I handed in an assignment in homiletics with these words: "Will this sermon do?" The professor replied, "Do what?!" That is the question confronting all preaching and all preachers: What will our messages do? A good practice is to write at the top of page one of every sermon manuscript the words: What will this sermon do?

Messages which are true to scripture and meet the needs of people include three elements: They are—biblical; relevant; persuasive.

Biblical Preaching

Preaching emanates from a Bible text. The word "text" comes from the Latin "texere" which means to weave. The fabric of the message has to hang together by the thread of eternal truth running throughout. This is not to conclude topical messages are erroneous; it is to emphasize sermons originate from scripture. "For since, in the wisdom of God, the world did not know God through wisdom, God decided, through the foolishness of our proclamation, to save those who believe." [8]

Robert J. McCracken cautioned, "...We shall do well to beware of what has aptly been called 'suburban' preaching, the type of preaching that is always out on the circumference of Christian truth. We shall likewise beware of flitting from text to text in the Bible according as casual interest, or idle fancy, or last minute desperation move us. It is our God-given duty to preach regularly and systematically about the basic and perennial themes——the Incarnation and the Atonement, (humankind's) exceeding sinfulness and God's exceeding grace, the life of faith and the life everlasting." [9] Great preaching proclaims great scriptural themes.

Relevant Preaching

Preaching is relevant when it sees life through the lens of God. Such authentic preaching maintains a proper balance between law and gospel. Marshall Wingfield wrote: "A good sermon cannot be made out of sanctimonious whining, bombastic bullroaring and declamatory tricks...A good sermon finds people where they live, and helps them to move on to better living, by feeding the mind, warming the heart, stimulating the imagination, kindling high resolutions, strengthening the will, and reassuring the soul." [10]

In the struggle for existence, people can lose hope and begin to question values. Pummeled by catastrophies to humankind heard and visualized around the world on a daily basis, struck by fear of foreboding doom, frustrated in the attempt to attain tranquility, shaken by economic instability around the world, society seeks an outlet and flirts with extremes in human behavior. The now has taken over. This age is bent on pleasure and expressions of suppressed inhibitions. Searching the scriptures for guidance in meeting these complex situations in life will necessarily drive the preacher back to the realism of the Christian faith. We do not have all the answers to life but we have enough answers to share God's great assurances. We can help give stability to life as we tell the News. Jesus makes sense in a senseless world.

In this realm of relevancy, we have a preaching heritage. The messages of Elijah, Isaiah, Jeremiah, Amos, and Jonah burn in our hearts. John the Baptist came preaching. Evidently John had a strong voice as his stirring messages sounded throughout the Jordan Valley. City-slickers left town to hear a person speak God's message. Because of his forthright preaching on the immoralities of the day, including the king's, he lost his life.

Paul was relevant as he dealt with the fallacies of human-made gods. He could not have planted all those Asia Minor churches without the ability of interpreting the times, exposing weak religious arguments in the light of the truth in Christ Jesus. He became the forerunner of inclusiveness, Gentile and Jew.

The whole Bible is a record of preaching truths applicable to life. After the Biblical preachers come Chrysostom, Ambrose, Bernard of Clairvaux, John Hus, Savonarola, Calvin, Luther, and a host of others—in the same vein.

Roland Bainton catches the significance of the sermon in Reformation times and how Luther felt about it:

"His pre-eminence in the pulpit derives in part from the earnestness with which he regarded the preaching office. The task of the minister is to expound the Word, in which alone are to be found healing for life's hurts and the balm of eternal blessedness. The preacher must die daily through concern lest he lead his flock astray." [11]

Bainton observed that Luther preached 2,300 sermons with the highest count for the year 1528, 195 sermons in a matter of 145 days.

And, there are those today who complain about not having time enough to prepare a solitary sermon for a Sunday! Put your heart into preaching the truths of God and something will happen in the lives of people who hear you.

Persuasive Preaching

Jesus was persuasive. Countless times religious leaders tried to put him into a corner, designing questions which they thought were unanswerable. Jesus saw through their trickery. He often anwered questions with a question of his own. For example, keeping every iota of the religious law was a hot issue in those days. Jesus asked: "Is it lawful to cure people on the sabbath, or not?" [12] The Pharisees and Scribes didn't know how to answer. Jesus insisted on an answer, after healing a man who had dropsy— a disease of an unnatural accumulation of watery liquid in some part of the body. He said, "If one of you has a child or an ox that has fallen into a well, will you not immediately pull it out on a sabbath day?" Scripture attests, "And they could not reply to this." [13] His way of answering questions reveals Jesus' persuasive power. He was crisp, concise, and clear in his teaching and preaching. There was no waffling. He taught and preached for a verdict. That was why Jesus was persuasive.

A persuasive preacher can expect a change of heart and mind among hearers. That's what happened after Peter's first sermon in Acts 2. His hearers were "cut to the heart" and asked "what should we do?" That sermon of Peter's changed thousands of lives.

In discussing this sermon with clergy, I point out that Peter's sermon was effective for five reasons: 1) He preached as if his own life and the lives of others hung in the balance; 2) He quoted scripture with a purpose; 3) He proclaimed the victory of God through Christ; 4) He preached for a verdict ; and 5) he kept to the point. Peter could have reviewed Holy Week events for hours. Instead, Peter preached for a verdict and people responded—"What should we do?" Peter didn't need to caucus the disciples for an answer. He simply said, "Repent, and be baptized every one of you." Peter's sermon prompted reactions like "More! More!" as Acts goes on to relate that " ...he testified with many other arguments...." and exhortations.

Analyze the sermons of great preachers in the Bible, especially Paul, and you will find those five ingredients. Study the manuscripts of great preachers who maintain listener rapt attention, and you will find those elements. Examine their craftsmanship. Take great proclaimers into your workshop. It is unnecessary to imitate their style; rather, digest their style of preparation and proclamation.

Robert Louis Stevenson, in one of his letters, wrote "I've been to church, and I am not depressed!" That's a chilly statement. Do church-goers expect to feel depressed after worship?! It need not be so. Go into the pulpit with the Good News, intent on redirecting lives, and expecting response.

At the bottom of the last page of every sermon manuscript write three questions: 1) Is this sermon from God's word? 2) Is it relevant, applicable to life today? 3) Is it persuasive, encouraging people to say "yes" to God in Christ?

*

Practice, Practice, Practice

Spend time practicing in front of a mirror or before a video camera. The fright of seeing oneself in action prompts a better delivery. There are pastors who preach with their hands and drive people to distraction. There are those who lack voice resonance and inflection, and congregations go away with the feeling there is no sure word from the Lord. The tone of voice, the excitement generated in hearing a person enthralled with the privilege of proclamation, can set a worship celebration on fire. LLoyd Ogilvie of Hollywood Presbyterian Church has a tone quality that makes people think God is talking! Try taping your message before you give it and listen to your own voice, detecting whether it is full of energy or if it has a tired sound. Wesley commented that people came to hear him because they wanted to watch him "burn."

*
Care For Your Voice

At one point in my ministry, I took the comment of a hearer seriously and went to a voice teacher. This teacher, an older lady in her eighties squinted with one eye, banged on the piano for me to follow with a sound, instructed me to put vaseline up my nose at night and "spit, Reverend Click, spit"! She gave me resonance. The congregation noticed the difference. James Mason, the actor, would often precede or follow me after a voice session. I asked him one time why he, an actor with such a great voice, kept taking these lessons. He replied that the voice always needed tuning. He further stated that he wished he could get his Church of England priest to take lessons!

It costs to take such lessons. This parishoner who gave me the suggestion also paid the cost. Regardless, I know that such an investment will pay dividends in the art of preaching. In 1991, I lost my voice for three months because of the removal of a malignant tumor on a vocal chord. During those months, I wondered whether I would ever be able to preach or teach again. I told myself that if I couldn't, at least I could write. Ah, the wonderful feeling when I could preach again! Thank God for the human voice. Cherish it. Take care of it. It is a gift from God.

*
Preaching Styles

Harry Emerson Fosdick revealed that in his earlier years he preached without notes. As the years went by he felt more comfortable with a full manuscript. Memory has a way of tricking us. If you saw Fosdick in action, however, you realized that he knew his manuscript so well that you could hardly tell he was reading.

Most preachers have tried different styles of proclamation. People love extemporaneous preaching and are fond of exclaiming, "He didn't have a single note before him!" That is commendable if the preacher has something to say and says it well. Too many times preachers have nothing to say and say it. I suspect a particular style of preaching is not all there is to it. The preacher, after thorough preparation, needs to feel comfortable as well as confident in delivery.

Some preachers have developed great memories and can give a sermon without notes. They work at it. It takes more time to give a sermon from memory than it does using notes or a manuscript. That's why most preachers do not preach without notes—because of the time element. Clarence Macartney wrote a whole book on this subject and entitled it PREACHING WITHOUT NOTES. One of the great preachers of America, Raymond Lindquist, when he was senior pastor of Hollywood Presbyterian Church, always amazed me by the way he preached from memory. We were members of the same Rotary Club, Los Angeles #5. Sitting next to him at a Rotary luncheon, I noticed he was writing furiously as the speaker was delivering his message, and the speaker was not one of our best. Supposing that he was taking notes, I said, "Ray, why are you taking notes? I haven't heard him say anything yet?!" Ray leaned over and whispered, "I am writing my sermon. I write it several times a day. It doesn't matter if I write it the same way. This is the way I get my message into my head. My memory is not all that great." That was his way of memorizing; he worked at it and it worked for him.

Bishop Fulton Sheen of the Roman Catholic Church was a communicator. He looked at ease before a televison camera. His chalkboard talks, with the "angel" erasing the board between television shots, were a delight for Roman Catholics and Protestants across the country. He was a forerunner of Vatican II. Protestants watched him with appreciation. He came across as human, one of us, which people do not always see in the clergy. His penetrating eyes reached people of all church persuasions. It might be a good idea to use a chalkboard for a Sunday message now and then.

Bishop Sheen and I used to cross paths on the way to work in New York City, stop and chat for a minute. We both wore clerical collars, and. homburgs! He knew I worked at the United Lutheran Church in America headquarters, 37th and Madison Avenues, in what was the old J. P. Morgan mansion. One spring morning, I asked him what he thought about Lent? He replied, "We have these three flights of stairs to climb to get to lunch, and frankly, during Lent it isn't worth the effort!" The Bishop had a great sense of humor. Appropriate humor has a place in preaching, changing the pace, reminding hearers that the preacher is human, but making a point. Scattered through the gospels are vivid illustrations of Jesus' humor. He said it was pretty difficult to push a camel through one of those Palestinian doorways!

There are preachers who need something before them. Billy Graham has his open Bible and notes which include quotes and paragraphs of paramount points he wants to make. During his New York City Crusade, during the fifties, our evangelism staff sat down with his people and suggested Billy go on salary, avoiding possible accusation that he was pilfering the crusade till. To Billy's credit, he did. To this day he is one of the most respected persons in the country. For decades the people of America, and people in countries around the world, have flocked to hear him proclaim the gospel. He is likely the most enduring and consistent gospel orator of this century.

It is not the purpose here to capsule the preaching style of all effective preachers. It is to say that we can learn from them. For example, Robert Schuler is a topical preacher with catchy (in the good sense) words and phrases that stick in the memory. He speaks to the needs of people, especially in the realm of mental health. His smile may appear forced; his style is not, however, for he communicates sincerity. He speaks with confidence and conveys possibilities. People drive for miles to hear a person like that.

Find a style of preaching that fits your personality. Several styles may be befitting. Congregations like variety. Try standing out from the pulpit and just talking with people. Try creating an outline that gives you more freedom than a manuscript. Try using a manuscript with as much hearer eye contact as possible.

There is an art in writing a message to be given orally. One of my seminary friends became a homiletical professor and wrote a book. Richard Carl Hoefler points out, "A good speech is like a bumble bee. It possesses five basic parts, each one playing a vital formation in the total process of the flight of the bumble bee: a head, a body, a stinger, legs, and wings. They enable both the bumble bee and the speech to get off the ground and into their work." [14] Maybe we need a few more "stingers" in our preaching to go along with the "soothers," especially when getting to verdict time.

Television has spoiled us. We wonder how politicians can look right at us, as if they are speaking without notes. Eye contact is essential in public speaking. They have teleprompters, of course. I often wonder why churches fail to use this device; preachers could look up instead of down. Evidently the cost has prevented us from doing it. Blessed is the congregation which invests in such an aid to preaching.

*

Sound Systems

With all our sophisticated electronics, there are still countless churches plagued with a hearing problem. What good for a worshiper to go to church and not be able to hear clearly? In churches where the preacher can be heard but not easily understood, attendances will falter and growth will be stymied.

There are church buildings better for music than for speaking, and others better for speaking than for music. Fortunate is the congregation with a building wherein both preaching and music can be heard and understood easily. Providing hearing aids for those who have difficulty hearing is a good thing to do, but too many people will let pride prevent them from requesting or using one. There is no substitute for an adequate sound system. Wise is the church which invests in the hearing of the gospel.

*

Evangelism is announcing God's victory through the life, death, and resurrection of Jesus Christ. In essence, this is the only message we have. Its announcement requires a response of "yes" or "no." God created the human voice, and its highest use is to proclaim this truth. How fortunate is any person, lay or clergy, blessed with a voice, commissioned to deliver this News!

Worship provides the setting for proclamation; it is evangelism time. Preaching is an evangelism voice, delivering the Good News— God's priority mail— in person.

*

The next chapter accents the role of the Holy Spirit as laity and clergy evangelize.

CHAPTER SIX

THE SPIRIT RECYCLES EVANGELISTS

"To evangelize ought to become in the believer a holy obsession, the essential atmosphere of his(her) daily living, the passion of his(her) soul, an unceasing exercise for the sake of his(her) own health."[1]

"One is Christianzed to the extent that he is a Christianizer. One is evangelized to the extent that he is an evangelist."[2]

What the Apostolic Church experienced, so should every church. THE ACTS OF THE APOSTLES, one of the most exciting books in all the Bible, is the record of what happened to the disciples after the fulfillment of Jesus' promise, "But you will receive power when the Holy Spirit has come upon you; and you will be my witnesses in Jerusalem, in all Judea and Samaria, and to the ends of the earth."[3] The record shows thousands came to believe as they told the story of Christ in the languages of the world.

They announced, "There is salvation in no one else, for there is no other name under heaven given among mortals by which we must be saved."[4] I don't hear the church talking like that today. Too often we sound as if we are just another religion in a long procession of religions. There are many imitations of Christianity; none can compare. God may be reaching people in other ways, even on other planets, but we do not know that. We do know salvation is through Jesus Christ. Jesus entrusted believers both past and present to say that. The apostles did and that is why the Christian church came into existence and thrived. They perceived the presence of God in their lives and went into action. Their experience in the upper room was passed on to others. "Awe came upon everyone, because many wonders and signs were being done by the disciples."[5]

The apostles understood what happened to them and knew it could happen to others. It never entered their minds to keep the Spirit (God) to themselves. If you have this Good News of Jesus, you intuitively pass it on. It is God's way of working through believers. In addition, when you act on the NEWS, something good happens to you—you are recycled by the Spirit. You come to realize God is in you, as he was in the apostles. For the apostles, Pentecost was not a one-act experience of receiving the Spirit and that is why they call the book THE ACTS OF THE APOSTLES. As the Spirit recycled the apostles, they were able to do great works for the Lord. Jesus told them that would happen: "Very truly, I tell you, the one who believes in me will also do the works that I do, and in fact, will do greater works than these, because I am going to the Father."[6] "Going to the Father" assured the coming of the Spirit. From that time on it meant the apostles, the early converts, and the Church throughout the ages including today, can receive the same Spirit. We are empowered by the triune God. The Apostolic Christian church was a dynamic force in the culture in which it lived because its members were energized by firsthand knowledge of God.

Schedules of churches can get so jammed with meetings and projects that it is easy for church people to equate activity with Christianity. Because the lights of the church building are on every night does not mean anything of consequence is occurring. Churches can deceive themselves by becoming engulfed in providing people with something for everyone. They can disillusion themselves by operating under the notion that if you give people what they want, they will keep coming. There is a concerted effort on the part of some mega churches to function on this premise. People may keep coming for awhile but it does not mean they are going anywhere in the kingdom. What people really want is a firsthand experience of God.

This firsthand experience of God is basically how the church thrives. If people go out the back door of a church, it is because they never really came in the front door—experiencing the Spirit. Or, entered a church by the back door or crawled through a window (accepted into membership with little or no teaching). The front door is to know God as a person even as we know one another as persons.

Non-believers ask legitimate questions: Who or what is the Spirit? How do you get the Spirit? How do you know when you have the Spirit? Why is it necessary to have the Spirit? What can the Spirit do?

Answers to these questions in clear and concise terms will meet the non-believer on his/her level. The Holy Spirit is the Spirit of the Father and the Spirit of the Son. You don't "get" the Spirit; the Spirit comes to you with the gift of faith. Those who are willing to trust God with their lives today and tomorrow and the day after are believers. The Spirit—God—can help any person live meaningfully and purposefully.

How do we retain the Spirit? We don't. God does. God recycles the Spirit in our lives daily, energizing our faith to act on his promises. This firsthand, front-door experience of God enables us to proclaim his presence.

Churches have difficulty motivating members to evangelize when they fail to teach people the basics: God made them; Christ reclaimed them; the Spirit enables them to tell others—"There is salvation in no one else...." If we are not passing on this News, we are failing God and people and ourselves. A Christian exists to tell the story of how God reconciles and recyles.

It is imperative that every Christian comprehend that once confessing Christ as Savior, there is the God-given responsibility to share this faith, and that by sharing the faith the Spirit recycles, renews our lives. To do this:

1) Teach people how to know God firsthand.

What good does it do to receive new members if we fail to teach them what it means to be Christian, which includes sharing the faith? It isn't enough to tell them about the nuts and bolts of the church's program, get their monetary pledge of support, enroll them in a class, and put them on a committee. The first thing we need to do is make sure they understand the faith. Nobody can give something away they do not have. Unless our new members are nurtured in the faith, they will be lost sooner or later. The key to the beginning of the Christian church was what they did after the baptisms. The new converts "...devoted themselves to the apostles' teaching and fellowship, to the breaking of bread and prayers." [7] People were added daily to the new church because the gospel was explained, illustrated, experienced, and then put into action. What is the good of truth if we do not share it?

2) Explain how the Spirit works.

God makes himself known throughout the ages, with the Bible being the beginning record. The New Testament makes it clear that the first business of Christian people was to tell others of Jesus Christ. When they did, something happened to them. The psalmist prayed, "...Do not take your holy spirit from me."[8] That is the only fear for Christians. If we lose the Spirit, we lose the zip and the zap and the zing and the zest for life.

Imagine a group of scientists upon discovering the cure for cancer or Aids or some other deadly disease. Would they stay in their laboratory and tell no one about it? Would they rejoice among themselves only, pop the cork and have a party? Of course not. They would call a press conference and announce to the world the results of their discovery. They would explain what can be done to eradicate the deadly disease and would tell it with excitement in their voices, consonant with first experience exhilaration, This good news would be too good to keep to themselves; they would have to tell somebody. The world would have to know. Then, they would get to work!

The Good News is far more beneficial to the world than the cure of cancer or Aids or any other disease which threatens human life. We dare not stay in our laboratories (church buildings) with our potluck suppers and programs. We dare not just sing our songs and say our prayers. We have to tell somebody that God has come in Christ; we have to tell it to the world, and, with enthusiasm.

The word "enthusiasm," from the Greek "enthousiasmos,"

is akin to the meaning of the Holy Spirit. It literally means being "in God." Strong excitement occurs with the coming of the Spirit. It rubs off on others. We become God's catalysts. It is as if heaven is poured into the hearts of believers. Enthusiasm is the yeast of evangelism.

3) Illustrate how this can be done.

Christianity is not complicated. It is telling another person how God makes contact with us and how we make contact with God.

When Lindbergh made his famous flight over the ocean to Paris, his single engine plane propeller had to be turned by hand in order for the engine to start. He had to say "Contact" which means the switch was on and the person on the ground could give the propeller a flip. It was only then that Lindbergh's engine started and kept going for the long journey to Paris. But, he needed the person on the ground to get him started. He flew alone. He didn't get started alone.

That's what we Christians are—people down on the ground turning the gospel propellers so that people can get their spiritual engines running for the long journey to be with God now and forever. We are the people who can help others get started on the journey of faith.

People can be taught how to do this during worship celebrations, at least once a month. On these occasions, illustrate how to invite another person to worship and to the INFORMATION TALKS FOR VISITORS (discussed in detail, Chapter Twelve).

An example: "Most people are brought to worship by a friend or relative. If that is true, and I think it is, you people are very important to God. God is depending upon you to invite others to 'come and see.' Members often ask how to do this. Do it your way, but here is an approach. Wherever you go ask people, 'What church are you a member of?' Assume they are members of a church in the area. If they are members of a church in the area, rejoice with them and invite them to share an idea or two about what is working well in their church. Share that information with your pastor or board member. If they are not members of a church in the area, invite them to worship the next Sunday. For example, 'Our worship celebrations are at 8:00, 9:30, and 11:00 a.m. Our church is located at....I can meet you in the narthex and we could sit together. After worship, I would like to take you to brunch or lunch. Which of the three times of worship is best for you?" Hand them The Card (your church card with the name of your church, address, times of worship, space for member to write their name.) Assume a positive answer. Of course, they can say 'no.' But, you have nothing to lose. Give it a try! If you can't afford brunch or lunch, omit that statement. Or, take the brunch money out of your tithe; it will be an investment. Moreover, you will feel good about issuing such an invitation and you will better understand how the Holy Spirit works through such invitations. The question is: Can God count on you to try?"

Just as one automobile can jump-start another, so Christians can be jump-starters for Christ and his church. Any church which teaches people how to be jump-starters will have few inactive members. This is one way the Spirit recycles people.

The Spirit recycles us, running enthusiasm through us again and again. God revs up our spiritual motors! This is how we keep spiritually healthy.

The Apostolic Church was exciting. Additions to the Church occurred every day. It had dimensions all its own. Think about them:

    1) They learned how to let the Spirit work through them, leading others to Christ and his church;

    2) They worshiped, prayed, recalled scripture, studied, listened, shared;

    3) They indicated by their attitude that they expected something to happen, as Jesus had promised (Acts 2:3-5);

    4) They accented prophetic proclamation, perceiving the times (a corrupt generation, Acts 2:40);

    5) They kept on target because people asked questions, "What shall we do?" (Acts 2:37) and they had ready answers;

    6) They knew how to sustain people in the faith (Acts 2:40);

    7) They had "koinonia"—a great friendship;

8) They were generous, happy, and not hung up on side issues (Acts 2:46);

9) They chose people to lead, after asking God's guidance, and didn't select people simply because they were available (Matthias, Acts 1:15-26);

10) They trusted each other;

11) They had few "collapsed members" (inactives who had lost the Spirit);

12) They were not caught up in competition (the Jews outnumbered them);

13) They were not consumed by social issues despite Roman oppression;

14) They did not have purchasing land and erecting buildings as priorities;

15) They praised God!

You can hide a church like that in an alley and people will find it. People were genuine. They had the Spirit. The preacher in GRAPES OF WRATH confessed he no longer preached because he lost the Spirit. Do you have the Spirit? Can God count on you to permit the Spirit to work through you by inviting others? People full of the Spirit, captured by the resurrection message, can fill the countless empty pews in the churches of America. And, God will fill such churches with the feeling of "awe."

An observation: If you have ever started, or been a member of, a new congregation, there is an outlook different from most established congregations:

* Enthusiasm is contagious;
* Reaching out and inviting others are common occurrences;
* Expectation of surprising new things to come to pass is readily understood;
* Strangers are welcomed;
* Everybody likes the pastor and one another.

A new congregation is dedicated to growth, not for the sake of growth but for the sake of the gospel, planting the seed of faith in the hearts and minds of others. It is a natural expectation. Talking to friends and strangers about God and his church becomes second nature.

Over the doorway of a church entrance (Dove of Peace, Tucson, Arizona) are these words: "Expect a miracle!" Churches which expect miracles, as the Apostolic Church, will experience them. The same power and the same Spirit are available to the church today, as stirringly as when the Christian church first began. God's power has not diminished. We are the ones who need recycling by the Spirit, again and again The Holy Spirit is always available in plentiful portions.

There are numerous ways the Spirit recyles us. I will demonstrate and document this in succeeding chapters.

CHAPTER SEVEN

THE TEAM SPIRIT: LAITY AND CLERGY

"A good objective for many local congregations would be to deploy approximately 50 percent of its leaders in mission and outreach in the community and the other 50 percent in the accomplishment of programs within the local church itself."[1]

In evangelism, both laity and clergy have the same role. Anyone confessing Christ as Savior is commissioned by Christ to make other disciples. Laity and clergy are responsibile for planting the seed of faith. God counts on both.

Call Committees (now dubiously labeled "search" committees, as if somebody is being hired to do something instead of being called by God in Christ to a specific parish) sometimes conclude that their job is to look for three characteristics in a pastoral candidate: 1) Can this candidate preach? 2) Can this candidate bring in more money? 3) Can this candidate bring in more members? Any candidate fulfilling that list of requirements is likely to be called. This is poor theology. It reduces a pastor to the level of a hired hand. It fails to sense what the church is in existence for and misinterprets the role of a pastor. It would be better if they included in their questioning a more penetrating question: Can this pastor teach people how to become evangelists? If a candidate indicates that evangelism is not his/her "bag," as one pastor told me, the candidate could do the church a favor by switching to another vocation.

A question could be asked of seminary administrators and

professors: Are you training potential pastors to teach church members the meaning of evangelism and how to do evangelism in a parish? Our Lord was primarily a teacher. It is the role of a pastor to teach evangelism.

During the depression of the 1930's our family moved to a farm, after a decade in a city. As a town boy of fourteen, I didn't have the first notion what it meant to be a farmer. In order to make ends meet and in addition to farming, my father drove a bread truck 150 miles a day. As the only son, it became my lot to help as much as I could, not only learning how to milk cows and slop the hogs, but to learn how to use farm implements and work horses. Since my father had to get up at 3:00 a.m., he would show me the night before how to harness the horses, work a plow or a disk or a hay rake. We couldn't afford a tractor, something new on the farm in those days. Dad would say, "If you have any trouble, I will explain what went wrong and how to fix it." Both my mother and father were mechanically minded. I was not.

We had two horses. One was blind; the other became the lead horse. One day I was at a neighbor's farm helping thresh, as farmers did in those days. The thresher was placed on an incline. I couldn't get Bill and Molly to pull my wagon, loaded with wheat, up to the thresher. I was embarrassed. Just then my father, home from the bread route early that day, appeared. He climbed up on the wagon, took ahold of the reins evenly in his hands, shouted in his gruff, authoritative voice a command to Molly and Bill that they must have thought was God's, whipped the reins over their buttocks, and away we went right up to the thresher. Afterward, Dad said: "Son, you not only have to get the attention of those horses, you have to get them to pull together. You had one horse going forward while the other was going backward. When they pull together, they can pull a big load like that, even if one horse is blind." I never forgot that lesson. Molly and old Bill and I ploughed many a field, planted acres of corn, operated a heavy manure spreader, and pulled wagon loads of hay into the barn.

Parenthetically, the laity and the clergy are like two horses. Together they can plough, plant, cultivate, nourish, and pull together so that the dear church reaps a harvest. When lay people and pastors hear the authoritative voice of Christ and work together as a team, the crop of evangelism can get to the "thresher."

The disciples didn't do evangelism all alone. They employed new converts to the faith; taught them how to plow, plant, cultivate, nourish, and pull together. This is the lesson we need to learn from Christ and the disciples, and never forget.

The Apostolic Church and the Early Church grew because their converts understood that the faith given to them was too good to keep to themselves and belonged also to others. That is the responsibility, heavy as it might seem, awesome as it is, of every Christian whether a lay person or pastor. No committee can hire somebody else to do what all of us are commissioned by God to do—to publish glad tidings.

1. The role of a pastor in evangelism.

The responsibility of a pastor is to teach parishioners the why and the how of evangelism, and to demonstrate it. A pastor failing to make evangelism the primary pastoral work, fails God and the flock. Single out any church that is growing and invariably you will find a pastor who believes in the first business of the church, and is doing something about it. Pastors who complain that they are not in a growing area and thus their church cannot grow give in too easily. There are countless people in the arena of the world lacking a loving relationship with God. Our job is to locate them. Church homeless people aren't likely to knock on our church doors, since they do not see the need of a church; we have to go after them. Thus, the pastor's role is to teach parishioners the meaning of evangelism, why it needs to be done, how to do it, and then work alongside members in reaching out to others.

The ministry is a wonderful vocation. God recognized that, if he was going to reach all people in the world, he would need people like John the Baptist to prepare the way. John didn't pretend to be somebody he was not; he knew who he was—a forerunner. As Isaiah points out "...prepare the way of the Lord, make straight...a highway for our God" and make "...the uneven ground...level."[2] The pastor, then, is no more and no less than a pick-and-shovel person, preparing the way for our King.

a) Reexamine your ordination rite.

A pastor is an evangelist by the nature of the call to the ministry. Read Jeremiah 23:1-4, Romans 10:6-15, Matthew 9:36-38, John 21:15-17, Luke 10:2-11,16, what Paul said to Timothy (I Timothy 3:1-7), and what Jesus said to the disciples after his resurrection (John 20:19-23). Recall the prayers said on your behalf at the time of ordination. A portion of the prayer at my ordination were these words: "...We heartily pray Thee, give Thy Holy Spirit plenteously to these Thy servants, to us, and to all who are called to the Ministry of Thy word, that we, with a great company, may be Thy true evangelists, and continue faithful and steadfast against the world, the flesh, and the devil, that Thy Name may be hallowed, Thy kingdom come, and Thy will be done...." [3] Those words still make my spine tingle! And assuredly, you noted, the phrase about being "...Thy true evangelists...." Written in old English style, the words still leap out at any servant of the Word. In your ordination rite, you were called to be an evangelist. That is your first business. Evangelism is the heart of a pastor's role.

b) Illustrate what it means to be an evangelist.

A Methodist pastor-friend gave me a bit of advice: "Dale, they may not remember your sermons; they will remember your hospital visits." There is insight. After that I never missed any person hospitalized, especially on Christmas, Good Friday, and Easter.

Making direct contact with people, by telephone or visit, is imperative. It is good to proclaim the gospel from a pulpit; it is also obligatory to hit the road, as Jesus did. Our role is to demonstrate the gospel.

c) Manage time for evangelism.

If time manages pastors, they become clock-watchers instead of soul searchers. Many church boards require a monthly written report from their pastor indicating the number of contacts (telephone calls, interviews, counseling sessions, home visits, hospital visits, meetings, etc.) made. That practice may or may not give the board insight as to how the pastor spent time. A better question would be: How many segments of time (mornings, afternoons, evenings especially), did the pastor spend in evangelism inreach and outreach?

Church business hours are day and night—we never close—but especially during three crucial hours at night, six-thirty to nine-thirty. Pastors who spend an evening or two each week keeping in touch with members by telephone, will discover previously unknown personal concerns and needs, and thus become more effective. Pastors who work two evenings a week telephoning POSSIBLE members will witness church growth. The telephone saves time, an antenna which indicates whether a personal visit is required. In these days, the automobile allowance of pastors might very well include a telephone in the automobile. Sales people and executives know such an instrument multiplies their energy.

Clergy unwilling to spend three or four evenings per week contacting people individually, readily complain they don't have time because of countless meetings and other duties. It is a matter of deciding which is more important—individuals or the machinery of the church? If administrative duties are preventing a pastor from making necessary personal contacts, invite the laity to share their management skills. The laity do many things better. Trust the laity. Ministers who do enjoy mutual trust. One way to utilize pastoral time in reference to committee work: schedule one monthly meeting for all committees. At this monthly get-together of committees, go from one committee to another, sharing ideas, asking and answering questions. In addition, prior to committee meetings, have a telephone conference with each committee chairperson concerning special issues that may come up.

d) Exemplify what it means to be a whole person in Christ.

There will be pastors unwilling to spend the required number of evenings on inside and outside evangelism because they want to be with their families at night. Such ministers might very well revise their schedules so they get to the church at noon and spend the mornings at home; or, do church work in the morning, home in the afternoon, and church work at night. Any minister who spends five nights a week in the Lord's work will be a blessing to others. Night shift pastors are in the people business!

It usually takes at least 60 hours a week to do an ordained ministerial job. Business executives consider 60 hours a week rather normal. We don't have to be glued to the job. We can, however, make time count. God gives us the gift of time to make a difference. We have only a limited number of pulpit appearances in a lifetime, a limited number of days and nights to reach people.

Make time count for the Lord and his church. A typical pastor's schedule for a week could be organized along these lines: 20 hours for research, writing, and preparation for delivery of messages and teaching opportunities; 20 hours for reaching people by telephone or in person (including counseling, hospital and home visits); 20 hours for administration. Look for the balance in your schedule. An imbalance can disrupt the rhythm in your ministry. How blessed pastors are to have such a varied schedule. Most of us have little direct supervision. How we spend our time is mostly up to us. Where in the world can you find another job like that?!

I must confess that in my early ministry, when the telephone would ring around 6:00 a.m., I would literally jump three feet out of bed and get to the telephone before it rang twice. I was afraid my parishoners would find me in bed at 6:00 a.m.! I always thought I had to be up and at 'em even if I had been up until 3:00 a.m. with some disconsolate soul. Yes, it was a sense of insecurity. It was necessary to work that out so that I could feel good about the way I spent time. When I shared these feelings with the church board, explained how I spent my time, how I felt about keeping a balance of time among those three areas of research (including prayer), people, and desk work, they were overjoyed. They were not so keen about pastoral reports including all those statistics of how many of this, and how many of that. They appreciated a responsible sense of time, used in the most fruitful way. When I took time to play golf, I didn't feel guilty about it and my game improved! I wish for every pastor, especially the younger ones, a kind of schedule wherein they feel comfortable about how time is spent on church work. Sixty hours a week for the work of the Lord and his church is an approriate amount of time. What doesn't get done (and all of it never gets done), leave in the hands of the Lord. Trust God about time. He knows you need time for family and time for physical exercise. He knows you need time for reading, soaking up the scriptures, and time for prayer. After the church work of 60 hours, you have 108 hours of the week left. Getting proper sleep means another 56 hours. You have 52 hours left to eat, keep the body clean, spend time seeing a movie or watching some televison or going to a ball game, mowing the lawn and making repairs, or doing whatever you desire. Now, don't you feel better already?!

Enroll in a Time Management Course, if you feel the need. How time is spent is serious business. Even people in the ministry have turned to alternatives (alcohol, drugs, etc.) in order to survive the pressure. Working out a time schedule that meets your needs contributes to a sense of well-being. Jesus took time to be whole. He liked to do many things: sailing; fishing; preparing breakfast on the beach; eating lunch or dinner with somebody; walking; telling stories; visiting in homes; healing; stopping to talk to somebody on the street; asking questions; sharing truths; praying; going off alone. He made time count. In three years he turned the world around. God only gives us so much time for kingdom work. We can make the most of it, feel good about the wonderful work entrusted into our hands, and enjoy life with all its blessings. A whole pastor helps make whole people.

e) Expand your evangelism library.

Pastors have hundreds of books. Authors are friends. Scan through your library. What proportion of them are on the subject of evangelism? Are there old and newer books on evangelism? When did you share one of these books with your evangelism chairperson and committee? Have you given the church library a list of evangelism books?

At the back of this book is a list of evangelism books for further reading. Authors come from different churches, offering varying points of view. They provide new insights, different ideas for church program. They help us delve further into the subject of evangelism. As long as a person searches for understanding, ideas will come. Pass the list on to your people. Call attention to books by listing them in the bulletin and newsletter. Publish an evangelism book review. Quote them in messages. Help the laity to understand something of the depth, breadth, and length of evangelism.

f) Write a course on evangelism for your people.

Try it. You will discover how much you do and don't know about evangelism. Pray about how you might be instrumental in motivating people to embrace evangelism as a way of life. Give them a good taste for the word evangelism. Teach the theology of evangelism, evangelism in the Bible, and how they can get power for their lives. Relate to them the story of the Christian church, how the church has remained in existence because people passed the message on. Review the ministry of Jesus Christ, how he involved people in his plan of redemption, and what his plan is for us today. With the laity, work out a plan of evangelism for your parish. Pray with them about it. By the power of the Spirit, stir people into action.

II. The role of the laity in evangelism.

Every Christian is an evangelist since we testify to our beliefs by what we say and do. The church member who goes to worship without endeavoring to retrieve people for Christ is missing the reason for existence. People say, "I don't know why I was ever born." "I don't have any real purpose in living." "I don't know why God lets me keep on living." "I feel lost." "I don't belong in this world." "My life doesn't amount to much." "I feel useless." All of these weary people can find new meaning in life when they start being "Retrievers." Even a dog can learn to fetch a stick and take it to his/her owner. God sends us out to retrieve people he has made, bringing them back to be in touch with him, bringing them back to new life in Jesus Christ. All of us have been retrieved by God. Now, we are RETRIEVERS for God!

There are eighteen specific ways the laity can be evangelists:

1) Read what the Bible says about the people of God as evangelists: Proverbs 14:25, Isaiah 52:7, Daniel 12:3, Matthew 4:19, Matthew 28:19, Mark 13:10,11, Mark 16:14,15, Romans 1:16, Ephesians 4:11, II Timothy 4:5.

These references pertain to laity and clergy. Clergy are simply full-time (usually) servants of God in the church. We are all full-time Christians, given the responsibility of announcing the Good News.

2) Study books on evangelism. They will broaden your view of what evangelism is and what is entailed in carrying out the thrust of evangelism in your parish. These books will help feed your soul and give you more confidence as you endeavor to motivate and inspire others in becoming evangelists. An informed laity can help return any church to its first business. Your pastor will appreciate the fact that you have done your homework, especially if you tell him/her that you want to be one of God's evangelists.

3) Suggest to your pastor that he/she preach a series of messages on evangelism. Offer to participate in a dialogue sermon. People listen to lay people when they preach, too.

4) Propose to your pastor that he/she teach a course on evangelism. Be a jump-starter by helping to enlist attendees. Offer to assist in the teaching. People like to hear members teach also, especially when there is evidence of research and solid preparation.

5) Go with your pastor to the church board and present the need of an EVANGELISM OUTREACH COMMITTEE and an EVANGELISM INREACH COMMITTEE, if you do not have these. (See Chapter Nine, WHERE TO BEGIN, for details.) Suggest that the Board review the talents of the entire congregation and select those members who might best serve as evangelists on these committees. Offer to help enlist these committees.

6) Be a "LOOKOUTER" for visitors in worship. Look for visitors at worship time and encourage other members to do the same. Without being aggressive, aid visitors in following the worship format and help them to feel at home. People do react positively to attention and genuine friendliness. When I contact first-time visitors, I listen for that word "friendly." If a visitor exclaims "unfriendly," the next Sunday I tell members what the visitor said (without the use of a name, of course).

7) Seek instruction on how to visit POSSIBLE Members. (How do you know whether you can do this without trying?) Learn

how and if it works out, volunteer to instruct others. (See Chapter Eleven for details.)

8) Serve as a telephoner of first-time visitors. Thank visitors for the privilege of worshiping with them (not the other way around!) and write down their first impressions of your church. If they are members of another church, ask them what is working well in their congregation. If they are without a church home in the area, tell them about the next INFORMATION TALKS FOR VISITORS (see Chapter Twelve).

9) Give a temple talk on members becoming evangelists. For example: "How I Found Something I Have Been Looking For All My Life!"? (What you found, of course, is that God calls every Christian to tell others about God in Christ.) Relate how God has redirected your life since this discovery.

10) Be a "LOOKOUTER" for Possible Members. (You will find help in Chapter Eleven.) A hundred pairs of eyes are better than the pastor's one set. Your eyes and the eyes of the parish are to be on the lookout for people without Christ and without a church home, beginning with our own family and friends. There are church "homeless" people out there.

11) Help new people become adjusted in their new church home. (See Chapter Fourteen). Samuel Chadwick, saddened by how he and his church permitted new members to lapse (I call it "collapse"), made a startling statement: "It was like putting a baby in the arms of a corpse." We need churches that are alive and care for all people, members and new members.

12) Set aside one evening a week to be an evangelist. Any lay person who will set aside at least one evening a week in either outreach or inreach evangelism, will see his/her church grow in strength. Not only sing "O For a Thousand Tongues to Sing" but "O For a Thousand Lay Visits or a Thousand Telephone Calls Made"! People want to know these days how they can make a difference. This is one of the ways.

13) Look at your church's list of Possible Members and pray over each name. What does this do? It frames the mind in thinking "people" and reminds you that these are real people who

need Christ and his church. Moreover, it is a way of inviting God in on your evangelism thrust.

14) Invite people to worship and to the INFORMATION TALKS FOR VISITORS. Chapter Twelve details how this fourteenth point can be accomplished. It is the responsibility of all members to invite and take people to the INFORMATION TALKS FOR VISITORS. As an evangelist, you will want to make a point of doing this prior to each new series of the INFO TALKS.

15) Walk your neighborhood and find out who does not have a church home, invite them, and give the names, addresses, and telephone numbers to the EVANGELISM OUTREACH COMMITTEE. Learn how best to approach your neighbors. (See Chapter Ten—Good Neighbor Visits.)

16) Be responsive to people in daily life, their needs and feelings, and give encouragement to become followers of Christ. You, along with St. Paul, are not "...ashamed of the gospel; it is the power of God for salvation to every one who has faith...." [4]

17) Sense the joy of being an agent of Christ and that your life is important in extending the kingdom. "The seventy returned with joy, saying, 'Lord, in your name even the demons submit to us!'" [5]

18) Realize that evangelism for the Christian is as natural as breathing and that you have been sent into the world to announce God's story. "Then I heard the voice of the Lord saying, 'Whom shall I send, and who will go for us?' And I said, 'Here am I; send me!'" [6] "Go therefore and make disciples of all nations...." [7]

If you do your homework, you will think of many more ways that will be applicable to your congregation's evangelism. As a member of Christ's church, you are an evangelist.

*

The laity and the clergy, joining efforts to reach out to people and combining to sustain members in the faith, are God's team. There isn't a better team in the NFL or the NHL or in the Olympics. Both the laity and the clergy have similar responsibilities. In some churches, laity are commissioned to take The Lord's Supper to the shut-in, a vital part of evangelism. The church that has a team spirit will make evangelism the first business of the church, doing what comes naturally for Christians.

*

The next chapter considers the equipment evangelists need.

CHAPTER EIGHT

EQUIPMENT FOR EVANGELISM

"We should be clear that when we speak of mission and evangelism, we are not speaking of some variables that might belong to this or that model of the church constructed by the theological imagination. Mission and evangelism are invariable structures of the church, firmly embedded in the apostolic traditions of our Lord's final summons to his disciples."[1]

No church or evangelist in history possessed better evangelism equipment than the modern church. Can't you just hear the disciples exclaim, "Lord, why didn't we have computers, laser printers, fax machines, and telephones? Why didn't we have automobiles and airplanes? Televising our messages could have changed the Roman Empire within our lifetime!" You and I have access to the miracles of communication in this last decade of the twentieth century that first century Christians never dreamed about.

The Lord changed water into wine. We changed the clock by electronics and engineering, enabling us to accomplish more in less time and traveling faster than any generation in history. Jesus and the disciples walked everywhere on dusty roads; we have autos to whisk us from place to place. We fly. From this side of the ocean, we can watch worshipers celebrate Christmas in Bethlehem at the site of the manger. We can telephone thousands of miles in seconds; even talk to people on the telephone while riding in an automobile, or see people on the other end of the telephone. We can send a complete set of plans via fax. With all these capabilities people declare, "Who needs God?"

All of this has happened in a lifetime. My mother died January 1, 1993, after 108 and a half years of life. She saw the Wright boys fly a fragile piece of fabric called an airplane; abandoned her horse and carriage for one of those Model T Fords; heard about Lindbergh crossing the Atlantic over a crackling crystal set called a radio. When she saw her son on television she marveled exclaiming, "It's a miracle." She saw and heard rockets launched into space, noted the staggering advancements of humankind in a single century; but, she never asked the question: Who needs God?

The modern evangelist, dependent upon manufactured skills instead of God's creative Spirit, will fail to communicate the Good News. In order to evangelize, we need the source of all energy—God's Holy Spirit.

l. The evangelist needs the Spirit, before any of the miraculous gadgets.

Paul said we are to "...equip the saints for the work of ministry...."[2] First on the list of equipment is God's gift of the Holy Spirit. (I emphasized the power of the Holy Spirit, especially in Chapters Two and Six.)

The Holy Spirit enabled the apostles to go into all the known world and make disciples. He does the same for us. The pastor or lay person who goes evangelizing without depending upon God's help, however, will fail. The church that doesn't have anything with which to evangelize except worn-out traditions and frail faith will fail. We cannot do it on our own. Every Christian has to have the Spirit in order to evangelize.

The apostles unlocked the upper room door, walked out and faced a hostile generation, a generation that killed the Savior and accused them of being drunk, because the Holy Spirit unlocked their hearts and minds. They were changed from coward-likeness to Christ-likeness. This generation is hardly different.

The Holy Spirit is a gift to all believers. He comes as we set about doing evangelism. The church or person who wonders where the Spirit is need only try making disciples. The Spirit comes as we endeavor to draw people to the Savior. It doesn't matter what kind of building we worship in; it does matter if those inside the building have the Spirit. Even a poor church building will not turn everybody off if the congregation has the Spirit. Those who have the Spirit will draw others to the Savior. Ask yourself the question: Do I have the Spirit? Ask another question: Does the congregation have the Spirit? The explanation to the third article of the Apostles' Creed (Luther) might very well have an addendum: "I cannot by my own understanding or effort bring others to Christ and His church. But the Holy Spirit has called me to plant the seed and nourish it." It is the Spirit who "...calls, gathers, enlightens, and sanctifies the whole Christian church on earth...."

God's presence—the Holy Spirit—is our first need. There is ample supply. The Bible promises, "...he gives the Spirit without measure" (John 3:34b). God never withholds the Spirit from any evangelist.

2. The evangelist needs the Bible.

Ministerial students in the past were required to take Hebrew and Greek, languages of the Bible. They were trained to translate from the original tongue and to do research, digging out the insights of scripture for the benefit of hearers. As in Reformation times, when the Bible was chained in the library and only priests and scholars read the scriptures, pastors of the recent past were reported to be keepers of Biblical kernels of truth. When it came to understanding the Bible, the laity were dependent upon pastors.

All that has changed within the last few decades. A ministerial student today may not even take Hebrew and Greek, although there is explicit value in doing so. Now laity and clergy have available a multitude of translations to choose from, helpful in comprehending God's message. The NEW REVISED STANDARD VERSION of the Bible, published in 1990, takes out the sexist language and thus, we have a Bible that is used in many of our churches. The discovery of manuscripts (Dead Sea Scrolls), the painstaking research over many years—help us all to understand the Bible better. Commentaries, concordances, dictionaries, and maps aid the serious student of the Bible. There is no excuse for not knowing what God has to say to every generation. Chapter Three emphasized the importance of the Bible in evangelism. It is our tool to tell God's story.

3. The evangelist needs evangelism courses taught by people who know the why, what, when, and how of evangelism.

The disciples had an advantage with Jesus as their teacher. They didn't learn evangelism by having a fast food supper, a brief instruction, shoved a handful of 3x5 cards, and told to go out and make disciples. Even the "seventy" (Luke 10) were given detailed instruction about going in pairs, how difficult it might be, what to take with them, where to go, what to do when they got there, and how long to stay at a place. Jesus even told them, in specifics as well as in a general way, what to say and how to react when not well received. The scriptures attest that when they returned, they "...returned with joy,"[3] surprised that Jesus' instruction worked so wonderfully! How did Jesus react? He "...rejoiced in the Holy Spirit"[4] and gave thanks.

The point is: there was some solid teaching given before any of these people went out to make friends and influence people for Christ. There was nothing haphazard about it. The disciples had three years of intensive evangelism instruction. The "70" had less time. In both cases, however, people were prepared to evangelize.

The church needs people who can teach others how to evangelize. A far too repeated pattern in the church is for the pastor to round up the usual few who do this kind of thing, read a Bible verse or two, pray a little, give them a few minutes of instruction, and send them out calling on those who attended worship one Sunday. In contrast, the Kennedy program in Florida, designed to have an experienced visitor take along an inexperienced caller, demonstrating techniques, has a lot of merit. This helps some overcome fear about making home visits. The fallacy in the Kennedy program is that the presentation can become canned.

If we are going to develop a number of communicators of the good news, we will need to start by offering people courses on the meaning of evangelism. It is not just a matter of technique; it is a matter of understanding why we are doing evangelism in the first place. Offering courses with real substance on the subject of evangelism, without any obligation to make calls, can plant seeds in the minds and hearts of believers for the necessity of sharing the good news, whether in formal calling or informal evangelism. Providing a plan of evangelism education can make it possible for a large percentage of members to comprehend the basics of evangelism.

4. The evangelist deserves the best up-to-date equipment.

Church administrators can learn from business what equipment can best serve the church in reaching and sustaining people in the faith. In most churches, there are members able and willing to share their expertise (if invited). Yet, why is the church slow in obtaining equipment to do the best job possible, in the quickest and most efficient manner? We know the answer: it is because church boards are notorious for not spending money on equipment. Board members will use nothing but the best in their own business and yet shortsightedly settle for less for their church. The smaller church is usually penalized here. Wise is any church board which sets aside investment money for equipment. Just as Jesus needed a colt for his ride into Jerusalem, so the church needs equipment to reach the hearts of people in the community. As quickly as possible, equip your church. The following are the A,B,C's of present-day evangelism equipment:

A. Copier(s). (Facilitates the production of the bulletin, provides material for meetings, keeps people informed.)

B. Computer(s). (Enables tracking of member attendance, tracking of Possible Members, accumulates and assimilates talents in the congregation, provides data about giving habits, serves as a word processor, makes library lists, stores inventory data, plus stores records of your choosing.)

C. Telephones. (A bank of telephones for member and Possible Member calling. In a world of busy people, one of the best ways to communicate.)

5. The evangelist needs a library.

Books are expensive. The evangelist, however, needs to know what others are thinking and doing in evangelism. If you are serious about being an evangelism person, you will haunt the library and accumulate books for your home library. One of the best things a church can do is to stock up on evangelism books. Give people necessary knowledge on the first business of the church.

*

There is the basic equipment for evangelists: the Spirit of God, the Bible, evangelism courses, copier, computer, telephone, and an extensive library. Where money is required to obtain them, smart saints will find a way.

Part III, beginning with the next chapter, portrays how evangelism in a parish can be started and accomplished.

PART III

OUTREACH EVANGELISM

CHAPTER NINE

WHERE TO BEGIN

"Evangelism is not a thing in itself; rather it is the by-product of the Church being the Church."[1]

    If you were starting a new congregation, there would be no question about where to begin. An organizing pastor would first go from house to house knocking on doors, hunting for people without a church home. After finding "seventy" (or whatever number a church body might require) willing to "come and see," an opening worship date would be scheduled. Letters of invitation would be sent to all on the Possible Member list. Prior to the great day, every household in the area would receive a telephone call reminding them of the opening worship. It would be important to have a sizeable crowd in attendance on that first day, giving credibility to the need. Among the 70 will be those willing to make contacts also. The more people involved, the more they feel a kind of ownership—a responsibility for the new church's birth. You, as the "Jump-start" pastor, know that you cannot do this alone. You invite people into your home to pray about the opening day.

    Of course, it would be necessary to spend money to advertise the event—"New Church To Begin This Sunday." You would give a little background of who you are and what church body you represent, if any. It doesn't matter that there is no church building; it doesn't bother the 70 either. There is something exciting about starting a new congregation. The 70 broadcast the news, person to person. You get on radio and television as a part of the station's public information, arrange an interview with a newspaper editor, and get your picture in the newspaper. You and the 70 really get pumped up about the opening. Nothing is left to chance. Posters are made up and businesses invited to display them in a window. Calling cards are printed and prior to the opening, you and the 70 give them to people, even in the supermarket! All of you try to think of ways to announce the good news that a new church is about to begin.

You and the 70 make up a special bulletin for the first Sunday of worship. The Service is printed out so that any new person can follow it with ease. Nursery care is arranged so that parents coming with infants and toddlers will be able to concentrate on worship. A pianist is recruited and a volunteer offers to sing, and another to play an instrument. You make up a children's message that will get their attention. You write the main message in such a way that anybody coming to worship for the first time will know what you are talking about and will want to come back. No talk about a beautiful building because you don't have one. No word about how friendly the people are in the congregation because there isn't one yet. You talk about God's plan for every human being and how God demonstrated who he is in Jesus Christ. The message needs to come from the heart, you conclude. Eye contact will be important. You decide to lay aside the carefully prepared manuscript, stand in front and talk. You ask God to help you to be winsome without appearing clever, convincing without seeming manipulative, loving without being gushy. You pray for genuineness on that opening day.

The great day comes! Only twenty-five percent of the people invited come. Some of the 70 had a conflict in schedule. Nevertheless, there was a beginning. And, the work of contacting more people day in and day out consumes the major portion of your time. No board meetings or committee meetings to attend. However, as time goes on, there is the need to appoint a steering committee, before organization day looms. New people to the Christian faith are instructed. More messages are prepared, bulletins produced and printed, and publicity goes out. And, of course, if you are connected with a national church body, you have to give reports. But, your main goal right now is to reach as many people as you can so that you will have at least one hundred charter members for organization, in a matter of months. Organization day comes! The 70, and many more, rejoice that a church is born. All of the effort was worthwhile.

Now, take a look at this imaginary congregation twenty years later. There is a building to keep up and debt payments to be made; a church board to placate from time to time; money is tight; more teachers for the Sunday Church School are needed; youth programs need help; and, the neighborhood is changing. The percentage of older people has increased; few charter members remain; a handful of the 70 are still around and conclude that it is time for somebody else to pitch in and take over the church chores, because the same people have been doing almost everything for years. The church grows but the number of people who leave makes the membership stay almost the same. The new people haven't been in on the beginning, and haven't caught the old spirit. You are getting tired of pushing things and you feel like the pastor who went through the woods, sat down, and watched the train go by, thankful to watch something he didn't have to push. Everybody seems to leave the job of church growth in the pastor's lap. Nobody seems to have any time to make visits. There are personalities in the congregation who seem to control things and want their way all the time. Few want to try anything new. The old traditions are worn out but nobody seems to notice. The building needs repair. You begin to feel that you have done all you can for that congregation. Inside yourself, thankful that you were the organizing pastor, you hope you will be "outta here" before the twenty-fifth anniversary rolls around. Things are going downhill and the congregation may fold before that time. You better get out while you can. After all, you need to guarantee your future and have some feeling of security for your family. You are ready for a call to "St. Elsewhere".

Let's look back at that imaginary congregation and its imaginary pastor and see what has happened. Notice that at the beginning there was enthusiasm and expectation, and the focus was on reaching out to people. After some years, the focus was on surviving. The illustration is stretched but describes what can happen to a congregation when the first business of the church is set aside. What do we learn from it?

1. Start with focus.

A congregration needs focus. Ask questions: Where is my congregation going? Where has it been? What do we stand for? What are our emphases? What are our strengths and weaknesses? On what are we spending our energy and resources? If someone were to take a picture of our congregation, what would it look like? For what are we known? An adjustment of the lens may be in order.

For example: A member asked a pastor, "When are we going to stop bringing in all these new members? I don't want our congregation to get too big because then I won't know anybody"! The member was out of focus on several counts: 1) Our perennial God-given responsibility is to reach out to "church homeless" people and receive new members; 2) Knowing everybody in the congregation is not the top priority. What matters is that we try to know as many people as we can and count some as friends. The focus of the well-meaning parishoner was distorted. The parishoner needed a wider lens. Such a parishoner would have not felt comfortable in the crowd of thousands when Jesus fed them with a few loaves and fish.

Nobody is to fall between the cracks. Jesus spoke sharply to the disciples when they tried to discourage children from coming to him (Matthew 19:13). The parable of the lost sheep (Matthew 18 and Luke 15) is another example of how our focus is to be on people— the lost and the saved, the old and the young, the up-and-outer and the down-and-outer, all sorts and conditions of people, and those who become lost on purpose. The responsibility of any congregation is to focus on people.

How can a congregation get on automatic focus with a wide lens for people? It is not easy. Research, wisdom, winsomeness, and stick-to-it-iveness are involved. It takes, in essence, leadership.

People in the United States these days do not have much confidence in their leaders in Washington. Members of a church tend to react to their leaders similarly. Why? Call it the personality quirk syndrome or the Pharisee and Scribe in us; whatever it is, we need leaders who have sound scriptural insights, motivate people to seek others without a church home—leaders of faith who can articulate the reason a church is in business, and leaders unafraid to listen to the heartbeat of the present-day church and to take stands and to make recommendations. Yes, people will listen and respond to such leaders.

Let's begin with the opportunity of a new pastor or a new member, both leaders, coming into a well established congregation, yet a congregation out of focus. Consider these concerted actions:

a) Express appreciation for past pastorates and responsible lay leadership through the years, and all people who helped the congregation throughout its history (even if some of these leaders were out of focus!). Gratitude links you to the past. Genuine praise paves the way for a fresh beginning.

b) Exercise leadership. At one time leaders were called enablers. Such leaders were supposed to stand beside us or behind us. As a result, congregations became confused—didn't know who was in charge, and were reluctant to take a step forward. Pastors, afraid of being interpreted as authoritative, abdicated their leadership role, and as a consequence countless churches retreated. Instead, real leaders relate what Christ expects of Christians, what their hopes and dreams are for the congregation, and how they see their role—as an eastern shepherd—leading the way. Leadership which does not usurp authority yet displays a definite sense of God's direction, gives hope for the future and influences members to hear God's call. This type of leadership is sorely needed in the church, as well as in the nation.

c) Ask the church board for the authority to bring together one leader from each group in the church (Church board, organizations, Sunday Church School, committees, choirs, youth, etc.) for the purpose of getting their ideas about what they think is the first business of their church. Give the group meeting a name or simply call it a "Task Force on the First Business of the Church." Make the group responsible for making recommendations to the church board. Set a date and time for the Task Force meeting far enough in advance so that excuses for not attending can be kept at a minimum. In fact, if the head of a group cannot attend, ask that another representative be selected. Alert all attendees to be prepared to discuss only one subject: "What is the first business of our church?" Allow at least two hours for the meeting. In some instances, more than one meeting may be necessary. At the initial meeting of the Task Force, invite attendees to select their own leader and recorder. Encourage everyone to take notes. State that the only agenda for the meeting is to discuss the subject: WHAT WOULD CHRIST WANT THE FIRST BUSINESS OF OUR CHURCH TO BE? That question could be put at the top of a blackboard or turnover chart. Point out that the Task Force's summations and suggestions can be a catylist for the implementation of Jesus' statement, "Very truly, I tell you, the one who believes in me will also do the works that I do and, in fact, will do greater works than these...."[2] Invite them to sit back and take a look at their congregation from their vantage point, in relation to the one question they are to discuss. An opening statement by attendees about what they feel is the first business of the church will get things rolling.

    Listen carefully to what is said. Wait until they ask for your ideas (and they will as long as you are patient). You can state, carefully and genuinely, that the first business of the church is evangelism. Observe that every phase of the congregation represented could make evangelism a priority and, if that were done, they would see spiritual growth, as well as numerical additions. Designate two or three people to go back to the church board with their summations and suggestions. At the conclusion of the Task Force meeting, thank each person for attending and sharing.

    From the Task Force meeting, at least four things will be obvious: a) ideas that have held the congregation captive; b) ideas that have been waiting to be born; c) personalities who are roadblocks, and d) personalities who are roadways. Write down your conclusions immediately. Give your summations time to mature. Then sit down with the representatives of the Task Force and formulate an approach to the church board. Place on the next church board's agenda a report from the Task Force on THE FIRST BUSINESS OF OUR CHURCH, concerning their findings and recommendations.

2. Let the Task Force lead the church board toward concerted action. Their approach to the board could include these beliefs:

a) We believe that scripturally and theologically the first business of our church is evangelism. We suggest this fundamental principle be included in our mission statement.

b) We are convinced that Bible studies on evangelism, offered to all members, will educate the congregation on the meaning of evangelism and help equip everyone with biblical insights.

c) We contend that courses on evangelism offered to members will educate us in the what, why, when and how of evangelism.

d) We recommend that all phases of the congregation's life be focused on evangelism as the first responsibility (church board, Sunday Church School, organizations, committees, choirs, etc.).

e) As a first step in this direction, we recommend a CALENDAR DAY beginning with a force field analysis. (See Chapter Seventeen for a description of this procedure.)

f) We suggest the appointment of two committees: 1) An Evangelism Outreach Committee (see Chapter Ten for a description); and 2) An Evangelism Inreach Committee (see Chapter Fourteen). We also suggest that the chairpersons of these two committees be given positions on the church board. (Procedures, of course, will vary from congregation to congregation. Whatever arrangement, this tandem of committees is ideal, enabling the Outreach Committe to focus on reaching people without a church home, and the Inreach Committee to focus on keeping people in the church home, full of faith, alert, and spiritually healthy.)

In order to begin making evangelism the first business of a congregation, start from the ground up. That is why the following actions are essential: 1) The appointment of a Task Force to assist the church board in visualizing evangelism as the first business; 2) Education throughout the congregation as to the meaning and purpose of evangelism; and 3) Two committees, headed by chairpersons given the status of church board positions, in order to set in motion responsible evangelism in and through every facet of the congregation's life. Go and evangelize your own people to be evangelism-minded.

*

Congregations which worry about survival thwart the power of the Holy Spirit. Congregations do need to concentrate on responsibility. The church is not responsible for results; only God can bring an increase in membership. What God expects of his people is to plant seeds. It is foolhardy to set annual membership goals because we have no control over that; we can set goals as to the number of telephone calls and visits that are to be made upon people without a church home.

Whether you are a pastor or a lay person, start in your parish from the ground up. Redirection (change) may be necessary. Evangelism generates enthusiasm in a congregation as members discover the reason for not only their church's existence but their own existence.

The next chapter describes a plan for through-the-year evangelism.

CHAPTER TEN

CREATE YOUR OWN THROUGH-THE-YEAR EVANGELISM PLAN

"The Locked Out...give evidence of feeling not wanted or of being excluded from the fellowship of the churches they have known. The Floaters have found worship services dull, repetitious, and unexciting. The Pilgrims crave dialogue encounter and fault the traditional authoritarian style of Christian proclamation. The Boxed In react negatively to what they perceive to be the church's emphasis on dependence and submission."[1]

Creating your own Through-The-Year Evangelism Plan facilitates the Holy Spirit's work in and through people of God. A thoughtful plan sets the stage for the work to be accomplished. It can point to possibilities, signal pitfalls, serve as a track guide, and gauge performance.

We have discussed the context for evangelism and the preparation for evangelism. No one should attempt to create a Through-The-Year Evangelism Plan without that background. And, no one should launch a plan without parishoners fully understanding the meaning of and place of evangelism in the life of a parish, and what that involves. If you do, the "homesteaders" as Lyle Schaller calls them—the old timers in the congregation—may rise up in rebellion about all these new people coming in and disrupting everything!

The agreement of the pastor(s) and leadership (board, school, committees, organizations, etc.) that evangelism is the first business of the church will eradicate friction and prepare the congregation for action. The defining of the congregation's mission statement and adoption by the congregation is a necessary step.

Ascension Lutheran Church, Thousand Oaks, California,

has an exemplary mission statement, worthy of any church:

"As members of Ascension Evangelical Lutheran Church, we believe that we are a family of God's chosen people— chosen by the grace and mercy of God through baptism and strengthened for our faith walk by Word and Sacrament.

"We further believe that we have a mandate—set forth for us in the Great Commission (Matt. 28:19)—to fully equip ourselves to be GOD'S CARING PEOPLE and to proclaim his love, justice, and forgiveness through effective witness and service. To accomplish these goals we strive to nurture and encourage one another through worship, study, and prayer."

After the mission statement has become a part of the life of a congregation, members are ready to create their own plan of through-the-year evangelism. A sound plan:

1. Sharpens pastoral preaching.
2. Stretches the faith of God's people.
3. Announces to the world that this church cares for people.
4. Focuses the parish program on people.
5. Enlarges the capacity of the congregation to embrace all sorts and conditions of people.
6. Increases pastoral and lay person contacts with people.
7. Creates an attitude of growth.
8. Nurtures and sustains people in the faith.
9. Quickens member capacity to be a viable part of God's church.
10. Gives the Holy Spirit opportunities to work in and through precious lives.

Those are ten good reasons for planning through-the-year evangelism, as follows:

1. Create an Evangelism Outreach Committee.

A detailed description of this Committee's responsibilities for Evangelism Outreach is the next rung in the ladder. (Amendment to the constitution may be necessary.) Adoption of such a description will minimize misunderstandings. Write your own. Here are some ingredients:

a) The Evangelism Outreach Committee will be responsible for writing a through-the-year plan of evangelism, each year.

b) The Committee will be responsible for enlisting and providing instruction for potential evangelists making home visits and/or telephone calls upon Possible Members.

c) The Committee will be responsible for creating, maintaining, and monitoring the Possible Member List. (The number of Possible Member households on file needs to be one and a half times larger than the number of member households—discussed later in the chapter.)

d) The Committee will oversee the INFORMATION TALKS FOR VISITORS (discussed in Chapter Twelve), the Orientation and Reception of new members, (in concert with the Evangelism Inreach Committee).

e) The Committee will oversee evangelism communications in the bulletin, newsletter, letters to Possible Members, periodic saturation mailings, newspaper, radio, and television announcements.

f) The Committee will prepare and oversee an annual retreat on evangelism for selected leaders but open to all members.

g) The Committee will prepare and oversee an Evangelism Mission Week to be held annually or at least every two years (explained in Appendix #4).

h) The Committee will consist of representatives from the various facets of the congregation's life, with different ages and emphases represented. (For a smaller congregation, three to five persons will suffice to serve on the Evangelism Outreach Committee.)

2. Enlist and Educate Evangelism Outreach Committee Members.

There are five steps in enlisting such a Committee:

a) Go over the entire membership list and select the best Andrew type of people you can find, people who like to invite others to worship. Or Peter people—those who like to speak out and stand for something. Or, James and John people—those who like to see something happen. Or, Philip and Nathaniel (Bartholomew) people who learn to introduce friends to the living Christ as easily as you introduce a new friend to a long acquaintance. Or Thomas—people of courage and who must think things through before they can say, "Let us also go, that we may die with him." Or Matthew— people who may not always be accepted by others yet have a contribution to make. Or, Simon, the Zealot; James, the son of Alphaeus; and Thaddaeus—those who are not "yes" people and are eager for an enterprise bigger than themselves. Or, Mary Magdelene—people who care about the Master and are not easily turned away. Steer clear of the Judas type, who look upon new members as added revenue for the church's treasury.

In today's jargon, we are talking about sales people, communicators, organizers, and people of commitment who like to get things done. Frequently, the evangelism committee of a congregation ends up with those who agree to be on the committee because nobody else wants to do it. Be as selective as Jesus was in choosing his followers.

b) Telephone these potential committee members for an appointment. (It is best for two people to visit together.) Your approach might be like this: " Ruth, there is something good going to happen in our church. Frank Mead and I need to sit down and talk with you about it. It is not about money. We can't do justice to this matter by talking about it after church or at a committee meeting. We need a leisurely and uninterrupted time of about thirty minutes. After we have explained it, if you don't think it is a good idea, there is no obligation involved. Which would be better for you—Monday or Tuesday evening of next week? (If neither night is acceptable, ask what night Ruth has open and then bend your schedules to suit. Listen to the reply. If negativism is expressed, you may have made a bad selection. Go to the next name. If interest is expressed, continue....) Would 7:00 or 8:00 be best for you? Thank you, We will be there on time and look forward to talking with you!"

c) Visit your potential Evangelism Outreach Committee member(s). Hand Ruth the written description of the Evangelism Outreach Committee responsibilities. Explain that evangelism is not the only business of our church but that it is the first business. Go over what is hoped to be accomplished in fulfilling these Christian responsibilities, as we reach out to others. Relate how her name was selected—as carefully as Jesus selected one of his immediate followers. Invite Ruth to an "Exploratory Meeting of the Potential Evangelism Outreach Committee" on a date scheduled far in advance. Assure her that there will be other learning times for all committee members, following the "Exploratory Meeting." Detail the amount of time required and the length of the appointment to the committee (for example, two hours a week, on an average, for one year). Indicate to Ruth that she can make up her mind about becoming a member of the committee *after* the "Exploratory Meeting."

All you are trying to do at this point is to get an affirmative response to attend the "Exploratory Meeting." If there is any hesitancy whatsoever, tell Ruth that you will telephone her in two or three days for an answer. Conclude with a prayer that lifts up Christ and his church. If Ruth's answer is negative, remember you are not responsibile for results, only for planting the seed in a brother or sister member. If you planted the seed, you were successful. Go to the next name and follow the same procedure. You are going to get "yes" answers!

d) Write a letter to all potential attendees for the "Exploratory Meeting of the Potential Evangelism Committee" and in that letter express thanks for their participation, and enclose the agenda with a reminder of the date and time.

e) Include these components in the "Exploratory Meeting" beginning with refreshments:

* A Bible study on evangelism.
* A review of how their names were selected.
* A presentation on the hopes and dreams for the committee, carefully explaining the main responsibilities of the committee.
* Time for questions and answers.
* Announcement of the date and time for the first meeting of the Evangelism Outreach Committee.
* Distribution of a page wherein they can write their name as desiring to be a part of the committee.
* Time for prayer.

If you are faithful in following such a procedure, almost always you will be successful. Even a negative response may be a positive way for a member to share personal concerns that give you an opening to help. Remember, a person has a right to say "no". It takes time to enlist the members God wants for a committee. Shortcuts only make the job difficult. Those who think these steps are unnecessary invite failure.

Note well that an Evangelism Outreach Committee is not to do the work of evangelism for the congregation, a common misunderstanding. If a Committee operates that way, it conveys the impression that it is doing evangelism on behalf of the congregation, when in fact every member in the congregation shares this responsibility. Evangelism experience should be a requirement for any elected board member or leadership position.

In essence, this Committee is to study, plan, and implement evangelism in and though the congregation. It will endeavor to sound the heartbeat of the gospel, serve as the conscience of the congregation, and activate the spiritual drive of the congregation as it reaches, even stretches for people who have yet to hear the story.

Impress upon Committee members, in their beginning work, to differentiate between results and responsibility. As has been stated, we are not responsible for the number of new people brought into the family of God in a given year. We are responsible for planting seeds and nurturing people. Only God can give faith. Results, therefore, are in God's hands; responsibility is in our hands. We are responsible for making home visits, telephoning, inviting people, developing church program, and sharing the Word. God will bring the growth.

3. Teach members to think "people" and how to invite people to worship.

Everybody can be an evangelist in one sense or other. In conversation with people wherever we are, without being pesty, we can inquire about a person's church relationship.

For example: Ask, "What church are you a member of?" or "Of what church are you a member?" (The former, although clumsy English, seems the easier way to ask the question.) Assume people are members of a church in the community. This is an important question. They will readily tell you if they are not members. If they are members of a church, rejoice with them and share ideas. If they are not members of a church, invite them to worship with you. (Give all members "calling cards"—a card on which lists the church's name, address, telephone, times of worship, and a line for members to write their name. "Don't leave home without it"!) Make a date to take the unchurched person(s) to worship or arrange to meet them in the narthex, and sit with them in worship. Tell them you would like to take them to brunch (lunch) after worship, if they can spare the time. Business people do this all the time. Take the cost out of your tithe money, if you like. As we know, more people become members of a church because of friends than of any other way despite great preaching and beautiful music.

This teaching, described above and referred to earlier, can be done during worship, at least once a month. Repetition is good. We hear the same television commercial again and again. Do this teaching at the time of announcements or in place of the announcements. (Which is more important?!) Visitors appreciate a church that is reaching out to others.

This same teaching can appear in bulletins and newsletters. After awhile, members get the idea that you are serious about this matter of reaching out. (Churches that host regular brunches or lunches after worship celebrations make it easier for members to seek out visitors.) Give first-time visitors a flower or ribbon or some identification as a first-time visitor. Invite visitors to stop by the INFORMATION DESK and pick up a free video about your church. (Place the video in an envelope with an invitation to the INFORMATION TALKS FOR VISITORS and list the date when the next series begins.) Invest in visitors. Too many of our worship celebrations allow people to come and go without making a connection. We tend to go fishing with all line and no hook!

4. Prepare a POSSIBLE MEMBER LIST, put it on a computer, and track the worship habits of visitors.

Instead of calling it a "prospective member" list or by some other business name, consider calling the list the POSSIBLE MEM-

BER LIST. It has biblical implications. The word "possible" carries connotations of anticipation and expectancy. We are inviting people to become a part of the Christian faith.

Where do we get the data for the POSSIBLE MEMBER LIST? As long as you are on the lookout for people, you will find them. Here are some clues.

a) Invite members to submit names and addresses and telephone numbers of people they know who are without a meaningful church relationship. Provide a form for members to do this. (See Appendix #1.) Suggest they start with their own family, often the most difficult evangelism job. One wife said, "I have been trying to get my husband into the church for twenty years! Was I suprised when he accepted the invitation from another member!" We all need to work together on this.

b) Provide a "Friendship Slip" with the bulletin (see Appendix #1), giving members and visitors opportunity to record their presence and other interests. Some visitors will not do this. That is their prerogative. Those who don't, don't! Those who do are saying in effect, "You can contact me." It is our responsibility to do so.

c) Write a letter of thanks to each first-time visitor and enclose an invitation to the next INFORMATION TALKS FOR VISITORS (discussed in Chapter Twelve). Include a picture of the church and worship schedule. St. Mark's Lutheran, Charlotte, North Carolina, takes a small loaf of homemade bread to every first-time visitor. Bread bakers and delivery people become evangelists!

d) On the Monday following the Sunday worship of first-time visitors, telephone and express appreciation for the privilege of worshiping with them. (Note that the appreciation was for the privilege of worshiping with them and not the other way around! It makes a difference.) After thanking them, say something like the following: "We are always interested in first impressions. What was your impression of First Church?" Listen. Ask, "What prompted you to worship at First Church?" Listen. Ask, "What church in the community are you a member of?" Listen. From these three questions you can determine if the visitor is a Possible

Member. If the worshiper is a Possible Member, tell him/her about the next INFORMATION TALKS FOR VISITORS. Assume that it is agreeable to send them an invitation to the next series of the INFO TALKS. If the first-time worshiper turns out to be a Possible Member, almost always the answer will be in the affirmative. If the first-time worshiper is not a Possible Member, again thank them for the privilege of worshiping with them and state that the arms of the church are always open to them.

  e) Obtain names from an agency that keeps tab on newcomers in the community. If it costs money, it is a good investment. Be sure to include this cost in your evangelism budget. Make telephone calls on these newcomers. "I am George Wieman of First Church, and our church wants to welcome you to the community!" Listen. "We hope the move was not too traumatic?!" Listen. "Where did you move from?" Listen. "What church were you a member of in Grand Rapids?" Listen. If they are Roman Catholic, give them the name and telephone number of a Roman Catholic Church in the community. If they are Jewish, give them the name and telephone number of a synagogue in the community. (Some will feel this is not a way to convert the Jew and it isn't. However, noting your fairness may cause the Jew to come to your church. It does occur.) If they are from a denomination different from yours, give them the church's name, address, and telephone number. The idea is to be helpful to new residents. We are not in competition. We need to assist people in making a connection. New residents will recognize your sincerity and offer of help. Of course, if they are of your denomination or have no church home, indicate you assume it is agreeable to send them information. Almost always they will be receptive. Put the name(s) on the computer and track to see if they come to worship. Write them a note thanking them for the telephone conversation. If they do not come to worship, follow-up with another telephone call with a specific invitation to the next INFORMATION TALKS FOR VISITORS.

  f) Make a list of members' spouses, children, relatives and friends who do not have a church home.

  g) Schedule GOOD NEIGHBOR VISITS. Stake out a section of the community (city or rural) and call on "neighbors."

These are doorstep visits. For example: "Hello, we are Bud and Ethel Brooks from First Church. Our church is your neighbor. We want to be good neighbors. We hope you have a church home, too." LISTEN. If they do not have a church home, follow the same sequence as in 3. The idea is to help people become connected with some church, even if it is not yours. In a Salisbury, North Carolina church, a family lived within one block of the church but no one had ever contacted them. A lay visitor, who happened to have a speech impediment like Moses, stopped by to see them. He began, "I, I, I, am, am, am, from, from, from, the, the, the chu, chu, church (pointing down the street) and the people shut the door in his face. The next day, the residents of that home telephoned the church, apologized for their rude response, and asked that the gentleman who stammered come again. The lay visitor did go back and the people enrolled in the INFORMATION TALKS FOR VISITORS. For fifty years this family had lived within the shadow of that church. They had never gone to the church because nobody invited them. God can employ any person as an evangelist, even a stammerer. Jesus beckons us to go around the block and invite people. GOOD NEIGHBOR VISITS can best be done on a Saturday or Sunday afternoon. Teach your people how to be GOOD NEIGHBORS.

h) Conduct a house to house or apartment to apartment or farm to farm survey occasionally. This is simply an extension of the GOOD NEIGHBOR VISITS.

i) Scan the pastoral acts (baptisms, weddings, etc.) for Possible Members. Churches are known to have weddings without inquiring of people in the wedding party, "What church are you a member of?" Wedding receptions are opportunities to find people without a church home. A man came up to me after a wedding and exclaimed, "Wow! That was some Service! I didn't know the church had changed the vows so much." Obviously, this man had not been in church for a long time. And, if people live at a distance and are not Possible Members for your church, write down names and telephone numbers. Make it a point to telephone them later, giving them information about a church close to their residence. Then telephone that church and give them the information.

All people are our business. Churches need to work together instead of just swapping members.

Wherever you go, have your church Calling Card and inquire of people, "What church are you a member of?" When Jim Frey was the Chicago Cubs Manager, he was asked how he learned to always give it his best. "When I was young, I sold insurance one winter. And a veteran insurance man told me I should get seven beans. He said, 'Put them in your left pocket and don't go home until they're all in your right pocket. Whenever you talk to someone about insurance, put a bean in your right pocket. Even if you don't sell anything, at least you gave yourself every chance for success. This game of baseball is the same way."[2]

Evangelism is the same way, too. Try talking to seven people each day asking the question, "What church are you a member of?" Give yourself every chance to be fruitful.

Tell the story of Jim Frey to your people. Give out beans at the end of worship! Encourage them to invite seven people to worship during the week (if, not each day), shifting the beans from one pocket to the other every time they ask the question, "What church are you a member of?" It will help members to think people. (Women will have to make a place for the beans in their purse!)

A Possible Member List needs to be at least one and a half times the number of households in a congregation. For example: If your congregation has fifty households, set a goal of accumulating and keeping at least seventy-five Possible Member households on your list. If your congregation has five hundred households, set a goal of accumulating at least seven hundred and fifty Possible Member households on your list. Why? Volume. Any business which sells a product has to have Possibles. Where do they get them? Everywhere. Sales people are trained to be on the lookout for potential customers, anywhere! The church is in the people business. The reason why some churches do not grow is limited volume. Their expectations are too low.

5. Make date lists for the INFORMATION TALKS FOR VISITORS, ORIENTATION SUPPER MEETINGS, and RECEPTIONS OF MEMBERS through the year.

Possible Members may not accept your invitation to the

INFORMATION TALKS FOR VISITORS the first time. When they ask you, and they will, "When is the next series of Talks?" be ready with the answer. When they ask, "When is your next reception of members?" have the answer. When they ask, "What do I have to do to become a member?" know the answer. A year's schedule will give the Evangelism Outreach Committee an orderly work load and will give the pastor(s) a planning schedule. It will also give Possible Members the impression that you expect to be receiving new members!

A schedule of the year could look like this:

Series 1 of the INFORMATION TALKS FOR VISITORS (five Talks all on Sundays at 9:30 a.m. in the Church Lounge)—

    March 1 — Talk Number One on the subject of....
    March 8 —Talk Number Two on the subject of....
    March 15—Talk Number Three on the subject of....
    March 22—Talk Number Four on the subject of....
    March 29—Talk Number Five on the subject of....

(Please note: Lately I have repeated each TALK on a Tuesday evening following a Sunday, with some success. You may want to try it.)

Orientation Supper-Meeting on Sunday, April 5, 5:00 p.m. in Parish Hall, for those who decide to become members of the First family.

Reception of New Members on Palm Sunday, April 12, at all three woship celebrations.

(List Series 2,3,4,5,6 in the same manner. Six series are about all that can be fitted into a year's calendar.)

6. Schedule letters, visits, and telephone calls on Possible Members.

    a) Two weeks and a half prior to the beginning of a series of INFORMATION TALKS FOR VISITORS, write an invitation letter to Possibles. (See Appendix. #2.)

    b) Two weeks prior to the beginning of an INFORMATION TALKS FOR VISITORS, schedule instruction classes for evangelists in preparation for making visits, and make those calls, whether home visits or telephone.

c) One week prior to the beginning of an INFORMATION TALKS FOR VISITORS, telephone Possibles about the INFO, reminding them of the date, time, and place.

7. Widen the sphere of your church's influence via good public relations efforts.

Public relations is a partner in evangelism. If we minister only to those who appear at our door, our evangelism efforts stop short. Try asking strangers in a store or on the sidewalk close to your church if they know the location of your church and they may not know your church exists! Public relations, telling the story of Christ and his church through press, radio, television, and mailings, for example, extend our sphere of influence. Public Relations is proclamation.

Dr. Franklin Clark Fry, president of the Lutheran Church (ULCA, LCA), 1944-68, advised our LUTHERAN EVANGELISM MISSION in the mid-1950's: "News of the church should tell an honest story of what the Christian religion is all about....Our job is not to try to pass off as news propaganda that which is not worthy of the name 'news'—but to take the news that honestly does exist and turn it into a window that looks into the heart of the Christian religion." Good public relations is an evangelism window "...into the heart of the Christian religion." Consider these possibilities:

a) **During the week prior to an INFORMATION TALKS FOR VISITORS, place an ad in the newspaper, such as this sample.**

HOW TO SHOP FOR A CHURCH

Most people just go around from church to church to see if they like the pastor and/or the atmosphere. There is another approach which makes a lot of sense. Find out what a church believes before making a decision. How can you do this? Ask a church where you can get this information.

That's why First Church periodically provides INFORMATION TALKS FOR VISITORS. The next series of INFO TALKS begins Sunday, March l, 9:30 a.m. in the Parish Hall (building to right of worship center). You will be given a notebook and if you must miss any of the five Talks, you will be lent an audio or video tape and given an outline of the missed session.

The INFO TALKS are specifically designed to assist people in coming to grips with their beliefs in God, as well as illustrating how a person can embrace the Christian faith.

Attendees are under no obligation whatsoever. The invitation is simply to "come and see." All pastors of First Church give the TALKS and lead in discussions.

It needs to be noted that the INFO TALKS are an update on the world of religion. So much has changed in the last few years, including publication of entirely new Bible translations, that the INFO TALKS will benefit everyone whether they have a church background or not. It is the perfect setting to get answers to your thoughtful questions.

Here is a list of the Talks on succeeding Sundays at 9:30 a.m. beginning on March 1 —

Talk Number 1 - BELIEF IN GOD. (Step by step on how a person can come to know God.)

Talk Number 2 - HOW TO GET A HANDLE ON THE BIBLE. (Six ways of settling the matter of interpretation, plus a listing and description of books which will aid you in home study.)

Talk Number 3 - THE SACRAMENTS. (What is a sacrament? Are they hocus-pocus or what?)

Talk Number 4 - THE STORY OF THE CHRISTIAN CHURCH. (When and how the church got its start and what it is today.)

Talk Number 5 - WORSHIP. (What is it? How do you do it? What's in it for me?).

Check it out and enroll now by telephoning (213) 495-0406. Or, simply mail or bring this slip with you on Sunday, March 1, 9:30 a.m. sharp. Welcome!

Name_____
    Telephone ( ) _____
Address_____
    (street and number)   (city and zip)
Mail to First Church, 138 First St., Dayton, Ohio 45402. Thanks!

If you run this ad in the sports section on a Wednesday or Thursday prior to the beginning Sunday of the INFORMATION TALKS FOR VISITORS, you will get results. If you run this ad periodically, prior to the beginning of each series of the INFO TALKS, you will get better results. People shop for a church. Acknowledge it. Meet the "customers" where they are in their thinking. They check us out. One man told me that he and a friend went from church to church gauging the effectiveness of pastors and churches. It was a kind of hobby! They had a little game evaluating the sermons and the prayers, the openness and friendliness of the people, on a scale of 0 to 10. They compared notes over Sunday brunch. They even chose a "church of the month"! How would you and your church have fared?!

People do shop for a church. When I asked this man and his friend for a report on our church, I was shocked. When I invited them to the INFO TALKS and to appraise it on the same scale, the rating was not high. Nevertheless, I am happy to report, they stopped shopping and became members of our church. The hobby stopped. They took up something bigger and became members of the Evangelism Outreach Committee. They were a real asset because they saw things through the eyes of church shoppers. They were the best "shoplifters" I ever encountered! They brought ideas from their experience—what turned them on and what turned them off. They became servants of the Savior.

b) Spend money on saturation mailings.

Periodically, invite the youth and others to distribute "flyers" in neighborhoods within a five mile radius. Set aside money for "saturation" mailings (employ an agency to do it or rent a reverse telephone book and enlist volunteers to do the mailing) over a wider area and do it periodically. There are three times in the year when this works to advantage: 1) Prior to the fall program kick-off, usually around Labor Day; 2) Prior to Christmas; 3) Prior to Holy Week. A fourth time could be prior to Pentecost. Still another good time is before the Fourth of July when freedom of worship is stressed.

It is a myth to think that everybody goes away for the summer. Many cannnot afford it. Churches which decelerate during the summer to the point of having little or no music during summer worship celebrations, turn visitors off. People shop for a church in the summer—the curious who are looking for change; the newcomer just settling in before school begins for the children; those who resolve to do things differently before fall and want to get a jump on what is happening in the world of religion.

c) Write a weekly column.

I tried writing a weekly column for the local newspaper entitled "Keeping In Touch" with my picture ("vanity of vanities says the Teacher"—Eccl. 1:2), the name and location of our church, the times of worshp, and telephone number. At first we paid for the column and ran it on a Wednesday. I wrote about the implications of the Christian faith and commented on local events, careful not to cause controversy. People began to stop me on the street, exchanging ideas, etc. Visitor attendance increased. Try it!

d) Prepare spot announcements for radio and television.

Many churches do not have money for radio and/or televison, unfortunately. We leave this to the big-timers.

Yet, there is free time available in many communities, especially radio. It takes time to go to these stations, become acquainted with the manager, find out the "ropes", and supply them with cogent writing. There is much to gain by not only tickling the imagination of the community to be aware of your church, but also to lift up the Christian faith as a representative of the churches in your community.

Television is different. Few television stations offer community service except for announcement of coming events. Do not let this stop you. Inquire about the cost of a fifteen-second or thirty-second announcement. Hire a professional to help prepare and present such announcements, or, take lessons on how to do this. Television is a window for the church.

The image of Christianity across the nation needs enhancing. National church bodies should set aside sizeable sums for televising the Good News. What about a CHRISTIAN HOUR on television? Why don't churches pool their resources—Roman Catholics, Orthodox, and Protestants together—and tell the story of Christ? That would shake up the nation! It could be done for the sake of Christ. This unity in Christ could be the anthem for the next new century. Think of it—all of us together, evangelizing together, with the announcement "Go to the church of your choice and worship!" Even groups of automobile agencies advertise together! This whole matter of working together, called ecumenism, needs to be thought through again in the arena of evangelism. At least, we could do "one thing" together, couldn't we? Anybody listening?!

Evangelism without public relations is like an automobile without wheels. Public relations in evangelism is establishing a rapport with people at large. Hearing again and again the message of the Christian churches, some seed will fall on good ground.

e) Make a video of your church's spirit and life.

Millions of households today own a television set and VCR. Make and use a video of your congregation's life and witness. In the making of a video, sort out what is important in your church's life. Evaluate just what is the spirit of your church? Whether homemade or professional, there will be positive side effects in producing a video. Take it into the homes of Possible Members. Lend or give it to first-time visitors.

A professional video will pay dividends. It could be that there is someone in your church who will see a video as an evangelism tool and pay for it, as occurred in the church where I now serve. It cost $10,000 in 1991 and was worth it. This video is good enough to show on television.

Whether professional or homemade, a video is a valuable evangelism tool. It can be used in six specific areas: 1) Lay visitors can take the video (supply a VCR when necessary) to Possible Member homes, remain while it is being viewed or leave it and pick it up later, and answer any questions; 2) Show it at the Orientation Supper-Meeting for new members; 3) Offer it to members for purchase or loan (encourage them to invite neighbors to their home to see the video, or to lend it to a church homeless neighbor); 4) Arrange for your video to be seen on local television (if it is of professional quality); 5) Lend or give it to first-time visitors; 6) Use in stewardship emphases, group meetings, growth groups, etc.

8. Lead a series of Bible studies which illustrate evangelism

Not everybody in your church is going to take evangelism efforts seriously. You can get the hook into them and fish them out of the water of indifference by offering them Biblical courses on evangelism. Church people respect courses on the Bible, competently taught. Your goal is to educate people on the biblical implications for evangelism. It is all a part of the stream of the Spirit making his way into the hearts of church people. It will help answer their questions about evangelism:

    a) What is the authority for evangelism?
    b) Why is evangelism urgent business?
    c) What is the breadth of evangelism?
    d) Are our evangelism methods consonant with Scripture?
    e) What phases of evangelism ought we to be engaged in now?
    f) What does God expect of me?

God's yearning for evangelism is evident in many scriptures that can be studied in these courses. Here is a sampling:

Proverbs 25:8-28	John 1:19-51
Isaiah 40:1-11	Acts of the Apostles, especially the translation of J. B. Phillips
Isaiah 50:1-9	
Isaiah 52:7-12	Romans 1:1-17
Isaiah 6l:1-11	Romans 10:9-21
Daniel 12:1-3	I Corinthians 5:1-34
Matthew 4:18-22	II Corinthians 4:1-6
Matthew 28:16-20	Ephesians 4:1-32
Mark 13:9-37	Colossians 1:21-29
Mark 16: 9-20	I Thessalonians 3:1-13
Luke 1:5-19	I Timothy 1:8-20
Luke 2:1-20	II Timothy 4:1-5
Luke 8:1-18	

If we are to hold the people we have, if we are to help the people we hold, if we are to add people to our church community, Bible study in evangelism is a requirement in congregations.

9. Provide a section in the Sunday bulletin entitled "Visitor Information."

Let visitors know you are interested in them by capsuling items in your bulletin that concern them. For example: a) A welcome; b) Location of parking and how to get inside the worship center; c) Location of restrooms; d) Location of nursery; e) Where "Friendship Time" is located; f) Information about tape and video ministry; g) How to get children's bulletins; h) How to get hearing helps; i) Where they can get more information.

Repeat this section in the bulletin every week. Visitors will thank you.

10. Prepare a cost proposal for your THROUGH-THE-YEAR EVANGELISM PLAN.

In looking over countless evangelism budgets for congregations all over the country and in other countries, I was constantly astonished that many congregations expected to do evangelism for little or nothing. Church boards rarely thought about a budget line for evangelism. Shocking when the God they proclaim gave his life to bail them out!

What should go into the annual proposal for evangelism? Consider these line suggestions, without amounts, acknowledging that size of a congregation will be determinative:

- a. Staff person assigned to evangelism, even part-time. (This really pays off.)
- b. Office person assigned to evangelism (computer, letters, mailings);
- c. A computer and printer.
- d. Cost of office materials, mailings, saturation mailings, etc.
- e. Mileage allowance for those who make home visits (volunteers included).
- f. Telephones.
- g. "Calling Cards" for evangelists (all church members).
- h. Videos and audio tapes about the congregation and the INFO TALKS.
- i. Public relations (newspaper, radio, television).
- j. Cost of agency providing new resident information.

k. Retreat(s).
l. Mission Week (missioner, public relations, etc.)
m. Information Talks For Visitor cards and materials.
n. Brochure describing your church.
o. Church library books on evangelism.
p. Evangelism conferences.
q. Special speakers on evangelism.
r. VCR.
s. Video equipment.

Complete the list with your ideas. In order to reach people without Christ, the wise church will set aside funds for evangelism. The fact that increased membership increases a congregation's income is not the reason for doing evangelism. We do not look into the eyes of new people and see dollar signs—more income for the church, as some church boards tend to do. No! We need to see the sign of the cross in their eyes because these are people for whom Christ died and rose again from the dead. This is the rightful motive for evangelism.

11) Set times for enlisting, teaching, and retooling evangelists.

This is the subject for the next chapter.

CHAPTER ELEVEN

ENLISTING, TEACHING, RETOOLING EVANGELISTS

"....The ordinary members of the Christian Church cannot hold back from evangelism while they wait for a re-statement or for new strategy. They are confronted in their daily lives by men and women who they know need God and need Him desperately. If they have the eyes of Christ they see these people involved in a matter of life and death....For such ordinary Christians, if they are awakened to their duty, evangelism is something which must be done, and done to-day—not to-morrow."[1]

There is the story of Satchel Paige, the Hall of Fame baseball player, in the days of the Negro League World Series. Paige was pitching in the deciding game. His team was ahead by one run. It was the last of the ninth inning and the bases were loaded. There were two out. Paige told the left, center, and right fielders to come on in. Paige proceeded to strike out the next batter and won the series!

I always wanted to do that as a preacher. I wanted to tell the church council to come on in! Treasurer, come on in! Stewardship chairperson, come on in! And then proceed to make a pitch to the congregation about the need for putting a million dollars in the offering plate that day and get it! Such is a preacher's dream.

Pastors and evangelism committees, tempted to do evangelism by themselves miss the mark. Jesus proved that personal spiritual growth occurs when believers tell the God-story when he sent seventy people out to witness and they returned pumped up with enthusiasm and exclaimed, "Lord, in your name even the demons submit to us!" [2] The church grows as proclaimers grow. First, the apostles, then the seventy, and then the thousands on Pentecost. The Apostolic Church kept growing after Jesus' death and resurrection and ascension because members had the Spirit. The Early Church kept growing after the apostles died because church members were active evangelists. Christians do not reach spiritual maturity until they plant the seed of faith in the heart of another. Evangelism is God's way of life for believers!

Furthermore, well-meaning pastors and evangelism committees who endeavor to do evangelism by themselves without involving others prohibit congregations from reaching their potential. After baptism—given the Spirit (the source of our new life), and charged with the responsibility to live as a person of God—what are we expected to do? "Proclaim the praise of God and bear his creative and redeeming Word to all the world." [3]

We have the habit of sticking new converts on committees thinking that if we keep members busy doing some kind of church work, they will catch the Spirit. It is the other way around! The Spirit claims people as they proclaim the Good News. Jesus made a similar point to Nicodemus, an old hand at church work. Realizing something was missing in his life, Nicodemus sought out Jesus one secretive night and was told he must be "...born from above." [4]

Before we get into the area of organized evangelism, however, consider how the Holy Spirit works through people in unorganized ways.

Unorganized evangelism is believers, evangelists all, conversing about Christ and his church as easily as talking about sports or the theatre or business concerns. Chapter Ten illustrated teaching people to ask: "What church are you a member of?" It sounds simple. It is! Do not underestimate unorganized evangelism. It is effective. Every time I begin a new INFORMATION TALKS FOR VISITORS, I note enrollees who had been invited by members of the congregation, and I didn't even know about it. Members had given THE CARD to others, explained the INFO TALKS, and invited them. Often such members accompany the visitor(s) to the

INFO. Challenge all members to set an annual goal of bringing at least one other person to the INFO TALKS. Encourage new members to do the same. New members are enthusiastic evangelists. They know what appeals to a person without a church home. Unorganized evangelism is productive.

Enlisting evangelists (and congregational workers in general)

Organized evangelism employs selected members in the work of evangelism. Every congregation, regardless of size, reaches more of its potential by enlisting a selected corps of evangelists for these purposes: 1) To create and sustain a list of Possible Members (prodigals, lost sheep, the unconverted, church shoppers); 2) To follow-up worship visitors, either in person or by telephone; 3) To make concerted efforts to enlist Possible Members for each series of the INFORMATION TALKS FOR VISITORS. It is important to select and enlist three different groups of evangelists for these assignments.

Congregations rightfully expect members to share responsibilities. Everybody can serve; not everybody will. In order to reach the quantity and quality of people needed to do organized evangelism, originate some kind of **Employment Agency** within the church. Commission this agency to list jobs in the church and who does them, and to make another list of unemployed members, those who have no specific responsibility in the church. Determine the percentage of unemployed in your church!

I estimate that in the average church 70% are unemployed. The government worries about the unemployment rate if it gets over seven percent. People capable of work (including the handicapped and disabled) need a job to have a sense of worth and to meet financial needs. In the church, members need a sense of spiritual worth. This is not to suggest that the only way a person can be Christian is to take up some job in the church; it does propose that Christians can increase their spiritual vitality by serving in some capacity, especially as an evangelist, whether in organized or unorganized ways. Anybody who has water poured on his/her head (or is immersed) is expected to serve and not be on Christian welfare—letting the Andrews do all the evangelism work. This includes children and youth, as well as adults. Do not overlook children and youth—it is second nature for them to invite and bring friends to church.

Churches are prone to produce "Help Wanted Ads" in newsletters and bulletins or make verbal announcements inviting volunteers to fill job vacancies in the congregation. The result? A small percentage of people end up carrying the largest percentage of the work load. Burnout occurs, that exhaustion of physical or emotional or spiritual strength. Members become discouraged and drop out. It doesn't have to be that way.

An **Employment Agency** in the church can solve this dilemma. Business pays employment agencies to find the right person for the right job. Individuals hire an executive search firm to find a position worthy of their talent. We can do the same in the church without cost! The EMPLOYMENT AGENCY (or call it whatever you want) can do several things: 1) Compile a detailed list of responsibilities with job descriptions; 2) Make a list of the unemployed in the church and match people with jobs open; 3) Select, enlist, and instruct people how to make interviews; 4) Interview jobless members who have been matched with job opportunities, explaining why they have been chosen by the Lord's church, what is involved, the amount of time required, and the length of service expected on the job; 5) Provide on-the-job help for people who accept the challenge of an assignment.

*

Think on this: There are multiple education courses in our churches. Where are the courses to help people do the work of the Lord?! There are manuals describing what boards and committees do. Where are the manuals which teach people of God, a) why they need to work in the kingdom, and b) how to work in the kingdom? An enlarged curriculum is in order for the churches of America.

*

Newsletters, worship bulletins, verbal announcements, telephone calls, tapping somebody on the shoulder after worship—all of these methods are more convenient than taking the time to sit down (either at their home or at the church) to talk with people at length about what is needed, why it is needed, and how it can be done. Because the idea is prevalent that getting volunteers is difficult, especially in this age when people equate time with money, churches opt for the easiest methods and do not reach their potential. As a result, the church fails both the Lord and members. There are numerous people out there who need to serve for their own spiritual well-being and are willing to serve but have never been approached in a suitable way.

It takes time to do it right the first time. There is no shortcut. Lou Holtz, Notre Dame football coach, catches what is wrong when he says, "We have instant coffee, instant tea, and instant restaurants. Everybody looks for a quick fix. There isn't any. You build it every day. You don't panic....If you preach the same thing over a period of time, they're going to believe in you or they're going to leave." [5]

The matter of carrying out the Great Commission is connected with the way volunteers are enlisted. There is no short fix.

The **Employment Agency's** work of enlistment can be accomplished by following these guidelines:

1) Identify and list occupations (skills and training) of church members, reflecting their interests and capabilities.

2) Discover and list member interests in working for the Lord, and match that interest with a position in the church. If there is no such position, create one! There may be no corollary between what people do for a living and what they are interested in doing for the Lord. For example, there are teachers who prefer a change of pace and opt not to teach Sunday Church School. We can honor these feelings.

3) List positions available and print what is entailed for each position.

4) Select people to conduct interviews for open church positions, and teach them how to do it.

5) List members unemployed in the church.

6) List members employed in the church's work, how long they have been on the job, and evaluate their effectiveness.

7) List those who have more than one job in the church's work and what they do. Be on the lookout for burnout. Strive to keep members from having more than two jobs. Spread responsi-

bilities around; it makes for a happier and more wholesome church atmosphere.

8) Match people with positions open.
9) Interview people for positions open.
10) Instruct people how to do the job they have accepted.
11) Accept and respect a "no" answer. (However, people do not always mean "no" and may require more motivation and nurture.)
12) Report to the congregation what is being done and by whom.

Set aside a Sunday in the year when all people with church jobs are honored. Announce the total number of volunteer hours given, and describe a variety of accomplishments. Translate this into total dollars saved for the Lord's church at an average wage per hour, even minimum wage per hour. Figure the total hours given and how many staff persons it would have required to do the equivalent work; e.g. 200 volunteers at 1 hour a week = five staff persons. Set up booths for members and visitors to view after worship which list jobs now being done, and another list of open job opportunities. Consider calling this event— PRAISE THE LORD AND PASS THE COMMENDATIONS SUNDAY. It is, after all, evidence of God working through people.

The above is a general description of how to select and enlist people for kingdom work.

*

Now let us be specific about enlisting people for organized evangelism.

1) Select, enlist, and teach people how to make a Possible Member list. (See Chapter Ten for instructions.) Two or three people can accomplish this work and keep it up-to-date. With a computer, they can track the worship habits of Possible Members.

2) Select, enlist, and teach people how to make telephone calls on first-time visitors. These telephone calls need to be made regularly on Monday evening, with follow-up on Tuesday and Wednesday evenings when necessary. For example: some calls will result in no answer or an answering machine. The purpose of such telephone calls is to discover Possible Members. Personal visits need not be made until such determination. To make personal visits on worshipers prior to finding out whether they are valid Possible Members (unless there is an unlisted telephone number), wastes person power and time.

3) Select, enlist, and instruct people how to make visits on those who have been determined as Possible Members. (See content of instruction later in this chapter.) This is a seasoned group who have a high sense of God's call and understand how the Spirit works through them. Although telephone calls and home visits are targeted to enlist people in the next INFORMATION TALKS FOR VISITORS, these home visits may include a) identification calls (determining if a person is a Possible Member), b) cultivation visits (people who rightfully require personal touch which a telephone call may not satisfy), c) people who have no telephone listing or who have not been at home when the Monday callers telephoned, d) repeaters— people who worship but have not taken an advanced step and need personal contact. Note: There will be people who make their entry into the congregation via Growth Groups, Prayer Groups, Bible Study groups, etc. However, they will need the INFO TALKS to prepare them for membership. There are also congregations which feel formal membership is unimportant, content to build up worship attendance, a worthy goal in itself. Somewhere along the line, however, commitment to Christ and his church is necessary. Those who take what the church offers without a willingness to make a commitment, consider church membership just a piece of paper. Baptism is more than a sheet of paper! The INFO TALKS can be the turning point in the life of a person.

4) Select, enlist, and instruct two groups of members to make, a) telephone calls, and b) home visits prior to a series of the INFORMATION TALKS FOR VISITORS. Two weeks prior to the beginning of the INFO TALKS, home visits are effective. One week prior to the INFO, telephone calls are necessary, as a follow-up.

The number of Possible Members on file will determine how many people are needed to do this. The number of telephone callers needed obviously will be fewer. Home visitors are more effective as a team (two). It takes three to five cards (names, addresses, telephones of Possible Members) for a team of visitors to work through in an evening, since some Possibles will not be home. Note: Lay visitors need not make appointments prior to making visits; doing so runs the high risk of turn-down.

Remember to include children and youth among home visitors. Families calling upon families make a lasting impression. Teach childen and youth how to make visits. Include them in your instruction. Help the children and youth to grow up being evangelists!

Teaching evangelists.

"I run out of gas, out of material for instructing my evangelists" stated one pastor. "Give me some ideas." Here are some:

Whether you can make it a requirement for all potential evangelists or not, it is a good idea to have all telephone and home visitor evangelists experience the INFORMATION TALKS FOR VISITORS. If they are going to invite people to it, they need to know first-hand what it is. The INFORMATION TALKS FOR VISITORS, discussed in detail in Chapter Twelve, is a series of talks by the pastor(s) which give attendees a basic understanding of Christianity. Evangelists are not required to know the Bible from cover to cover, to give an answer to every question asked, or to be a walking encyclopedia on the Christian faith. The evangelist invites people to "come and see" as Andrew brought his brother, Simon Peter, to Jesus. Therefore, look upon the INFORMATION TALKS FOR VISITORS as basic training for the evangelist. It is boot camp!

Inform your evangelists-in-training that they are one of millions selected by Our Lord through his church to contact Possible Members. Naturally, they want to know what to do and how to do it.

Remind your evangelists that they are not asked to "win" anybody. Only God can win. They are not expected to be super salespeople, clever conversationalists, overwhelming people with witty words in favor of the kingdom. So, what are they supposed to do? They are to plant seed and water. Saint Paul gave this open secret of evangelism in I Corinthians 3:6, "I planted, Apollos watered, but God gave the growth." We need not worry about results. In fact, even the people you contact cannot of themselves decide to become Christian. It is the Holy Spirit who gives faith. Throughout the INFORMATION TALKS FOR VISITORS the Spirit will be at work. The Spirit will be at work through evangelists, even giving them words to say and the spirit in which to say them, as they issue invitations to attend the INFO TALKS.

Tell your evangelists that witnessing to the truth in Christ is the Christian's natural responsibility. Peter and John and the other disciples discovered this at the time of Pentecost. Claimed by the Holy Spirit, they spoke with simple clarity and conviction, and thousands believed. That is what we attempt to do in the INFORMATION TALKS FOR VISITORS. During the INFO TALKS the Holy Spirit will move among attendees. Not all attendees will accept. That is their prerogative. They are invited to come, without obligation. Inviting and bringing people to the INFO TALKS is a way to open the hearts and minds of people who have yet to make a decision for Christ and his church. God will take care of the decisions as the Gospel grips the hearts and minds of believers.

Implant in the minds and hearts of your evangelists that they are part of a great stream of witnesses through the centuries (Hebrews 12:1), and that Christ gave to the disciples, and through the disciples to us, the responsibility of proclaiming the Good News. No one can transfer this witness to someone else. You cannot pay someone to do it for you, not even your pastor. Every Christian is an evangelist. By the nature of your belief in God, you are an ambassador for Christ. Because you claim Christ as Savior, Christ claims you as witness. God is depending upon you. If you are his, you are his witness.

Clarify for your evangelists the words "witness," "ambassador," and "evangelist" and that these words are used interchangeably. In the New Testament, witness means to bear testimony. An ambassador is one sent with a message to deliver. An evangelist is one who announces good tidings. As the seventy, we go out and come back with joy!

Emphasize that evangelists have a unique witness which only they can give. It is a scientific fact that no two people are exactly alike, not even identical twins. No two people have the same spiritual experience with the Savior. Only you, in your own way, can tell the story of what Christ and his church mean to you. Whether you are a recent convert or have been a Christian all your life, you have a witness to give. All the experiences of the believer—catechization, Bible study, prayer—are now brought into action for God. Your witness is as unique as your fingerprints.

Caution evangelists that the starting-place in making contact with Possible Members is on their knees. We visit with God before we make visits. "But you will receive power when the Holy Spirit has come upon you; and you will be my witnesses in Jerusalem, in all Judea and Samaria, and to the ends of the earth." [6] Before his ascension Christ instructed the apostles to remain in Jerusalem until they received that power. After they went to the upper room, they devoted themselves to prayer. Here the Holy Spirit spoke to the apostles and translated belief into action. These apostles acted for Christ because they were acted upon by Christ. You and I cannot speak, either, until we have been spoken to, and we cannot act until we have been acted upon. The evangelist goes forth after quietly yielding to the power of the Holy Spirit.

Point out to your evangelists that they will go out in faith and fear. Yes, of course they will! We will go out in faith assured that God is with us. "...Remember, I am with you always...." [7] And we go out in fear, too. Everyone who does calling experiences fear. It is natural. Without such trepidation, we go depending upon technique and personality to carry us through. Go in faith and fear, depending upon God's guidance. He will bless our witness.

Just out of seminary and in my first church, I visited one evening a man who had attended worship. He had told me at FRIENDSHIP TIME that he was the west coast director of Buick Division. I was impressed; it didn't take me long to decide to zoom out to this man's home! As I drove toward his house, I soon realized I was coming into a plush area. Suddenly coming into view was this big, beautiful house. I began to think in these terms: "What could a young squirt just out of seminary say to such an important man living in a house that must have servants!" I became fearful and zoomed right past his house! As I circled the block, I became ashamed of myself. "Didn't the Lord tell you that he would be with you always?!" Finally, I got enough courage to stop my cheap little auto in front of his enormous house. I was actually trembling. I prayed for help. Gradually, I opened the car door, got out, ambled slowly up the steps and long walkway and arrived at the door. "Suppose a servant answers the door? What do I do? Hand him my hat?" I rang the doorbell. After it had rung, I wanted to run away. I prayed that nobody would be home! Then the door opened and here was this man himself smiling and welcoming me into his home. I discovered, as important as he was, that he was just like any other human being. He didn't talk down to me. We had a delightful conversation. He introduced me to his family. They became members of our new church family.

That man, George, was responsible for over fifty people becoming a part of our church. Often have I said to myself, "Suppose you had let your personal fear dominate and you never visited that man. You would not only have missed George but over fifty people!" So, I know what fear is like, and I now know what faith is like.

Outside a louvered window, birds make a nest each year. They are finches. It is intriguing to watch the little babies grow and finally fly away. Before the babies are old enough to fly, their parents and other finches fly back and forth in front of the nest attracting the attention of the baby birds. The older birds put on a flying demonstration for the babies. They fly back and forth and then perch, giving the babies the idea of what they can do. Finally, one of the baby birds gets the idea, ventures over the side of the nest and begins to fly. One by one the babies understand they are made to fly and tumble out of the nest!

It is something like that for us as beginning evangelists. Hardly do we know we are born to be evangelists. Once we venture to fly in faith, we never go back to nesting in the parish. We begin to understand we are made to be evangelists.

Teach evangelists that they cannot lose. Whenever people go out in the name of Christ and under the influence of the Holy Spirit, something good is bound to happen. Not always will people agree to attend the next series of the INFORMATION TALKS FOR

VISITORS. The influence of your call may not become evident for weeks, months, years, perhaps never. However, as a representative of the Christian church, your testimony is an important part of the evangelization of a person whether he/she is immediately receptive or not. The idea is to plant seed!

The teacher of evangelists, whether a pastor or lay person (both can be equipped to do this), will want to emphasize and review these concepts over and over again. Use scriptural illustrations, as well as your own. Spend time in prayer with your evangelists. You will never "run out of gas" again.

*

After an evening of calling by evangelists, invite everyone to return to the church for dessert, and conclude with a Report Meeting. (In large cities this may not always be feasible.) Record how many visits were completed, how many people were enrolled in the INFORMATION TALKS FOR VISITORS, etc. (See Appendix #1 for a form.) Give evangelists time to talk about their visits, without the use of names (we do not want to be categorized as gossips). Let evangelists tell their stories, as the seventy did. Think through questions the Possibles ask. Talk over how to meet obstacles. Formulate answers that help. Analyze approaches. What works—keep; what doesn't work—throw away. There isn't just one approach. Every person is like a country with different customs. You may have to make more than one visit to a country to understand what the different customs mean. So it is with people we visit—other visits may be necessary.

*

A seasoned member of a church cornered me with a question: "I have served on Council, taught Sunday School, and gone to church all my life. Yet, I'm not sure what to say to these Possible Members. Can you give me some pointers?" I was grateful she did not say, "Tell me what to say!" Below are some specifics.

After receiving oral instruction and an assignment packet containing calls you are to make, visit two by two. Actually, you will visit three by three, for Christ leads the way. "...He is going ahead of you to Galilee...." [8] as the angel told the women on resurrection day, and they told the disciples.

Memorize the information on the Possible Member Data card before each call. (See Appendix #1 for sample.) The Possible Member is not to see the card or other evidence of instruction. Decide which of you will take the lead in the conversation. Keep only one conversation going during the visit, although each of you shares in the witness.

Final Instructions

1) Know the location, dates, and times for each of the sessions of the INFORMATION TALKS FOR VISITORS, and the nature of the instruction. Those who attend are under no obligation to unite with the church. (Avoid the term "join." People join clubs. People unite with Christ and his church.)

2) Acquaint yourself with the program of the church, the hours of worship, the time of Sunday Church School, the various opportunities for Christian growth.

3) Know when your congregation was organized, and how many households are in the membership now.

4) Familiarize yourself with any printed material you are to distribute, especially the card entitled AN INVITATION TO THE INFORMATION TALKS FOR VISITORS (See Chapter 12). Be selective of any printed material you leave, usually not more than two pieces. People pitch it if there is too much to read.

5) Endeavor to enroll Possibles in the INFORMATION TALKS FOR VISITORS.

6) Learn how to assist Possibles in filling out these forms: "Individual Information Sheets For The Church Files" and "Request For Letter Of Transfer." (See Appendix #1 for samples.) The "Individual...." form is for people who indicate interest in uniting. When they so indicate, be ready to seal the membership decision with the form "Individual...." The form "Request...." is for those who are members of another church and are eligible to transfer.

7) Pray as you reach each Possible Member home, that God will speak through you and that the Possible(s) will be receptive.

8) Determine who will be the lead visitor.

9) Expect a positive response.

10) Remember the pointers on how to start, continue, and conclude a visit.

Pointers

Like the birds falling out of a nest and learning to fly, so people learn to visit by visiting. Confidence is reinforced by experience. Evangelists are eager to tell others of Christ and his church.

Now you are at the door! Your finger presses the doorbell. Your heart beats with uncertainty. Suppose these people are unfriendly? Suppose you fail and falter in telling the story? Don't worry.

Pointer Number One. You are going to make mistakes. Even the most experienced evangelist makes mistakes. Be able to laugh at yourself, even in front of a Possible Member. On the whole you will find an overwhelming majority of Possibles to be friendly. Few people are seemingly unfriendly. Disinterested? Maybe. Unfriendly? No, for the most part.

Pointer Number Two. The door opens and the lead visitor makes the introduction. "I am Jack Andrew, and this is my wife, Jane Andrew." (You have stated your name twice in the event it was not heard distinctly the first time!) "We are from First Church, and we have come to express appreciation to you for the privilege of worshiping with you recently." You smile and have an expectant look on your face. You do not put your foot in the door. but your body has that forward look!

In the event the Possible Member has guests, excuse yourself and suggest another time when it is more convenient. (Have a day and time in mind.) "Would tomorrow evening at 7:00 be convenient?" (If not, tell them you will telephone for an appointment.) You cannot do justice to a call when a disinterested party is present. If the Possible Member(s) is dining, the same procedure prevails; excuse yourself and make an appointment.

You are invited into the house! How do you start the conversation?

Pointer Number Three: Be observant. Survey the room and look for items of interest as conversational pieces. Children are starters. Unusual pictures or gadgets furnish ideas for questions. Or, just ask about themselves: where home was, their occupations, how long they have lived in the community, and like questions. Tell them something about yourself, too! The beginning conversation need not take long.

Pointer Number Four: After five minutes, try to get to the point of your call. But suppose the television set is on, or the stereo is in high gear? A convenient way to handle such a situation is to speak in such a low voice that you cannot be heard. Somebody in the household will catch the cue and turn the noise off. If the set is not turned off, indicate that you are having some difficulty hearing. Be courteous and polite in your tone of voice.

How do you channel the general conversation and get to the point of the call?

Pointer Number Five: People like to talk about themselves. After your genuine expression of interest in them, conversation flows like water in a flood. The intent is to turn the conversation into the direction of Christ and his church.

Perhaps you will have been talking about things which you have in common. Therefore, you could begin by saying: "We have so many things in common. There is something else we have in common, too, and that is our belief in God. (There will be rare occasions when the person(s) does not profess belief in God. If talking to a disbeliever, when you begin talking about the INFORMATION TALKS FOR VISITORS, you can point out that that is where the INFO TAKS begin—as if no one believes in God.) Let the Possible Member talk about his/her belief, if inclined to do so.

Pointer Number Six: Be a good listener.

Pointer Number Seven: Be a good announcer of the INFORMATION TALKS FOR VISITORS. You could begin, in another approach different from above, by saying, "It has been delightful talking with you and becoming acquainted, but as you may have guessed, we have come for a specific purpose. Periodically our church provides a series of INFORMATION TALKS FOR VISITORS. These TALKS are designed with people like yourselves in mind. People shop for a church. People have questions about what a church teaches and believes. We think that is an intelligent way to approach things. That is why the INFORMATION TALKS FOR VISITORS is important. We give you a notebook with outlines for each of the five sessions and by the time the INFO TALKS are completed, you have a brief summary of what we believe and teach. Hundreds of people have found that the INFO TALKS help them get a handle on things. Since there is no obligation and it is free, we invite you to the next series of the INFORMATION TALKS FOR VISITORS which begin Sunday, June 28, 9:30 a.m. in the library. The library is located next to the worship center One more thing, in the event you must miss one of the five TALKS, we provide you with an audio or video tape and outline of the session missed so that you can keep up to date. Sounds good, doesn't it?!" (This is said in an affirmative tone of voice, expecting a positive response.) Listen.

Pointer Number Eight: Take people where they are in their religious thinking. We cannot hope in one visit to correct misconceived notions about God. The INFO TALKS are designed for this.

Pointer Number Nine: Do not argue. You can discuss Christianity without insisting on your viewpoint. Your job is to tell the story of the INFO TALKS. Endeavor to place Christ in the heart and mind of the hearer.

Pointer Number Ten: Tell what it means for you to be a part of the Christian faith, as:

+ I receive a Christian education through the teaching of the Bible.

+ I hear the Word of God which feeds my Christian faith.

+ I learn to trust and love our Savior more in the church.

+ I realize all over again my unworthiness in God's sight and his marvelous mercy toward me.

+ I receive forgiveness of sin and strength to live the Christian life through the Sacrament of The Lord's Supper.

+ In the company of other Christians at worship, I am drawn closer to God.

+ I participate in God's commands through the church and help tell the story of Christ in all lands.

+ As a Christian, I want to be a part of the church, for Christ established the church and his Spirit guides the church.

+ In our church we pray for each other and take a special

interest in one another. I would be dreadfully alone without this fellowship.

+ Christ died for me. I want to live for him in the company of his followers, sensing God at work in my life, and guiding me into his future.

Pointer Number Eleven: Be a closer. Take out the card, INVITATION TO THE INFORMATION TALKS FOR VISITORS, and place it in the Possible's hands. Be sure they understand what the INFO TALKS are. Then ask, "May we count on you?"

If the answer is "yes" have the Possible fill out the card, tear off the bottom part and return it to the church, leaving the description of the INFO TALKS with the Possible Member. Have available the dates and times of the INFO TALKS and give that list to the Possible Member. Tell them that you look forward to seeing them at the first session of the INFO TALKS beginning on Sunday, June 28, 9;30 a.m., and that you will be there to greet them. Ask them if there is any transportation needed and if so, offer to take them to the INFO TALKS.

If the answer is "no" to the invitation to attend the INFO TALKS or the Possible Member is uncertain, state the date of the next series of the INFO TALKS. Always leave the Possible in a friendly way. Prayer may be appropriate, although not always. If the invitation has not been accepted, thank the Possible Member for his/her time and consideration. At the same time, never let a person feel that he/she is justified in remaining outside the Christian church. Always plant the seed for the next series of the INFO TALKS.

On Telephoning Possible Members

This section on specific instruction concludes with a few comments in reference to the use of the telephone. The telephone is not a substitute for home visits. However, the telephone is an effective way of contacting Possible Members. I have found Monday, Tuesday, Wednesday evenings, and Saturday morning as prime times.

There are three benefits to using the telephone from the viewpoint of the Possible Member: 1) They do not have to worry about how the house looks; 2) They can control time; 3) They can be themselves and say what they want to say without becoming involved.

I must confess most of my contact with Possible Members these days is by telephone. Try spending Monday, Tuesday, and Wednesday evenings of each week (especially between the hours of seven and nine) telephoning Possible Members. It will pay off. One of these days it will be by videophone!

Here is a telephone example in contacting people who are first-time visitors. "Hello, Leila Brown (I use both first and last name as a matter of identification), this is Pastor Click from First Church. We want to thank you for the privilege of worshiping with you on Sunday. We are always interested in impressions of first-time visiitors. What was your first impression of First Church?" Listen. "Thank you! We are all the time trying to improve and comments such as yours are taken seriously. What prompted you to attend First Church?" Listen. Usually a friend invited them or they rode by the church and wanted to see what it was like on the inside or just felt like going to church that Sunday. "Wonderful! We are so pleased that you took the time to worship. That says something good about you. What church are you a member of?" If they are members of another church—"It is good to talk to another Christian. What is happening in your church these days? Got any ideas for us?" Listen. Some will share ideas. Some will give you the hint that they feel they are not being fed and are looking around. This is a delicate situation. Encourage them to try again with their church. At the same time, assure them that your church is open to them.

If they are not members of another church and/ or are church shopping, describe the INFORMATION TALKS FOR VISITORS. "We have something just for you. It is called INFORMATION TALKS FOR VISITORS. It is a series of five Talks by the pastor(s) designed for visitors, such as yourself. It is actually an update on the world of religion. No obligation is involved. It is free. We give you a notebook and an outline of each session. If you must miss a session, we provide you with an audio or video tape and outline so you can keep up. Sounds good, doesn't it?!" Listen. Expect a positive answer. "The next INFO TALKS begin on Sunday, June 28, 9:30 a.m., in the Library. The Library is located to the right of the worship center, on the first floor. If this interests you, and from our conversation I detect some interest, I will send you a reminder of the when, what, and where of the INFO TALKS." Listen. People do respond affirmatively. Yes, they may not follow through. But, you can follow through with another contact prior to the actual beginning of the INFO TALKS. By such a conversation, you have good ground on which to build. If there is hesitation, thank them for their time. By the tone of their voice, you can determine whether to put them on the list to be contacted for the succeeding INFO TALKS.

You can instruct people how to make telephone calls on Possible Members by giving them an example in writing, as above. They do not have to follow the exact words. But if you analyze the words in the example given, there are insights on what to say and how to say it which will help Possible Members respond in an affirmative way. Instinct, as well as instruction, goes a long way in developing successful telephone evangelists.

Retooling Evangelists.

One of the problems businesses face is keeping their employees enthused as well as informed. Businesses pay big fees to motivators—successful people who go around the country telling about their keys to success. Red Auerback of the Boston Celtics is one.

"'How did you keep your players motivated?' That's the number one question I get when I speak before management groups. Managers must think I used some magic formula to roll to 16 world championships, nine as coach, seven as general manager and president. Well, I didn't.

"You can't motivate a team or a group. You have to motivate an individual. What gets one person going can turn off another. There's also no quick fix when it comes to motivation. It's a gradual process that starts in the initial recruitment of an employee or a player and builds through a career.

"The key to motivation is attitude. If a player doesn't have the right attitude, he isn't going to play for the Boston Celtics. Period."[9]

Auerbach is right. Sit down with your evangelists one by one and talk about attitude. Evangelists can become as discouraged as anyone. In addition, bring in specialists, as business does, to give your evangelists new perspectives.

ABC televised what they called SPORTS SPECTACULARS which featured stars from various sports competing against one another in specialties foreign to each. A fighter, a pole vaulter, an automobile racer, a tennis player, a baseball player, a basketball player, a football player—all were pitted against one another in several events whether pingpong, bowling, batting a ball, weight lifting, a dash, a run, bicycle riding, golf, and the like. Regardless of age or height or weight—all competed against one another.

It was surprising that the pole vaulter could lift more weight than a world boxing champion and could go on to win the marathon-like event. But the pole vaulter freely admitted he could not last very long in the ring. There was one thing he could do better than anybody—he could pole vault.

There is one thing you and I can do better than anybody else. We can introduce others to Jesus Christ and his church. In fact, we are the only ones who can do it.

Tell these things to your evangelists as you endeavor to motivate them in groups and one on one. Daniel Hudson Burnham (1846-1912), architect and planner of cities stated: "Make no little plans. They have no magic with which to stir (people's) blood and probably they themselves will not be realized. Make big plans; aim high. Remember that our (children) and our (grandchildren) will do things that would stagger us. When you create a situation that captures the imagination, you capture life, reason, everything." [10]

In evangelism, if you reach for the stars, you may not make it, but at least you won't come up with a handful of mud.

The key to motivation and having the right attitude is having something of the mind of Christ in our minds. Christ made big plans—"Go into all the world...."

Retooling evangelists involves giving evangelists a steady diet of insight, information, and inspiration.

Types of People

Evangelists will meet many types of people as they visit. It is good to be prepared for them. Try to see through excuses and proceed to the point of the call—to enlist the Possible Member in the INFORMATION TALKS FOR VISITORS. The following illustrate some types of people you will meet!

You will meet the gentleman who confesses that he is good enough. "Why, I am better than most of your church members who go every Sunday. I haven't run over my neighbor's lawn mower lately, and I don't beat my wife. I feel that I am getting along quite well, thank you. I haven't done anythng of which I'm ashamed. I'm a pretty good citizen. I try to do my part for the betterment of the community."

Well! What is **Mr. Good Enough's** problem? As an evangelist you understand that a person does not become a Chistian until he/she first recognizes that he/she is a sinner. But Mr. Good Enough wouldn't understand if you told him bluntly he was a sinner, so you keep that to yourself. What he is lacking is a personal, close relationship with God.

"Of course, you are a good person! Probably better than I'll ever be. But you know, Mr. Good Enough, it is not enough to be good. Christianity is more than a set of moral standards. It is a way of looking at life through the eyes of Jesus. You could be missing something. The church is a caring community, like a familly. Try the INFORMATION TALKS FOR VISITORS and then make a decision."

Mr. Sympathetic is glad to see you. "My, I think it is wonderful what you Christians are doing! I read in the newspaper about the various church doings and I watch Robert Schuller on television. You Christians are to be commended. You know, I wouldn't live in a community without a church. I'm sympathetic with what you are doing. But, well—I'm just not a churchgoer!"

Mr. Sympathetic doesn't realize that Jesus is not interested in sympathy. Christ wants the whole person. "Whoever is not with me is against me...." [11]

As long as you know the Possible Member's problem, you can talk more intelligently with him. Do not blurt out his problem and make him face it! Try to get him to face it by indirect reasoning.

"We surely are delighted to hear you say such nice things about Christians and about our church. We work mighty hard to honor God. But you know it goes deeper than that. We believe Christians exercise their belief through the church. Your sympathetic views are valuable. You love your wife, don't you?! She is not primarily interested in your sympathy, is she? She wants your love. So Christ wants your love expressed in the Christian church. Besides, how would you feel if overnight the churches would disappear?"

There is no short-circuit of conversation in this visit. **Mrs. Hypocrite** uses the direct approach on you. "Why, there are too many hypocrites in the church! I wouldn't think of going. I can live without those fakers."

Hypocrites in the Church

Explain to Mrs. Hypocrite the meaning of the word "hypocrite." "I hear what you are saying and have similar feelings. That's why I looked up the meaning of the word 'hypocrite' and this is what I discovered. The word 'hypocrite' does not mean an individual who goes to church, worships God, and then fails to fulfill all of the teachings. That is a description of a sinner. The church is full of them. A hypocrite does not really believe in Jesus Christ. A hypocrite may put on an outward show to please his wife so that she won't nag him into going to church, or a hypocrite may think it is good for her business to go to a church. Church-going may even soothe his/her conscience and boost his/her spirit. A hypocrite is a pretender. Actually, I suppose only God knows who the hypocrites are. Since a hypocrite is a non-believer, Mrs. Hypocrite, I am sure you do not mean to say that you would let a non-believer keep you from participating in God's commands?

"Of course there are hypocrites in the church! What better place for a hypocrite to be than in the church! At least there a hypocrite is exposed to the Word of God, and there is the good chance of his/her accepting this Word. We worship Christ, the Head of the church. We neither worship nor neglect worship because of people or their religious failures. There are hypocrites in a movie theatre or at a ball game. Do we stay away?!"

Another character you will contact is **Mr. So-What**. After you have told your story so beautifully and feel that you have made your best presentation, a look of disinterest appears on the face of this individual, and he says, "Ah, so what?" It is apparent that Mr. So-What has not been listening, so you will have to go back over your story very carefully. Try to change the quizzical "what" to the "Who" in his life. This individual may have no anchor in life. He is not bound by conventional values. His knowledge of the Christian faith is limited. Invite him to the INFORMATION TALKS FOR VISITORS, so he may have a basis on which an intelligent decision can be made.

Mrs. Too-Busy immediately gives you a long list of her activities. "You know, I'm in too many community activities already. Besides, I do work, you know, part-time in a Lab. Every Tuesday is the bridge club, and on Thursday I have my hands full taking care of the Cub Scouts! The children's schedule is so irregular, and my husband is so demanding! You can see that I'm just too busy at this time to think of uniting with a church."

Explain to Mrs. Too Busy how you can relate to what she has said and then zoom in on the meaning of the word "worship." "Wow! You and I are in the same boat. I just can't get around to doing everything. Then one day I began to think about what I was actually saying to God. Of course, I didn't mean to imply, 'Well, God, I just don't have time for you.' That would have been disrespectful. I suppose what we mean when we say we are too busy is that so many activities consume our time that there is so little time left over. I had to re-think my choices, and 'seek first His kingdom and His righteousness.' That makes sense, doesn't it?!"

Mr. Too Much Religion says: "When I was a kid, my parents made me go to church morning, noon, and night. I made up my mind that, when I became a man, I wouldn't have anythng to do with it. I had too much religion when I was a kid."

Too Much Religion

You might be tempted to ask this person, "If you had so much religion when you were a child, where is it now?!" Naturally, you do not say this to him! You need to draw this individual into a consciousness of the fact that we can never get enough of Christian education and experience of God. Besides, Christianity is a demanding religion. God expects the life of the believer to be completely devoted to the Savior. In business we cannot expect to develop just by living on past laurels. We must continue to learn in our business. Christian experience parallels this. We have to work at Christianity or waste away. The real fact of the matter is that Mr. Too-Much-Religion never really got it in the first place. In the INFORMATION TALKS FOR VISITORS he will have opportunity to recognize his immature beliefs and will be given the opportunity truly to accept Christ as Savior.

Willing—

Mr. Willing is the individual whose response gladdens your heart! You will have the pleasure of visiting him more frequently than you think. "We are surely glad you came tonight," Mr. Willing exclaims. "We were hoping someone from the church would come. It has been many years since a representative of the church has been in our home. That INFORMATION TALKS FOR VISITORS you mentioned sounds like a good idea and will give us the opportunity to gather pertinent facts about the Christian faith. We might as well get started going to church right away." Yes, you will meet many people ready and willing to accept the invitation which you give on behalf of our Lord and his church. Although America has a large percentage of church members, there are millions of people in the wilderness waiting for us to contact them.

*

Retooling evangelists is a continuing responsibility. The word "retooling" means "to reequip" or "reorganize." Both meanings apply to evangelism. Whenever evangelists feel they have enough instruction and experience in contacting Possible Members, watch out! It is easy to depend on your own cunning, instead of on the power of the Holy Spirit.

We need prayer, the Word, the Spirit in us—a renewing sense of purpose in life, if we are to make an impact. There is no short-cut. It is hard work, but the prime privilege of the Christian church. Rejoice, evangelists, for you have a vital part in extending the Kingdom of God!

THE INFORMATION TALKS FOR VISITORS is the target of our invitation to POSSIBLES. It is the subject for the next chapter.

CHAPTER TWELVE

THE INFORMATION TALKS FOR VISITORS

"Despite their differences on many matters (church people) through the centuries have held tenaciously to the divine origin of the Word, its veracity and authority, the fulfillment of prophecy in Jesus of Nazareth, and the focus of faith in Christ as the basic New Testament witness."[1]

The INFORMATION TALKS FOR VISITORS is a series of talks, usually by the pastor(s), on the main tenets of the Christian faith. Such TALKS are designed for non-members. (Members are encouraged to attend also, as a refresher course. Youth and adult classes of the Sunday Church School, one after another, could attend a series as a matter of information as well as serving as a support group.) Visitors attend without any obligation whatsoever. After attending the series of TALKS, visitors may or may not make a decision to unite with the congregation. The INFO prepares them for church membership, if they feel led by the Spirit to do so.

Encourage those who are uniting with your congregation by letter of transfer to attend the INFO TALKS, for four valid reasons: 1) An update on the world of religion. (For example, there is another Bible translation— NEW REVISED STANDARD VERSION—published in 1990); 2) A comprehensive presentation of the Christian faith which can serve as a springboard for a deeper understanding; 3) An opportunity to become acquainted close up with the pastor(s) and other leaders in the church. 4) A chance to associate with people who are also searching.

From the viewpoint of the church, there are other reasons why transferees need to attend: 1) You do not know the status of a person's faith; the INFO TALKS can ferret out incomplete or erroneous information. 2) Everyone who attends the TALKS come into your church on a similar level of Christian understanding. 3) An updating of information is necessary since change is constant inside and outside the church.

How did the INFORMATION TALKS FOR VISITORS get its name? I created it (as I did The Pastor's Class) and have used it for over a decade. Visitors appreciate TALKS designed for them alone, TALKS which purport to give them basic information about the Christian faith. The name tells visitors the church is interested in them. Try it!

How many sessions in a series of the INFORMATION TALKS FOR VISITORS? That's your decision. Some pastors require a half dozen or more. Visitors can feel threatened by too many sessions. Others require only two or three sessions. There is danger in giving too little information. The INFORMATION TALKS FOR VISITORS is the opportunity of a lifetime to plant seed. It is conversion time, the Holy Spirit's work.

Therefore, every person who gives these TALKS needs to take preparation seriously. The teacher needs to know the material so well that he/she can sit in a chair, surrounded by visitors, and talk as one on one. What could be more exciting than sharing the Christian faith? Thus, the teaching needs to wring out of you every ounce of belief and feeling. People who attend need to sense your sincerity as well as your ability to tell the story. Talk as if your life depends on what you say, and the lives of your attendees, whose spiritual lives may hang in the balance.

What kind of demeanor will the teacher have? A humble attitude. An authoritarian approach turns people off. Tell them: "These TALKS are designed to be helpful to you. At the conclusion of each TALK (or if something is burning in your heart and you can't wait that long—blurt it out!) questions will be invited. If I know the answer, I will be glad to share it with you. If I don't know the answer, I will be honest and say 'I don't know' and together we will find the answer. Remember, too, there are questions which have no answers. If we had all the answers, we would be God. I, or the church I represent, do not have all the answers to questions about life. We do have enough answers to help people have a right relationship with God and people. Does that sound fair?!" Right away people catch something of who you are and where you are. They realize you are searching along with them. That is important.

What subjects to cover in the INFO TALKS? That, of course, will be up to you. Here are mine.

TALK Number One: BELIEF IN THE TRIUNE GOD.
(Step by step on how a person can come to know God.)
TALK Number Two: HOW TO GET A HANDLE ON THE BIBLE.
(Six ways of settling the matter of interpretation plus a listing and description of books helpful in home study.)
TALK Number Three: THE SACRAMENTS.
(What is a sacrament? Are they hocus-pocus?
Only an historical drama?)
TALK Number Four: THE STORY OF THE CHRISTIAN CHURCH.
(What and How the church got its start and what it is today.)
TALK Number Five: WORSHIP.
(What is it? How do we do it? What does it do for you?)

*

It is vital to know the religious background, if any, of attendees in order to teach effectively and to reach these people. At the first TALK, invite people to share that information; they will be delighted to know that others in the TALKS are searching, too. Take nothing for granted: begin as if no one believes in God and go on from there. A great percentage of visitors attending today have little knowledge of the triune God or the Bible. That is particularly true of the so-called BABY BOOMERS (people born between 1949 and 1969), although not restricted to them. In one TALK two older people remarked, "You talk about Matthew and John. Who are they? We don't know."

In a little book which I hope to complete entitled, THE INFORMATION TALKS FOR VISITORS, written from the viewpoint of Lutheran theology, each session will contain the full manuscript. It is sufficient here to provide general outlines as starters:

*

TALK NUMBER ONE - BELIEF IN THE TRIUNE GOD
Introduction

The possibility of God's existence (or whatever you choose to call that someone or something more powerful and knowledgeable than human beings) exists whether we believe it or not.

As children, we were taught a fable about the cow jumping over the moon. We laughed. Only a few years ago, it was just as incomprehensible to believe a human being could travel to the moon and back. Since it has been done, we acknowledge this possibility existed all along, even in the time of Columbus, whether human beings believed it or not.

Likewise, there is the possibility of God's existence, whether we believe it or not. In considering this possibility, whether to accept or reject someone or something beyond ourselves, we land in the realm known as "belief" or "faith."

I. How a person can approach believing in God.

a) Settle who is in charge—human intelligence or an intelligence beyond ourselves? Adam and Eve in the book of Genesis depict our situation. They wanted it all. We are like that; it is called original sin.

b) Acknowledge that the combined human intelligence of the ages is limited. We are finite. God is infinite. There never was a time when God was not (Genesis 1:1). God always was. is now, and always will be.

c) Contemplate how God put life together. If we were in charge, we would have done it differently! Questions keep coming into our minds. Earnest and sincere questions are good. Discovering how God put life together is a continuing quest. The ten commandments, for example, teach us something of how life is put together. Ignore any one commandment and life can get mixed up. For instance, morality is a matter of responsibility. We are our brother's and sister's keeper. To ignore God's commandments is dangerous.

II. How people have tried to relate to God.

    a) Erected altars and made sacrifices (possessions, animal, human) to express what is inside of them in order to reach out to what is beyond them, thinking to appease the creator, especially when the elements of nature threatened existence. For example: burnt offerings were supposed to be pleasing to the nostrils of God.

    b) Endeavored to be on a par with God, striving for excellence, called Eros, a Greek word for upward love (a love that begins and ends with us).

    c) Created religions (systems of belief) of their own with adherents claiming a relationship with God.

III. Christianity is God-given, declaring belief in the triune God, who initiates contact with his creation.

    a) The Old Testament (testament—a covenant or promise by God to people) is the written (scripture) record of a progressive revelation of God, in and through the lives of believers in one God. Because he is our creator, we call him—Father.

    b) The New Testament verifies the coming of God to this earth in person, given a name—Son, Jesus Christ.

    c) The Holy Spirit is God's presence today, at work in and through believers.

    d) This triune God is omnipotent (all power), omniscient (all knowledge), and the source of all—the God of creation.

    e) Christianity does not know (nor does anyone) why creation came about, how creation took place, and how long this earth we live on was in the processs of formation. Christianity only asserts who created it, as the first words of the Bible declare, "In the beginning...God created the heavens and the earth...."[2]

    f) Christianity asserts that in the beginning God provided all the necessities of life on this planet. Human beings have difficulty sharing and distributing to all persons these necessities. Human beings, left to their own desires, follow a basic drive inherent in human nature which allows the strongest to survive.

    g) Christianity contends that God did not create and then desert his creation but that he continually keeps contact. We call this Agape—a Greek word for self-giving love—God coming to us with the gift of faith.

h) Christianity believes Jesus Christ is the answer to the human quest to know God, for Jesus demonstrated in human flesh what it means to be human in the best sense of the word and to be God in the only sense of the Word—love.

IV. How God continues to make contact with people today.

a) Creation is not only a past tense activity of God but a present tense reality.

b) Jesus Christ is not just an historical figure but is alive today.

c) The Spirit of the Creator, the Spirit of Jesus Christ, the Spirit of God is forever creating and renewing.

d) God creates groups of believers and gathers them into the church (Matthew 16:18; Matthew 18:17; Acts 2).

e) A believer is a person who has settled the matter of who is in charge of his/her life and who is in charge of creation, accepting the faith offered by this triune God and his plan of salvation.

f) Christianity relies heavily upon a word that is not in the Bible—Trinity—that conveys God's three distinct persons. This is to say that God is one and makes himself known in three different personal guises: Father, Son, and Holy Spirit. Another explanation is to say God is Creator (like a good parent); Redeemer (Christ makes us good as new when we fail to love God and one another); Sanctifier (Holy Spirit aids us in daily living). God is all this. He loves us and that is why we love him. Thus, the Apostles' Creed which Christians confess, expresses who God is and announces his plan of salvation.

Conclusion

Belief, the gift of the Triune God, is the recognized action of God in human life.

*

TALK NUMBER TWO - HOW TO GET A HANDLE ON THE BIBLE

Introduction

The church uses a word which deserves explanation and that word is "grace," which means God's love given to us without our deserving it.

Two ways God's love comes to us are: 1) The Word, and 2) The Sacraments.

When there is a capital "W" in the first letter of "Word" it means Jesus Christ, from the Greek "Logos" (Word) as in John 1:1 "In the beginning was the Word, and the Word was with God, and the Word was God." It could be translated, "In the beginning was Jesus Christ, and Jesus Christ was with God, and Jesus Christ was God." Since Jesus Christ is God, he existed from the beginning. In time God came in human form and was given the name "Jesus" which means he will save his people.

Three ways in understanding the Word are:

1) The incarnate Word (made into flesh) — the historical Jesus Christ.

2) The written word of God — The Bible.

3) The Living Word — The Resurrected Christ.

It is this written word we consider now. Many people feel embarrassed if they do not know much about the Bible or how to read it. If you have ever felt that way, this talk will give you the tools to help you read and understand the Bible. We are a generation blessed with a variety of accurate Bible translations that are affordable.

Unfortunately, Christianity is divided into its two understandings as far as the Scriptures (the writings) are concerned: 1) Literalism, and 2) those who employ Biblical Criticism.

1) The Literalists, sometimes called fundamentalists, take the Scriptures verbatim and hold to the inerrancy of the Bible. For example: the Creationists.

2) Biblical Criticism (criticism in the sense that you try to find out as much about the origin and history of the Bible as you can). They use, a) Textual Criticism, which seeks to ascertain as nearly as possible the exact words of the original writer, and b) Documentary Criticism, which seeks to shed light by background material.

Christian churches using either the literal interpretation or Biblical Criticism respect one another and work together in many, many ways through organizations of the Christian church in this country and around the world. This church teaches — (and here you insert your own understanding of the Scriptures). Include the purpose of the Bible, the relationship between the Old and New Testaments, and the principle that the Bible interprets itself.

*

Whether you are a literalist or an advocate of Biblical Criticism, provide a list of books for a basic home library. Provide copies of HOME LIBRARY SUGGESTIONS along with an order form listing prices. Display books and encourage attendees to browse before and after remaining INFO TALKS. Fill their orders. Visitors will appreciate this service.
Here is a possible list of books.
1) Two Bibles: a) New Revised Standard Version of the Bible;
b) Today's English Version.
2) The Harper Collins Study Bible.
3) A Commentary such as Harper's.
4) A Concordance such as Cruden's.
5) An Atlas such as Oxford (small) or Harper's (big and beautiful).
6) Helps for homes with children: a) Hurlbut's Story of the Bible or b) Egermeier's Bible Story Book; c) Walter Wangerin, Jr., The Bible For Children.
7) Helps for homes with children of a tender age, such as Tomie dePaola's Book of Bible Stories or My Good Shepherd Bible Story Book.

This session excites people as you help them get a handle on the Bible.

*

TALK NUMBER THREE - THE SACRAMENTS
Introduction

1) Define a Sacrament.

2) State why the Roman Catholic church has seven sacraments and why most Protestant churches have only two. (There were 49 sacraments in the Middle Ages.)

I. List the criteria for a sacrament to be a sacrament in your church.
II. Answer the question, "What is the purpose of the Sacraments?"
III. Give an explanation of Baptism.

a) Are children baptized or not? with an explanation of your church's stance on this matter.

b) Are people immersed, sprinkled, or water poured upon

the baptismal candidates? And why do you do what you do?

    c) What is meant by "born again"? since people ask this question all the time.

    d) Who can administer baptism in your church? and the reasons for your practice.

    e) What are the benefits of baptism?

    f) What is the duty which baptism imposes?

    g) What part does faith have in baptism?

    h) What good does baptism do?

    i) What happens to people who are not baptized?

    j) Why should I be baptized?

    k) Why was Jesus baptized and why didn't he administer baptism like John the Baptist?

    m) The thief on a cross next to Jesus wasn't baptized and never attended an INFO TALK. What happened to him?!

    n) How can baptism be a daily resource for Christian living?

Answers to these questions will give INFO attendees a view of your church's teachings. They want to know. It gives you the opportunity to relate what the Bible says about baptism as well as your church's teaching.

IV. Explain the Sacrament of The Lord's Supper?

    a) Why are there several names given to this Sacrament and what do they mean, such as Sacrament of the Altar, The Lord's Supper, The Table of the Lord, The Communion, Holy Communion, the Eucharist?

    b) Review the history of the Passover Supper and its connection with this Sacrament, as well as practices of Old Testament priests.

    c) At what age do you receive this Sacrament and why not at all ages?

    d) What happens to babies and small children during the administration of this Sacrament?

    e) Do you practice open or closed communion? Why?

    f) How is this Sacrament administered in your church and why do some churches have people go down front and others sit in the pews?

g) What elements do you use and why? What happens to these elements during the administration? Declare Christ's presence in the Sacrament. What happens to the left-overs?

h) Who can receive this Sacrament and why? Must I be baptized first? Why?

INFO attendees want to know if all this ado about Sacraments is necessary, why Christian churches differ, and does it make any difference?

*

TALK NUMBER FOUR - THE STORY OF THE CHRISTIAN CHURCH

Introduction

What the church is. It is not a building. The church consists of believers in the triune God as expressed in the Christian faith.

I. When was the church founded and why?

II. Is the church visible or invisible? Or, both?

III. If the church is one, as it claims to be, why are there so many churches, denominations, and sects? Recall the Nicene Creed "...one holy catholic and apostolic church."

IV. Why is the church called "holy"?

V. What is meant by the church as "militant" and "triumphant"?

VI. A glimpse of church history.

a) The Apostolic Church to 100 A.D. What was it like? e.g. Establishing new churches; New Testament writings.

b) The Ancient Church, 100 to 692. What did it accomplish? e.g. The creeds. The Canon. Organization.

c) The Medieval Church, 692-1517. What progress did it make and what difficulties did they encounter, and why?

d) The Time of the Reformation, the 16th century. Why was there a Reformation and what did it do?

e) How did Protestantism originate, why, and how did it get to this country?

f) Why do not the churches unite into one big church?

g) What is ecumenism? The National Council of Churches? The World Council of Churches? What good are they? (Attendees will be surprised to learn churches have more in common than they have differences.) State the difference between your denomination and other mainline churches.

*

This TALK gives you the opportunity to lift up Christ and his vision for the church throughout the world. It describes the wonderful work of the Christian church through the ages, what the canon accomplished, the value in the formation of creeds, how church government developed, as well as updating what is happening throughout the world of the church today. It invites the teacher to describe personalities that have dotted the history of the church. It challenges you to express your love for the whole Christian church and how we are not in competition with one another but brothers and sisters in Christ. The validity of various churches in existence today is in their love for one another, their ability to maintain their own beliefs and yet cooperate and respect others in their understandings of the Christian faith. Each church body makes a contribution to the picture of Christianity. Discussions between Roman Catholics and Protestant churches, and among Protestants have been going on for years and are bearing fruit. Together, we are lifting up Christ and his church!

*

TALK NUMBER FIVE - WORSHIP
Introduction

    a) The words "worship" and "worthy" come from the same root.

    b) "...Worship is growth in communion: it is apprehending more and more the presence of God." [3]

    c) Jesus' conversation with the woman of Samaria at Sychar: "But the hour is coming, and is now here, when the true worshipers will worship the Father in spirit and truth, for the Father seeks such as these to worship him. God is spirit, and those who worship him must worship in spirit and truth." [4]

I. There are churches which worship according to a church year of ancient vintage, namely Roman Catholic, Greek Orthodox, Lutheran, Episcopalian.

    a) A church year calendar revolves around the life, death,

resurrection, ascension, and the teachings and works of Jesus Christ.

    b) If you are one of the above churches, describe your worship calendar according to cycles, the meanings of the seasons, the colors used, and why.

    c) Describe principal festivals, lesser festivals, commemorations, and the dates assigned to each.

II. Describe your own worship practices and why, especially if you do not follow a church year calendar.

III. Why do human beings worship?
- a) There is an innate desire to give reverence to God.
  - —In ancient times the worship of nature;
  - —Sacrifices were made, both human and animal;
  - —Altars were built symbolizing God's presence;
  - —The building of the first Temple by Solomon;
  - —The significance of the Holy Land and sacred places;
  - —Cathedrals erected in Europe;
  - —Architectural designs of churches in the United States.
- b) Worship is possible anywhere, anytime.
  - —Alone;
  - —In a congregation ("For where two or three are gathered in my name, I am there among them" — Matthew 18:20);
  - —From the desert to the sea, wherever and whenever we stop to reverence God.

IV. The components of worship (see Worship by Luther D. Reed):
- —Obedience;
- —Reverence;
- —Communion;
- —Fellowship;
- —Sacrifice;
- —Celebration;
- —Education and inspiration;
- —Following the commandment to remember the worship of God;
- —Power;
- —Sensing the Spirit.

V. The equipment for worship.
>   —Liturgy, if you have one, citing scriptural references;
>   —Christian symbolism in your church building;
>   —The worship center in the form of a cross, if it is, and the explanation of church words such as chancel, nave, narthex, altar, pulpit, lectern, baptismal font, stained glass windows, carvings, etc;
>   —The history of your worship book and how to use it (with a worship book in their hands);
>   —Description of organ, vestments, communion ware—ciborium, paten, chalice, flagon, corporal pall, purificators, veil or fair linen, credence table, lavabo, burse, common purse, paraments (superfrontal, antependium).

VI. Why go to worship (church)?
>   —"I was glad when they said to me, 'Let us go to the house of the Lord!'" (Psalm 12:1);
>   —Jesus worshiped consistently (Luke 4:16);
>   —The practice of the Early Church (see Acts 2);
>   —The third commandment, "Remember the Sabbath day, to keep it holy." (Christians worship on Sunday because Jesus rose from the dead on the first day of the week; thus, every Sunday is celebration of the resurrection.
>   —Consistent worship says something about the faith of a worshiper;
>   —Worship as an expectation of the Christian;
>   —Attitude about worship, as the Psalmist exclaims about being glad to go to the house of the Lord—not a chore or duty only, but a privilege.
>   —Worship as a witness to what you believe, a demonstration of your love for God, an example for others, especially your neighbors.
>   —When you wake up on Sunday morning, there is no question about what you are going to do that day—going to church, as natural to do as opening your eyelids!

Conclusion

Distance to the church is as far as our appreciation, our

need, our longing for worship, our desire for Christian fellowship, our passion for Christian accomplishment.

*

You can cap off the INFO TALKS by giving attendees A VOCABULARY FOR CHRISTIANS, a listing and explanation of words used by the church. Physicians, engineers, woodworkers— all have words common to their profession. So does the church. Make your own list. Here is a list of some words and expressions Christians need to know:

God, Eros, Agape, Revelation, Creed, Father, Son, Holy Spirit, Creation, Redemption, Sanctification, Means of Grace, Incarnate Word, Written Word, Living Word, Law, Gospel, Synoptic gospels, Biblical Criticism, Textual Criticism, Documentary Criticism, Bible, Apocrypha, Aramaic, Septuagint, Bible Dictionary, Commentary, Concordance, Sacrament, Baptism, The Lord's Supper, Holy Communion, Sacrament of the Altar, Table of the Lord, Eucharist, Passover Supper, Instituted, Real Presence, Church, Church Visible, Church Invisible, Church Militant, Church Triumphant, Reformation, Ninety Five Theses, Catechism, Apostles' Creed, Nicene Cred, Athanasian Creed, Augsburg Confession, Apology of the Augsburg Confession, Smalcald Articles, Large Catechism, Formula of Concord, Name of your national church body, Synod, Bishop, Worship, Church calendar, Advent, Christmas, Epiphany, Lent, Holy Week, Easter, Ascension, Pentecost, Trinity, Symbolism, Altar, Pulpit, Lectern, Font, Chancel, Nave, Narthex, Liturgy, Liturgical Colors, Evangelism, Stewardship, Old Testament, New Testament, Jesus, Christ, Apostle, Disciple, Saint, Angel, Sin, Prayer, Confirmed, Affirmed, Repentance, Omnipotent, Omniscient, Heaven, Hell, B. C., A. D., Faith , Resurrection, Eternal Life, Salvation, Scripture, Office of the Keys, Paten, Ciborium, Flagon, Chalice, Fair Linen, Superfronal, Antependium.

*

Some Mechanics In Reference To The INFO TALKS

1) Determine the day and time when the INFORMATION TALKS FOR VISITORS will be offered. (I announce TALKS ten minutes early so that attendees will have time to register, get a name tag, grab a cup of something, and get acquainted. For ex-

ample, 9:20 a.m. with the TALK actually starting at 9:30. This helps give you a full hour for teaching, needed indeed.) Sunday morning is convenient for most Possible Members. It gets them going to church on Sunday morning. Many will worship and attend the INFO TALKS; however, there will be some not ready to handle a two hour Sunday morning, Do not worry if this happens, especially at the beginning. As the INFO progresses, encourage them to worship so they can get a feel for the church. Prior to the session on WORSHIP, suggest they worship as a group and bring their impressions to the TALK. When they have had the experience of worship, it is easier for them to make a decision about becoming a part of your church family (see 12 below).

The disadvantage of scheduling the TALKS on Sunday morning is that it restricts the pastor at the teaching hour, except when the INFO is not in progress. Since Sunday is targeted for the visitor, however, members will understand the importance of the pastor(s) teaching the INFO. I have tried morning, afternoon, and evening on Sundays and during the week. I have repeated the TALK on Tuesday evenings with some success. I have tried an all-day Saturday session. Sunday morning has been the most successful. (It also sets a pattern for attendees to keep coming at that hour for adult education courses and worship.)

2) Prepare outlines for each session.

3) Compile notebooks (inexpensive folder) for each attendee, and insert the first session outline, as well as blank pages for writing notes.

4) Appoint members to serve as receptionists for each series of the INFO TALKS (e.g. five TALKS in a series). Appoint young as well as older people, for obvious reasons. Receptionists greet attendees, help them register and obtain a name tag, give them refreshments, introduce them to each other, and escort them to a seat. Receptionists help attendees feel at ease. Another important factor: members become involved as they meet INFO attendees. (In some churches, adult Sunday Church School classes or growth groups rotate in attendance at a series, and serve as receptionists and as support groups.)

5) Provide registration slips (e.g. name, address, tele-

phone). For succeeding sessions have repeaters record their presence on a pad. This saves time. First-timers always fill out a registration slip.

6) Provide juice, coffee or tea, (doughnuts?!) on a table in the center of the room, and invite attendees to replenish any time.

7) Arrange chairs in a circle or rectangle, with the teacher sitting at one end with a clear view of every person. Although you give attendees an outline at each session, refer to it sparingly. Sit and talk with these people eyeball to eyeball. Urge them to study the outline during the week. At the close, share additional materials which amplify the subject for the day.

8) Introduce yourself at the outset of the first TALK—where you were born and reared, your education, and your religious background. Invite each attendee to state his/her name, where they came from, and what church background, if any. As stated earlier, if you know the religious background, you will know how best to teach. There are pastors afraid to ask about religious background out of fear of embarrassing an attendee. This is false timidity. Indicate that the INFO TALKS are for everybody and that we come from different backgrounds as well as from different locations. If they have no religious background you can say, "Many people in your particular situation have found the INFO TALKS especially helpful. I commend you for coming. We thank you for being here!"

Caution: Watch the clock! Time can escape without getting to the purpose of the session. The number of individuals in the INFO TALKS will be a guide as to the time available for this maneuver. There are instructors who spend more time relating to people than they do relating the message God has given them to share. There needs to be a balance. At the beginning of each TALK you can prompt attendees to talk about themselves. For example: TALK Two, ask attendees to state their name and vocation. TALK Three: their name and hobbies. TALK Four: their name and the name of another attendee (to see if the networking is taking place). TALK Five: their name and one thing they have learned in the INFO TALK that has been of significance.

9) Telephone each attendee during the week. Why? a)

You show an interest in each person. It encourages consistent attendance. No one is taken for granted. Occasionally, you will sense somebody is about to drop out and you can make suggestions. For example: "Thank you for sharing with me. It looks as if your personal calendar precludes finishing the INFO TALKS at this time. I suggest you put October 2 on your calendar. That's when the next INFO begins. You can begin again! I will send you a reminder. That sounds fair, doesn't it?!" b) It gives each attendee opportunity to share their feelings. Ask each week: "Do you have any questions?" This reassures attendees they can ask questions and get answers. It also lets you know whether communication is going on. c) Thank them for attending.

10) Provide a name tag that can be worn during each session. Instruct attendees to leave the tag at the end of a TALK and to pick it up at the beginning of each session. This helps attendees network and aids you in calling them by name.

11) Provide audio and video tapes, and outlines for each TALK. You can either record each TALK or make tapes at your own leisure. Keep on hand about ten tapes (for both audio and video) of each TALK. Pre-recorded sessions have an advantage: you can be sure all the information for each TALK is included, not preempted by time. Most people have a recorder and/or VCR. However, have available a recorder and a VCR that can be lent. Business people often listen to tapes in their automobile as they commute or are on trips.

Why have tapes of each session? a) If a person must miss a TALK (in this busy age some will), they can make-up by having a tape (audio or video). Instruct lay visitors to deliver tapes when attendees miss, along with an outline of the missed session. These casual visits give lay visitors opportunity to meet and greet attendees. If attendees know ahead of time a TALK will be missed, encourage them to take a tape and outline of that TALK. Attendees return the tape the following session. If anybody wants to buy a tape, set a minimal fee. You might be surprised how many people want to have a complete set of the INFO tapes. Video tapes are the most popular.

b) Providing tapes answers excuses for not being able to attend at specific times. Tapes and outlines also serve people who must work at the announced times for the INFO TALKS. On occasion, I have had some people go through the INFO TALKS entirely by tapes and outlines. Then, of course, I made appointments with them to make sure communication was complete. Make it easy to get the information but not too easy! There is no substitute for eyeball to eyeball communication concerning the Christian faith. But, if people can't come when we are available, we can make the information available to them.

12) Make your commercial to unite with your church toward the conclusion of the fourth TALK. Here is an illustration: "We are very pleased that you have taken the time and energy to be here for the INFO TALKS. At the outset, we said there was no obligation by attending and there isn't. At the same time, we want you to know the process in the event you feel Spirit-led today or next week to become a part of this church family. Feel no pressure about this. We are not interested in numbers. We are interested in people and want to be helpful. The INFO TALKS have prepared you for the next step. The next step is to go over to the table where there is a pad entitled, 'Yes, I wish to become a part of the First Church Family' and write your name on that pad. Also, pick up what we call is an 'Individual Information For The Church Files.' Fill it out and leave it on the table, or take it home with you and bring it with you to the next INFO TALK session. Prior to an Orientation, you will be assigned a sponsor or if you wish, select your own. Sponsors help new members settle in. On (date) there is the Orientation Supper-Meeting for new members. It is free and about the only free supper you will get around here! The Orientation will tell you about the nuts and bolts of the church organization and your part in it. One week after the Orientation, new members will be received. Welcome! Thus endeth the commercial. See you next week!"

Do not worry if some fail to put their name on the pad. You have opportunity during the week, as you telephone each attendee, to talk it through with each Possible. For example: "Your attendance at the INFO TALKS has been an inspiration to me. As you recall, there is no obligation involved. At the same time, we want to give everybody opportunity. What are your thoughts, at this juncture, about becoming a part of our church family?" If they are not ready, tell them it is o.k. and that their decision can come later. By the conclusion of the fifth session, when you will want to repeat the commercial, most if not all will have decided to become a part of your family. Those who don't, don't. Invite "undeciders" to the Orientation Supper-Meeting also. (Described in the next chapter.) Tell them to come to get the specifics concerning member privileges and responsibilities and then make up their minds. Get a firm commitment from them as to attendance at the Orientation so that you will have enough food. Indicate to the "undeciders" that no sponsor will be assigned to them and that only those who have decided to become a part of the church family will be introduced at the Orientation. Tell them they do not have to make a decision to become a member and that they do not have to attend the Orientation. Keep in touch with "undeciders" and they may say "yes" later on.

13) Announce in the bulletin and newsletter when a series of the INFO TALKS is closed and when the next series begins. Closing registration for a series prevents people from feeling they can just drop in anytime. A good time to close is at the conclusion of the second session. If people come into the INFO at the third session, unless they have reviewed previous tapes and outlines, they will find it hard to get the feel for the INFO. In fairness to everybody, close registration. It gives credence to the INFO TALKS.

14) Three weeks prior to Orientation, begin listing in the bulletin the names of people who have decided to unite. This encourages others to make a decision, too. Repeat this procedure each week with added names. There is another benefit: the congregation can start to become familiar with new member names.

15) Keep pew racks filled with cards describing the INFORMATION TALKS FOR VISITORS. Regularly refer to them in bulletins and announcements.

A Final Point

Make audio and video tapes describing the INFORMATION TALKS FOR VISITORS. In the narthex, have the video running at all times on Sundays. Provide modern-day home visitors with a supply of these tapes. If they cannot complete a call because it is inconvienient for the Possible Member(s) to see them (dinner guests, etc.), instruct home visitors to leave a tape along with a letter of explanation. (It is not a good idea to leave tapes on doorsteps of the not-at-homes.) For those not at home, the visitor can mail the tape, accompanied by an explanatory letter, inviting the Possible to return the tape the next time they worship— placing the tape in a designated box in the narthex. This procedure almost eliminates incomplete calls. It also prompts Possible Members to worship again. Possible Members, seven out of ten, will return the tape. If they do not, you have an excuse to visit again or telephone.

Following the INFO TALKS, come wonderful occasions— the ORIENTATION and RECEPTION of new members. The next chapter describes them.

CHAPTER THIRTEEN

ORIENTATION AND RECEPTION OF NEW MEMBERS

"When Martin Luther was most troubled by doubt and discouragement he would take a piece of chalk and write two Latin words on the top of his study table: Baptizatus sum — I have been baptized."[1]

THE ORIENTATION

The ORIENTATION SUPPER-MEETING FOR NEW MEMBERS follows the conclusion of the INFO TALKS, usually occurring the next Sunday, for four reasons: 1) Continues the momentum of the INFO TALKS which they attended five Sundays in a row. 2) Provides time to process membership papers; 3) Allows time to help some INFO attendees come to a decision; 4) Gives additional time to enlist sponsors, although the process of enlisting sponsors can begin as soon as someone decides to become a member.

The RECEPTION OF NEW MEMBERS can be one week after the ORIENTATION. Thus, if you are following a five week series for the INFO, it will take a total of seven weeks to complete the process.

To ORIENT means to face the east. If a church building is perfectly placed on a section of land, the chief altar is at the eastern end. It is symbolic— we face in the direction of the rising of the sun and thus herald the resurrection of the Christ at dawn. ORI-

ENTATION, too, means to face in the right direction, to get our bearings, to become acquainted with the existing situation, and to gather facts. ORIENTATION, thus, is introducing new members to the church of the risen Lord.

Make the ORIENTATION a gala affair! A Supper setting is ideal. For example, schedule an Orientation Supper-Meeting on a Sunday at 5:00 p.m. This time of day meets the needs of parents and their younger children, who go to bed early, and older children readying for school the next day.

The Orientation usually takes two hours and a half, including Supper (possibly less time for a smaller church). Make it a free supper! How? Ask sponsors to bring potluck, sufficient for themselves and a new member family. Sponsors are glad to do this and it involves them in a responsible way. The church can furnish beverage, tableware, and plates. Sponsors sit with their guests and become acquainted. Church representatives attend, such as the president of the congregation, presidents of organizations, chairpersons of committees, and the pastor(s). All members of the Church Board should be in attendance, denoting interest in the lives of new people. These representatives bring food also! Provide a nursery for babies and child care for young children. If you have a dozen new members, you will probably have forty to fifty people in attendance; if forty new members, over a hundred. It can be an exciting time! The ORIENTATION gives new members reassurance; it gives leaders a feeling of progress.

Who are the invited guests at the ORIENTATION? Those who have completed the INFO TALKS (or a previous series of the TALKS and now want to unite), and those who are transferring membership. It is best for transferees to attend the INFO TALKS, too. Be prepared for some objection if you make this a requirement. However, I do make it a requirement for transferees to attend the fifth session of the TALKS on WORSHIP. This session provides transferees opportunity to become acquainted with other possible members, and gives everybody needed information not covered in the ORIENTATION. Thus, in attendance at the ORIENTATION will be children and adults to be baptized, those who for the first time are becoming members of a church; those renewing their faith; and transferees. What a happy occasion!

Issue Supper invitations to the few in the INFO who have yet to decide about church membership. It is natural for some to want to know exactly what is involved in becoming a member of a church before making such a decision—the Thomases. After the ORIENTATION, follow-up. Be patient. No pressure. You have planted the seed. God will bring any increase. If you invite the "undeciders," remember to arrange for more food. It is a good idea to have "Stand-By-Sponsors" in the event someone decides to unite the following Sunday.

What is a sponsor and what does a sponsor do? A sponsor is a member of the church who is given responsibility for shepherding a new member(s) for a designated period, for example ninety days. Why ninety days? The first ninety days of a new member's church life are critical. If you do not get the new member connected in that time, there is danger the new member will be headed for the inactive (collapsed) list or lost. (See Part IV which addresses the matter of the collapsed). The beginning days of a new member's life are akin to that of a newborn baby. During the first ninety days of a baby's life, parents and physicians work closely together. For new members, sponsors are like parents and the whole church is like the Great Physician.

Prepare a descriptive list of sponsor responsiblities, distribute, and discuss in a planned meeting of all sponsors. Endeavor to enlist new sponsors for every reception of new members, with no repetitions for a year, if at all possible. Serving as sponsor recalls entrance into the church and refreshes the meaning of church membership. This is one way the Spirit recycles people, shrinking the number of collapsed members.

Duties of sponsors include: 1) Sit with new members in worship, or arrange for others to do so, during the ninety days. 2) Escort new members to Friendship Time (following worship) and introduce them to at least three other members, each of the Sundays. 3) Invite and take new members to an education course (Sunday Church School), at least twice. (Plant the seed for a two-hour morning, Sunday Church School and worship.) 4) Invite and accompany new members to at least one organizational meeting or

Growth Group. 5) Invite new members to their home or a restaurant for a meal, at least once during the ninety days. 6) Answer questions, and get answers when sponsor does not know.

The work of sponsors dare not be mechanical or doting. Sponsors are not to smother new members or force new members to do all that is described above. The level of Christian commitment on the part of new members can be raised when sponsors take their role as seriously as if a newborn baby had been placed in their arms.

Pairing sponsors with new members is a matter of judgment, usually selected according to age, education, interests, hobbies, location, etc. Not necessarily! For example, older people can sponsor younger people and vice versa. Having a right attitude toward new people coming into the congregation, exercising responsibility toward new members is far more important. Thus, make it clear to sponsors what their role is and what is involved. The job of sponsor is to aid new people in making a connection.

New members may select their own sponsor, of course. There will be other occasions when a change in sponsors may be necessary. It can be handled easily when explained to new members: "We like to have more than one set of sponsors for new members whenever practicable. John and Mary Smith will be your primary sponsors from now on. Isn't that great?!" It is a good idea to have a "chief shepherd" for sponsors, overseeing progress or lack of progress in this whole concept of sponsorship.

It is wise to make an agenda for the ORIENTATION-SUPPER MEETING, including the amount of time allotted for each segment. Here are two samples.

Orientation Supper Meeting For New Members
(Sample One)
Sunday, December 14, 5:00 p.m.

4:30   Tour of the church facilities for those who so desire, including an explanation of symbols. (Please note: if you do this, announce this opportunity ahead of time.)

5:00   Sponsors give New Members permanent name tags, packets, and escort them to location of picture taking for the

	church directory. While new members pose, sponsors arrange the supper.
5:15	Prayer prior to the Meal by_____
	Lineup for food - New members first along with their sponsors.
5:40	Video on "The Spirit of First Church" (shown during dessert time)
5:55	Reading of a scripture, and reading of congregation's mission statement in unison, led by the Evangelism Outreach Committee Chairperson.
6:00	Introduction of New Members and Sponsors (Children may adjourn to nursery after introductions, if parents so choose)
6:10	Welcome by the President of the congregation_____
6:13	What It Means For Me To Be A Christian Today by_____
6:16	What It Means For Me To Me To Be A Member of First Church by_____
6:19	What It Means For Me To Be A Pastor of First Church by_____
	Introduction of Pastors and Staff and Summaries of Responsibilities
6:25	Opportunities Galore! (One minute commercials by representatives of the Sunday Church School, Choir(s), Organizations, and Committees)
6:50	"Getting Settled Into A New Church Home: Seven Components For The New Member" by_____
7:20	Review of the Order for Reception of New Members, Sunday, December 21 (at any of the three worship celebrations), including where to check in before the worship celebration, where to sit, where to stand at time of reception, instructions for those to be baptized, how to give commitment (pledge) card, and where to stand in the reception line at the end of the Service.
7:29	Prayer, Benediction, and On Our Way Rejoicing!

Orientation - Supper Meeting Agenda (Sample Two)
For New Members, Sunday, April 18

4:30 p.m. - Tour of Church Campus led by Ruth Rust, Evangelism Chair
5:00 - Grace for the Meal by Jim Reese
5:35 - Video about the Spirit of First Church
5:50 - Introduction of New Members (children and adults) and their Sponsors
6:05 - Children of New Members and Sponsors exit to the Nursery and Child Care
6:10 - Introduction of First Church Leaders by the Pastor
6:15 - Music
6:20 - Group Discussions on "Getting Settled Into A New Church Home: Seven Components For The New Member" with an introduction by the President of the congregation, Carl Cohenour.
7:05 - Review of the Order of Reception of New Members, the arrangement of baptisms, and the determination of which worship celebration the reception will take place on Sunday, April 25.
7:20 - The Benediction and on our way rejoicing!

New Member Reminders

1) Please be in the west narthex fifteen minutes prior to the worship celebration so that the Evangelism Chairperson can check you in, give you a flower of recognition, and take your picture.

2) Please wear your member badge.

3) Please bring your commitment card and place it in the offering plate along with your offering.

4) During the last hymn, please follow the pastor(s) out to the west narthex and form a reception line. When people greet you, make it easy for them by extending your hand.

WELCOME!!!

In preparation for the gala event, the ORIENTATION - SUPPER MEETING, target these items:

1) Prepare packet for each new member household and include:

a) Agenda, b) "Getting Settled Into A New Church Home: Seven Components For The New Member", c) copy of church's organizational structure, list of church leaders, pastor(s), and staff, d) description of "Opportunities Galore....", e) a digest of church's financial picture, f) a commitment card with name of new member(s) on the card, g) offering envelopes, and h) church directory. (Make available the constitution, for those who desire one.)

2) Make permanent name tags for all new members, including children, to wear each Sunday. Attach a green ribbon (symbol of growth) to each name tag. Why? It will help members recognize new members and will assist everyone in becoming acquainted. At the next Reception of Members have these three-month old (approximately) members stand to be recognized and have their sponsors remove the green ribbon from their name tag, signifying that they have made a connection. In preparation for that occasion, alert these three-month old members and sponsors what will be done. This helps all new members feel that their reception into membership was not a routine matter and that they were not taken for granted. This ceremony recognizes "new" member progress in becoming settled into their new church home. It sends a signal to incoming members and the congregation that new members are not coming in one door and going out the other! It also increases worship attendance!

3) Enlist and instruct people who will give presentations at the ORIENTATION.

4) Print agenda in quantity for all new members, sponsors, and others who may be scheduled to attend.

5) Prepare personalized commitment cards for all new members, along with a brief description of how to fill it out.

6) Telephone each new member household prior to Reception, not only as a reminder, but to alert them to the importance of being on time, since there is a tight worship schedule.

7) Make arrangements for nursery and child care at the ORIENTATION.

What if a new member can be present for the Reception

but cannot make the Orientation Supper? Arrange for a private appointment during which time you can review the highlights of the Orientation, especially "Getting Settled Into A New Church Home: Seven Components For The New Member," the commitment card, arrangements, etc. This could be the dual responsibility of the president of the congregation and the pastor.

What if a new member can be present for the Orientation Supper but cannot be present for the Reception of Members? Receive the new member the Sunday morning before the Orientation or at a time convenient for the new member. Meet questions such as these with positive solutions. In other words, receive new members while they are hot but make sure they do what is expected of others. "No one escapes the ORIENTATION" is my motto.

We have mentioned the SEVEN COMPONENTS, which are described below. The COMPONENTS outline for new members how they can excercise their Christian privileges, as well as fulfill responsibilities. The SEVEN COMPONENTS are strong suggestions about how to get settled into a new church home. They are not laws, only opportunities. They help new members get connected. New members following the SEVEN COMPONENTS are unlikely to become lost or fall into patterns of inactivity. It is not enough to receive new members, as joyful an occasion as it is. Our responsibility is to give new members basic help in following the Christian life. Print the SEVEN COMPONENTS (or write your own), distribute them at the conclusion of the FIFTH TALK or mail them to new members and sponsors prior to the ORIENTATION, place another copy of the SEVEN COMPONENTS in the new member packet, and review (or read) each COMPONENT during the Orientation. This is the entree of the Orientation Supper! You will never have a better opportunity to teach people what it means to follow Christ. New members are open to the Good News. Serve it! Those in attendance, in addition to new members, will also benefit.

GETTING SETTLED INTO A NEW CHURCH HOME: SEVEN COMPONENTS FOR THE NEW MEMBER

Introduction

New residents walk into their empty house. It doesn't look like home at all. The moving van arrives. It is unloaded and familiar things fill the house. However, it takes more than the sight of familiar things, more than an arrangement of furniture to make them feel at home.

Taking up new residence involves adjustment. It takes some people weeks and months to feel at home. Meeting new neighbors can be intimidating, even frightening. Uncertainty can set in. Thoughts of needing to be sold a second time cross the mind. Was it the right thing to do, moving here?! When will I feel at home? There are some who never make the adjustment.

People uniting with a church for the first time or changing to a different congregation, even a different national church body, will find that after the excitement subsides, there is an adjustment to be made similar to moving to a new location. Finding your way around the church campus, endeavoring to make new friends, getting accustomed to the leadership, experiencing a different worship format, understanding the implications of the "mission statement," as well as the various programs and opportunities offered, involve adjustment.

Because you have made an important decision to become a part of Christ and his church in this place, we will help you make this adjustment. We cannot do it all. You have a responsibility, too.

Be assured that the excitement of becoming a member can continue. The Spirit (God's presence in life today) is always at work in believers. The promises of God are true. The joy of a right relationship with God and other people will contribute wholeness to your life. The News in the kingdom is always Good! There is nothing more spiritually satisfying than being a Christan, living in one of God's homes—with the Lord Himself as the head of the house.

The good adjustment, however, has much to do with your attitude and expectations plus your determination to make your membership meaningful. Involved is your commitment to the Lord and His church. Ask yourself: how serious am I about being a Christian today and becoming a blessing to others?

SEVEN COMPONENTS, when put together, comprise meaningful Christian living. They help deepen a person's faith. Nobody will make you embrace these COMPONENTS, not even God. God gives you the faith. His church offers the opportunities.

Component One. Worship consistently for ninety days. (Read the third commandment—Exodus 20:8, Deuteronomy 5:12-15; Psalm 122:1; John 4:24; Acts 2:42.)

After that stretch of time, you will feel the "furniture" is in place! You will be in the Christian life-style. If you travel during that period, worship in some church. If you are unable to get to a church for worship, take time for personal and/or family devotions. If you are ill, ask for a tape of the worship celebration. Jesus worshiped consistently. Christians worship the first day of the week because Jesus rose fom the dead on the first day of the week. Every time we worship, we are celebrating the resurrection.

Component Two. Set aside a percentage of your income and give it to the Lord and His church on the first day of the week. (Read Malachi 3:8-10; Luke 18:18-25; Matthew 6:25-34.)

The Lord's church gathers money from its members in order to carry out its mission. There is nothing wrong with money. "...The love of money is a root of all kinds of evil...." [2] God's church rightfully expects money from you as a belief response. No one else is going to tell the story of Christ except believers. This is our God-given responsibility and privilege. God has entrusted to his followers the work of reclamation. We all have been reclaimed at one time or another.

Now it is your turn to put this faith into action. God is counting on you—as he has every believer confessing his name throughout the centuries—to pass on his message of victory over evil and death through his church. This takes believer money.

Try tithing, a giving of 10% of your income. If you feel tithing is out of range right now because of the sorry state of personal finances, begin to rearrange your life-style so that you can do so in the future. Target a date when you will tithe. Meanwhile, set aside a specific percentage of your income for your church. Work up to tithing and beyond. Scripture holds tithing in high regard. Tithing does not make us Christian but is a prudent way of handling the resources God has put into our hands. Money, after all, is simply a reflection of our God-given opportunity and talent. What we do with our money has a direct relationship to how we feel about God. And, his church—your church!

We need to give money to Christ and His church consistently. If you go on vacation or out of town on business, give before you go! The cost of God's business does not stop because we do not show up on a Sunday.

It costs to be a believer. We do not skip over that part of church member responsibility or wink at this matter of giving money, as if it is too personal to talk about. That is why your determination to give a percentage of your income each week makes spiritual sense. We grow in faith as we joyously give from the heart of belief. Instead of something we have to do, it is something we need to do for our own spiritual balance. We are partners with God and with one another. Give and feel good that you have the privilege of helping the kingdom come!

In your packet is a commitment card. (Note to instructor: hold it up for everyone to see. Invite everyone to pull their card out of the packet and look at it. Explain how it is to be filled out.) Why do we need to fill out a commitment card? Because it helps church leaders plan program costs. Commitment cards can be revised at any time, upward or downward, by simply writing to the treasurer to change your commitment. Every commitment helps your church in mapping out its strategy. You do this with your own personal budget. For example, you want to know from your employer what you can count on so that you can determine how much you will have to spend on food and housing, transportation, health care, insurance, savings, school, and recreation. Oh yes, and what your church can count on from you! If you are self-employed, you can make a projection. As you count on your employer for a predetermined income or upon your self-employment projection, so your church needs to be able to count on you.

How do you figure out what to put on the card? How much should you give? Only you can figure that. You know what your income is; you and Uncle Sam! We don't need to know. That is your business. All your church needs to know is this: can you be counted on to be a part of the church's projection of income?

Remember, the widow's mite (Luke 21:1-4) was a larger percentage in giving than the rich people who plunked down coins that reverberated throughout the temple. The widow gave from the heart, Jesus observed. So, the amount of money is not the bottom line. The percentage you give of your income is the bottom line. It reflects your belief. Review your personal budget. List all sources of income. List your expenses. Talk with God about what percentage of your income you need to give. Start with a specified percentage.

Fill out your commitment card and next Sunday, when you are received into membership, place your commitment card in the offering plate as a sign that Christ and His chuch can count on you.

What happens if you do not make a commitment? A bolt of lightning is not likely to hit you on the head. The church treasurer is not going to hound you for it. It is simply a matter of trust. We can always count on God. God never fails the faithful. Let's just say God, too, counts on believers giving money to tell Good News to the world.

Note to instructor: Explain how new members receive offering envelopes. For example: once a month, by mail, and how to use them. (Churches who do this receive more offerings than those who distribute boxes of envelopes for the year!) List through the year designated appeals and what they are for.

Component Three. Enroll in a Bible study. (Read 2 Timothy 2:15.)

The INFORMATION TALKS FOR VISITORS was not a finishing school; it was a jump-start into the Christian faith and church. Learning is life's quenchless quest. Meet the people in the Bible as you endeavor to meet more friends in the faith. Get a handle on the Bible. Use the library resources of the church. Read. Study. The excuse of not knowing enough of the Bible and feeling embarrassed about it is not a valid excuse. The question you need to ask yourself is this: When am I going to do something about this?

The time is now! We never can exhaust the contents of the Bible. The church is the place to get spiritual food. We will provide courses to help you along the way. The best time to get at this matter of consistent Bible study is at the time you become a new member. Delay is deadly. Your spiritual life is at stake. Meeting "new neighbors" in the Bible is not as tough as you might think. The Bible is one way God talks with people and he has done this throughout the centuries. God talks with us today as we read his book. Listen in each day as well as on Sunday.

Component Four. Pray twice a day for ninety days. (Read Matthew 21:22.)

After such a period of time, you will see how vital it is to talk with God on a regular basis. Some people are like fish in a glass bowl, darting here and there, swimming in circles of frenzy. Some feel they must be on the go or they are not getting anywhere. Such people can land at a city dump, which one of my relatives did when he insisted he was headed in the right direction! Prayer points us in the right direction.

For our own good, we need to take time each day to sit absolutely still in silence. Some joggers and walkers have ear plugs belting out a tune, as if they can't stand silence. Bend your knee, if you feel comfortable. Above all, bare your soul to God. Say "Good Morning, God!" and "Good Night, God!" Read your Bible and get your bearings. We will provide you with guidelines.

Prayer is a miracle of life, a gift of conversaton with our Maker. Prayer helps keep us on track. Prayer sensitizes us to the needs of others as well as ourselves. Prayer gives us God's direction. Prayer is emptying the heart; it is being on the level with God. Prayer is simply talking things over with God, as you would with any good friend. "Whatever you ask for in prayer with faith, you will receive" Jesus promised. [3] Try it and you will be glad you did. You may even get healthier. Assuredly, you will feel on good terms with God and feel better about yourself.

Component Five. Serve in some capacity during your first ninety days of church life. (Read John 12:26.)

Of course, you can set aside time to serve God and his church, if you mean business with God. It is a matter of understanding who you are. Now you are part of God's people. It is natural for you to want to serve. Volunteer to serve in some worship capacity, especially if time is at a premium right now, because you are going to be in church on Sundays.

One of the easier ways is to serve as a greeter. Doing so helps you remember names and faces as the weeks go by. If visitors come to worship, you will be able to relate to them better than anyone.

Other immediate opportunities to serve are as an usher, lector (a person who reads scripture in worship), acolyte (lights candles, handles offering plates, etc.) communion helper, a "Circulator"——one who helps others become acquainted and is on the look-out for visitors— at Friendship Time, flower arranger, parking lot attendant, guide, or pew rack keeper. Say "Yes" and you will feel good about serving in the house of the Lord. If you sing, jump into the choir! On the list goes! You will feel "at home" more readily when you serve, especially in matters connected with worship. Try it!

Component Six. Invite and bring a church homeless person to worship and to the INFORMATION TALKS FOR VISITORS, within the next ninety days. (Read Acts 1:8.)

The last instruction Jesus gave to the disciples was to invite others (Matthew 28:19,20). It is the first instruction he gives to disciples today.

Try inviting someone else to take your place in the INFO TALKS. You know the nature of the TALKS better than anyone. Your experience can spill over into the life of another person without a church home. And, there is nothng like the feeling of seeing someone you invited to the INFO TALKS become a member of God's church! The Holy Spirit works through you this way. You are a disciple which means "learner." You can learn to invite others.

In your packet there is THE CARD; in fact, three cards. THE CARD lists the church's name and address, times of worship celebration, and a blank line for you to write your name. As American Express talks about their card, "Don't leave home without it"—DON'T LEAVE HOME WITHOUT YOUR CHURCH CARD. Here is a simple way to approach people and how to use THE CARD. Ask friends and relatives, even strangers on occasion, "What church are you a member of?" (Assume they are a member of a church!) This is an honest inquiry and shows concern for others. If they are a member of a church, exchange ideas. If they do not have a church home, invite them to worship the following Sunday (hand them THE CARD with your name on it) and promise to meet them in the narthex and sit with them in worship. Provide transportation, if needed. Spend money out of your tithe to take your worship visitor(s) to lunch or brunch! Such a gesture will indicate to your visitor(s) you are serious. It is an investment in somebody who needs God. (Business people dine clients; so should Christians. Zacchaeus did this in Luke 19:1-10.) During the meal, ask about the visitor's first impressions of worship. Exchange good feelings. Tell them about the INFORMATION TALKS FOR VISITORS. Relate your experience in the INFO — the way it begins as if nobody believes in God and continues by discussing the basics of the Christian faith. Promise to go to the first session with them. When they are received into membership, serve as their sponsor.

More people are brought to worship and faith in Jesus Christ by such contacts and follow through by the laity than by great organs and sermons. This is a fact.

Component Seven. Go to two or more GROWTH GROUP meetings. (Read II Peter 3:14-18.)

GROWTH GROUPS are groups of members meeting weekly in a home for Bible study, prayer, and exchange of feelings about God, his church, the world we live in, and what Christianity teaches.

If you attend at least two different groups, it is likely you will discover a congenial group with whom you can identify. GROWTH GROUPS are support groups, too. This does not mean baring our souls or gossiping; it means listening to one another about meaningful concerns. It is a good setting in which to meet and make friends. Try it! If you don't like it, try something else.

Conclusion

A little boy was asked how he fell out of bed during the night? He said, "I guess I went to sleep too close to where I got in!"

If you, a new member, will make a commitment to yourself to put together these SEVEN COMPONENTS, chances are good that you will not fall asleep too close to the time you got into God's church. If you equip yourself with these COMPONENTS, we are confident you will experience something of what God intends for your Christian life.

Note to instructor: after the above materials have been reviewed at the Orientation, invite new members to attach the following page to their refrigerator or post it at some conspicuous place, and review it daily:

**NEW MEMBER RESPONSE
TO THE SEVEN COMPONENTS**

(New Member—this is a commitment you make to God and yourself. If you feel you can do only some of them, start somewhere. Go for it! Do not return this form. It is for your use only.

( ) Component One. I will worship consistently for the next ninety days.

( ) Component Two. I will set aside a percentage of my income and give it to the Lord and His church on the first day of every week.

( ) Component Three. I will go to a Bible study.

( ) Component Four. I will pray twice a day for ninety days.

( ) Component Five. I will serve in some capacity over a period of ninety days.

( ) Component Six. I will invite somebody without a church home to worship and to the INFORMATION TALKS FOR VISITORS within the next ninety days.

( ) Component Seven. I will go to two or more GROWTH GROUP meetings.

Conclusion: You may very well be doing all these things. In that event, use this list as a checklist.

God bless you as you walk with Christ!

THE RECEPTION OF NEW MEMBERS

Strive to make each member reception a memorable event. Include some of these ideas:

1) Give each new member identification (a flower, for example).

2) Invite the Evangelism Outreach Committee chairperson to read the names of new members, and the Evangelism Inreach Committee chairperson to read the names of sponsors, and ask sponsors to escort the new member(s) to the front and to stand directly behind them at the time of reception. Thank the sponsors for their leadership and support.

3) Instruct new members to speak their words of affirmation as witnesses of the Lord, and to do it with the note of conviction.

4) Prepare a Reception Service that includes a witness by the new members, promises of sponsors and an affirmation response by the membership;

5) Give each new member a candle (some churches do this for baptisms only) and suggest to new members they light the candle each year on this date, as a remembrance of their church membership birthday.

6) Form a reception line, after worship, so that the congregation can greet new members.

7) Encourage the congregation to take time to greet new members and welcome them—they are family now!

8) Celebrate after worship with special refreshments. (For example, a cake decorated — "WELCOME NEW MEMBERS!")

9) Plant a tree or bush or plant, following the reception, with each new member planting something on the church campus (or a tree or plant in honor of a group of members), something they can see and remember, "I helped plant that tree the day I was received into membership years ago!" Or, make a circle of bricks or blocks with new member names. Or, stepping stones with new member names—anything which helps seal their membership and gives them the feeling of "ownership." "Now, I am part of the

church!" That's the feeling you want to get across.

The order of worship for the reception of new members can take many forms. Make it different at times. Look at this example:

Reception of Member Service

Evangelism Chairperson: Saint Paul writes in the Book of Romans (15:5-7), "May the God of steadfastness and encouragement grant you to live in harmony with one another, in accordance with Christ Jesus, so that together you may with one voice glorify the God and Father of our Lord Jesus Christ. Welcome one another, therefore, just as Christ has welcomed you, for the glory of God."

Friends, today we welcome into the family of First Church these believers in God the Father, Son, and Holy Spirit. They have been prepared for this occasion by attending the INFORMATION TALKS FOR VISITORS and the ORIENTATION SUPPER-MEETING FOR NEW MEMBERS, and are ready to make their commitment to God and his church. They will also be placing in the offering plate their financial commitment to the Lord's work through this church, just as you have done.

Pastor: New members, Our Lord Jesus Christ said: "Everyone therefore who acknowledges me before others, I also will acknowledge before my Father in heaven; but whoever denies me before others, I also will deny before my Father in heaven" (Matthew 10:32,33). Thus, you have opportunity now to acknowledge your belief in our Savior-God.

I, therefore, ask you: DO YOU BELIEVE IN GOD AS EXPRESSED IN THE CREEDS OF THE CHRISTIAN FAITH? (Opt for a full confesssion of one of the creeds at this point in the Service, e.g. The Apostles' Creed.)
New Members: I do.

Do you promise to abide in this belief, acknowledged in the gift of your baptism, and as a member of the Church, to be diligent in the use of the Means of Grace and in prayer?
New Members: I do, by the help of God.

Do you wish to be a part of this family of God, and do you promise to express your faith by consistent worship and study of the Scriptures, and by giving of your talents both in service and in financial support?

New Members: I do.

(Please note: If there are baptisms, insert rite at this point. In this event, at the outset, invite all new members to the baptismal font. It is a good idea to meet at the baptismal font anyway, inasmuch as it is a reminder of how we enter the kingdom.)

I ask you sponsors, will you faithfully care for these people and help them in every way as God gives you opportunity, enabling them to become connected in the life of our congregation.

If so, answer "we will, the Lord helping us."

Evangelism Chairperson: The congregation will rise.

Will you, members of the family of First Church, receive these believers as your brothers and sisters in the Faith? Will you be supportive of them, helping them to know your name, remembering them in your daily prayers, and aiding them in their growth in the Christian faith?

If so, answer, "We will receive them and love them, for Jesus' sake."

Pastor: Let us pray.

We give thanks to you, Lord God, for sending out the seventy, and for all in this congregation who go out from this church building planting the seed of faith. We are grateful that through the power of the Holy Spirit you have led these children and adults, all sisters and brothers, to our beloved church. Grant that those who are united with us and we with them, on this glorious day, may together grow in grace, be fruitful in every good work, and endeavor to serve you in the unity of the Spirit and in the bond of peace. Bless the whole Christian church around the world, as your Word is proclaimed and Sacraments administered, that together we may endeavor to plant the seed of faith in the hearts of all humankind. And, finally, may we all be welcomed in the Church triumphant, through Jesus Christ, Our Lord. Amen.

Evangelism Chairperson: Members in Christ, "So then you are no longer strangers and aliens, but you are citizens with the saints and also members of the household of God, built upon the foundation of the apostles and prophets, with Christ Jesus as the cornerstone" (Ephesians 2:19-20). In the Name of the Lord Jesus Christ, we welcome you into membership and extend to you the hand of friendship and love.

(Evangelism Chairperson and Pastor(s) grasp the hand of each new member and sponsor(s). If it is a custom in your church, invite the congregation to applaud as a greeting and a sign of affirmation, and let it be a lingering praise of God as well! Where practiced, the PEACE can be shared at this time.) Go in joy and peace!

Whatever Service of Reception you choose, invite the Evangelism Outreach Chairperson and the Evangelism Inreach Chairperson to participate, symbolizing the efforts of the laity in making this occasion possible. If you write a Service of your own, include these salient points as reminders to the congregation: 1) Every Christian is an evangelist; 2) God brings the increase; 3) Confession of belief in public is a privilege, as well as a responsibility; 4) Use scriptures which focus on being a part of the kingdom.

Post new member pictures in the narthex and reproduce them for the newsletter, with a paragraph of information about each, aiding the congregation in getting to know them. Before the next reception of members, remove the pictures and post them on a prominent wall reserved for new members received during that year.

Receptions of members take careful preparation with many people involved. Since there are only about five or six receptions possible in a year, based on a plan which includes the INFO TALKS and ORIENTATION, they are special occasions. Let them be highlights in your church year!

PART IV
INREACH EVANGELISM

CHAPTER FOURTEEN

NURTURING NEW MEMBERS

"'Conversion,' from the Latin convertere,'to rotate,' is not a leap, it is a turning. It leaves a person about where he was before, but now aimed in a different direction."[1]

It is relatively easy to receive new members by following a procedure along the pattern described in Part III. Receiving new members gives any congregation an upbeat feeling. Then comes the question: "What are we going to do with these people?" What happens to new members after they are received is an entirely different matter. Professional golfers claim there are two games in golf: hitting the ball on the green, and putting. Getting the ball in the cup is what counts, they say. Receiving new members is getting the ball on the green. Nurturing new members is putting commitment in the cup. It is the cup of blessing!

Nurturing new members is serious business. It takes more time and energy to retain new members than to receive them. Many congregations sigh in relief that the job of receiving new members is over, until the next INFO TALKS begin. It isn't over; it is just a beginning. That is why evangelism is like a coin with two sides: outside—reaching out to new people, and inside—reaching in to sustain people in the faith. The church that lets new members fend for themselves is like the hireling who flees from the sheep when the tending gets tough. The shepherding church helps the sheep detect the voice of the true Shepherd so that "No one will snatch them...." [2]

If we are going to shepherd people in the faith, another plan of action, as well thought out as the plan devised to reach new people in the first place is required—an EVANGELISM INREACH COMMITTEE. The chairperson for this committee is also to be a church board position. Thus, two people out of a dozen or so are readily available to remind the board to stay focused on the first business of the church.

Choose the chairperson for the EVANGELISM INREACH COMMITTEE as carefully as in selecting the person to chair EVANGELISM OUTREACH. Qualities to look for are: a) loves people, as the disciple, John; b) loves to listen, as Mary, sister of Martha in John 11:39); c) loves teaching, as Saint Paul in writing letters to new churches.

The same procedures in enlisting members of the EVANGELISM INREACH COMMITTEE apply as described for the EVANGELISM OUTREACH COMMITTEE (see Chapter Ten) and include: 1) Writing out EVANGELISM INREACH COMMITTEE responsibilities; 2) Requesting the church board to adopt the envisioned plan; 3) Screening the entire membership for the qualities desired in committee members, as listed above; 4) Making appointments with candidates selected for the committee and explaining what the work of the EVANGELISM INREACH COMMITTEE entails; 5) Calling an EXPLORATORY MEETING to outline the proposed committee's plan of action; 6) Starting to nurture new members.

Nurturing new members is akin to caring for all members, with these exceptions: a) It provides the glue for permanent church membership; and, b) It involves a time element (ninety days) to make a connection.

Responsibilities of the EVANGELISM INREACH COMMITTEE include:

1) Defining sponsor duties, providing written guidelines for all sponsors (described in Chapter Thirteen).

2) Overseeing the work of sponsors— enlisting, instructing, assigning, and guiding them.

3) Guiding new members' progress in the GETTING SETTLED INTO A NEW CHURCH HOME: SEVEN COMPONENTS FOR THE NEW MEMBER (see Chapter Thirteen). This does not mean policing their activity; it means encouraging them

along the way. Members of the committee are expected to become acquainted with new members and ask "How are the SEVEN COMPONENTS coming along?" This committee of five to seven people (or more) is to make sure some concerted connection is made with every new member. It is dangerous to assume other members make a connection.

4) Monitoring the spiritual health of every member of the congregation, tracking the habits of members in reference to worship, communion, giving, and participation, detecting inactivity before it becomes a habit; communicating with members who show signs of having the "wind" (Spirit) knocked out of them. (see Chapter Fifteen for more detail.)

5) Checking that new members are provided with opportunities to serve, as suggested in COMPONENT FIVE. (See the EMPLOYMENT AGENCY in Chapter Eleven.)

6) Communicating with the STEWARDSHIP COMMITTEE, to see whether new member commitment cards have been received (see COMPONENT TWO), and work with the STEWARDSHIP COMMITTEE in obtaining every new member commitment (this is vital not only for the stewardship health of the congregation but especially for the stewardship health of the new member).

7) Following through so that introductory biblical classes are provided new members, in consultation with the Education Committee. For the EDUCATION COMMITTEE this will involve printing an annual—a description of courses offered, a list of teachers, location of courses, dates and times of courses, and inviting new members to enlist in these classes. Later in this chapter a basic course for new members will be described, entitled "Through The Bible In A Year."

8) Providing GROWTH GROUPS (discussed in Chapter Seventeen), including format, procedures, and continuous instruction for GROWTH GROUP leaders.

9) Inviting these same new members to another SUPPER MEETING, three months following reception, and this time they bring the food for their sponsors! Discuss the import of the SEVEN COMPONENTS; receive their suggestions and comments about

what it is like to be a new member. Celebrate again their reception and express joy in being a part of the same church family. Implement valid suggestions.

10) Celebrating MEMBERSHIP DAY annually, honoring all new members received during that year, observing anniversaries of membership, highlighted by music and guest speaker on such subjects as "What It Means To Be A Christian In Today's World", "The Church of Yesterday, Today, and Tomorrow", "The ABC's Of The Christian Faith" etc.

11) Overseeing a Pictorial Directory which can be updated (looseleaf) at the conclusion of each reception of new members.

The EVANGELISM INREACH COMMITTEE has as big a job as EVANGELISM OUTREACH. Both activities dovetail. In business jargon, the EVANGELISM OUTREACH supplies the church with customers; the EVANGELISM INREACH supplies the customers with service. In church language, the EVANGELISM OUTREACH COMMITTEE is the Paul committee, planting the seed; the EVANGELISM INREACH COMMITTEE is the Apollos group, watering the new plants; and, God brings the increase in Christian growth, as always (I Corinthians 3:6).

Nurturing new members is more than what is sometimes referred to as "assimilation" or "integration." These terms imply a person is swallowed into a larger body and loses identity. We are not trying to absorb people into a church system. Blending in with a group of people is not all that is entailed in church membership. Church membership is not even the encompassing goal and end result of evangelism. Church membership is the beginning of the Christian life. We enter the church by baptism. The church is God's way of nurturing us in the Christian faith. The Spirit recycles us. It is what Brunner described, "The church exists by mission as fire exists by burning."

We nurture people in the faith. We are God's gardeners! A good gardener doesn't quit after the seed is planted. If the gardener quits, weeds take over and crowd out the new plants. The good gardener knows that planting is only the beginning. The good gardener is out under the sun supplying the plant with whatever it needs to grow—water, fertilizer, watchful tender care.

Computer tracking of people habits, endeavoring to keep members "in line" or living up to a constitution or a creed or keeping our church humming—this is not what it is about. Nurturing people in the faith is what it is all about.

The main complaint of disillusioned church members, as I have listened to them, is not so much about the personality of the preacher or the unfriendly people—it is, "I don't feel fed." If that is true, how do we answer that complaint?

I am a Lutheran. The Lutheran church was university born. We pride ourselves in emphasizing the Word and teaching it. We subject our young people to two or three years of rigorous training in the catechism. We have Sunday Schools for children, youth, and adults. Some of our churches have private schools, usually from kindergarten through the 6th or 8th grades. Many of our churches have weekly Bible studies. Our pastors are teaching pastors, in the pulpit and in the schools of the church. Comes the question: Why would anybody in such a church body complain, "I don't feel fed?" The answer: a sizeable percentage of our people do not have a handle on the Bible. They are illiterate concerning the Bible. What a travesty! How embarrassing to confess that thousands of our people are ignorant concerning the Bible?! And our business is to teach people the Bible! If our people are illiterate concerning the Bible, how can we expect the church to be a force in society? This must not continue or we fail to be the teaching church which we contend to be.

Where I served a suburban church, I discovered many of our people were going to the Baptist church for Bible study during the week. With all we had to offer, I wondered why? So, I marched over to the Baptist church to find out what was so great going on over there. My people were surprised to see me in a Baptist church! So was the Baptist pastor! I listened and I learned the answer. This assistant pastor, Alan Stringfellow, had developed a plan of Bible study entitled, "Through the Bible In One Year." It was a simple plan. 1) Reading an assigned book of the Bible before attending the lecture, a requirement; 2) Distributing an outline of the book which they had read, in suitable notebook form; 3) Outlining and describing the book in detail. Stringfellow was marching them through the Bible from Genesis to Revelation. On occasion, a couple of short books were considered at the same time so that all 66 books were covered in a year. He gave his people a handle on the Bible. I said to myself, "Why didn't I think of that?!"

Now Stringfellow has a Lit. D. degree and is known across the nation, producing with Virgil W. Hensley, Inc. two more books with similar approaches: Vol. 2, BIBLE CHARACTERS; Vol. 3, GREAT TRUTHS OF THE BIBLE. Those who embrace a more literal translation of the Bible will welcome Stringfellow's materials into their studies, churches, and homes.

It presented a problem for me, however, being under a different understanding of the scriptures. I couldn't use his material. But, I could use the pattern and create new materials. By this time I was in a large downtown church which was spiraling downward. My wife, whose major in college was Bible, agreed to write and teach a course acceptable to Lutherans. She spent at least twenty hours a week in research and preparation. We prepared the congregation for the course over several months, detailing the benefits, and emphasizing this was not a discussion course, but a course that would give them the basics of the Bible; in reality, a handle on the Bible. It was to begin in July. "You can't start something like that smack in the middle of summer," were some of the cries heard. We did. Over a hundred enrolled and continued throughout the year. She made tapes for those who had to miss a session but they were not allowed to have a tape unless they had read the assigned book first. An outline was given with the tape. Her sense of humor added to the good feeling in the class and helped keep people coming back week after week.

I am convinced this course was what turned that church around. Attitudes changed. They not only believed in the power of the Word, they began believing in themselves and their future as a bona fide people of God. The course was offered another year with remarkable attendance. People completing the INFORMATION TALKS FOR VISITORS immediately entered the course THROUGH THE BIBLE IN A YEAR. It was understood anybody could jump into this Bible course at any point since each lesson was on a separate book, providing they listened to the introductory tape and read the introductory outline prior to attending the course. This enabled new attendees to receive an overall view of what the course would entail. Youth were invited.

Many people read the Bible through for the first time. People understood what each book was about and could answer these questions: a) Who was the author of this book or was it written by an unknown person? b) When and under what circumstances did the author write? c) Where was it written? d) Why? What was the occasion for writing and what were the aims and motives? e) To whom did the author address these thoughts? f) What is the content, the outline, and the sources employed in the writing of the book? g) How does it apply to life today?

Write your own course of THROUGH THE BIBLE. Offer it perennially. Members are likely to comment, "This is what I have been looking for all my life!" They are likely to invite unchurched friends to take the course! The idea offers a unique opportunity to invite collapsed members to something that can make a difference in their lives. Strive to enroll all new members in this course. People are hungry to get a handle on the Bible. This is one of the better ways.

If it could be done, I would make it mandatory for every new member to take such a course. Certainly you can whet their appetite for the course by making a brochure describing the course and its benefits. Explain that they will feel comfortable in reading the Bible, after attending. Many people are embarrased about their sparse knowledge of the Bible. Tell them this course will cure that feeling. Some people will unite with the church because you have such a course. People shopping for a church often want to know what Bible courses are made available in your church. Start with this one!

The people who teach this course will find it demanding, preparing week after week. Only dedicated teachers need apply. Stock your library with those books which will aid in preparation, especially William Barclay's THE DAILY STUDY BIBLE series, HARPER'S BIBLE COMMENTARY and HARPER'S BIBLE DICTIONARY and ATLAS. Provide for a taping (audio and/or video) of each session, and make tapes available for people who must miss a lesson. Provide notebooks at cost. People pay for something they believe will help them. By the time the course is over, they will have a notebook of considerable volume on all books of the Bible. They will rely on these outlines in daily Bible readings, and when they participate in Bible studies offered in the congregation.

This is a basic course. Getting a handle on the Bible is the place to begin. The Holy Spirit works in people who have the biblical truth surging in them. Following that, you can, if you want, do what Stringfellow did: write other courses, on biblical characters and themes in the bible. Nurturing new members requires biblical reinforcement.

We turn next to the work of sustaining and strengthening all members.

CHAPTER FIFTEEN

SUSTAINING AND STRENGTHENING ALL MEMBERS

"Hold to the standard of sound teaching that you have heard from me, in the faith and love that are in Christ Jesus. Guard the good treasure entrusted to you, with the help of the Holy Spirit living in us." [1]

People, responding to the call of the Holy Spirit, attend the INFORMATION TALKS FOR VISITORS. The basics of the Christian faith are taught in those sessions. Led by the Spirit, many unite with the congregation. In turn, they are nurtured by the SEVEN COMPONENTS. Basic Bible courses anchor them. Strengthening members in the Christian faith is an ongoing strand in evangelism. "They go from strength to strength...." [2]

MOVING FROM SCRAPS OF FAITH TO MATURING IN THE FAITH.

What spiritual strength do new people have when they come into our congregation? These are several of their thoughts.

1) "I need to deepen my relationship with God. Most of my life I have had too much intellectual interference (mind static) to believe in God."

2) "A few weeks ago, it came to me that what I have had is spiritual emptiness. I have no belief system, no God. So I began to pray."

3) "I have little awareness of what it means to belong to a church."

4) "My life has been ragged, disjointed. I work hard and have a good job, but I lack something. I feel like I am in a black

hole and cannot crawl out."

5) "I was six when I decided I wanted to be baptized. I felt Jesus in my heart. But I did not believe in his promise of eternal life. Alone in my bed at night, I would become terrified of eventual death."

6) "It confuses me that people I know have such varying patterns of faith."

These are several theological concerns and personal longings by people who yearn to be filled.

Because of our sinful nature, we humans harbor doubts concerning God, ourselves, and other selves. Throughout life the Spirit of God in us fluctuates. We are severely tempted to "go with the flow" of our moods rather than the flow of the Spirit. Only congregations that understand and accept doubt as the dark side of faith are equipped to help people climb from weakness to strength in their faith.

People do come into church membership with different maturity in the faith. We shall identify several of these levels.

1) The First-Time Christian.

This level includes not only those who are newly baptized but those who were baptized as children but not reared in the faith. They need time and attention or they will slip away.

Too often the spiritually newborn are crushed under institutional wheels. The Apostolic Church paid attention to first-timers; they "...devoted themselves to the apostles' teaching and fellowship, to the breaking of bread and the prayers." [3]

2) The Returnees.

We rejoice that they are back in the fold, but they are cautious. They require understanding and love. Otherwise, they will fall away again.

3) The Inconsistent.

The inconsistent are with us always. They worship occasionally. They think they are doing God a favor. They adopt limited patterns of giving. They cannot be counted on to keep commitments. They are not in the church because they are not "in Christ."

The inconsistent haven't connected. Unless something is done to retrieve them, they will be lost. This field of evangelism is white unto the harvest in most churches. They are people for whom Christ died but they haven't been resurrected to new life.

4) The Collapsed.

These people are on the congregation's "inactive" list. Their faith has collapsed. They don't care about God or his church anymore. This is one of the church's largest fields for evangelism. Too many churches adopt the attitude that "nothing can be done with those people." They simply do not try to retrieve the collapsed. They write them off their membership roll without even giving them a second chance in a "new" church.

No church has a right to take people's names off a membership roll until it has done these things: 1) Talk in person with them; 2) Listen to their concerns; 3) Ask for their cooperation; 4) Pray with them. Some of the collapsed ones will "get it together." Others will not; encourage them to unite with another congregation. Christ calls us to help everyone to take his/her place in a congregregation somewhere.

5) Hearers and Doers.

James' exhortation "...be doers of the word, and not merely hearers who deceive themselves"[4] is taken seriously by many members. They realize the church is made up of sinners. They are slow to criticize, quick to commend. They accept Christ as the head of the church. They strive to grow in his likeness.

Members move in and out of these differing levels. We are called by Our Lord to be perfect; all fall short of that. "Saints are keenly conscious of their sins and grateful for a Savior—sinners are not. Evangelism cannot always go with the good news of salvation to those who know that they are lost; it must often go with the bad news that they are lost to those who think they are doing very well." [5]

All church members respond to the gospel on various levels and at various times in their lives: as a first-timer, a returnee, an inconsistent believer, as one whose faith has collapsed; and as one who hears and does the Word. Faith is dynamic, not static.

An Alban Institute study on the assimilation of new members concludes that: "In order for the assimilation to 'take' it will be necessary for the persons involved (both members and newcomers) to listen to one another, to have compassion for other perspectives, and to negotiate creative ways of programming and functioning so that differences can be enjoyed, or least become opportunities for growth and learning rather than dissatisfaction and pain." [6] Listening, showing compassion, negotiating church programing to meet the needs of all are ingredients in sustaining members in the faith.

How can the congregation sustain people in the faith?
1) Guard true faith.

People succumb to the temptation to embrace portions of different faiths, or, embrace spin-offs of religious ideas passed on by everyday associations. Faith can become diluted. A "personal" religion takes over. For example, some church members believe in reincarnation; whereas the Church teaches the resurrection. Some think of Jesus as only a person in history instead of the living Lord. Eastern religions, the sects, the "scientific" religions, endeavor to make Jesus only a figure in history. The Early Church had to confront Arius, a church leader, who claimed Jesus was neither divine nor human but something in-between. The church dealt with that issue in a forthright manner by compiling the creeds.

Guarding the faith today is just as acute a factor as in the Early Church. A warped religion will not stand the test of truth or time. From the pulpit to the classroom to small groups and group meetings in the church, the truths of Christianity are examined, mulled over, discussed, absorbed. As God's people we go from strength to strength as we go from truth to truth. Throughout life our shared responsibility in the church is to help one another see and experience the truth in Christ inasmuch as all of us are going to be "...afflicted in every way, but not crushed; perplexed, but not driven to despair; persecuted, but not forsaken; struck down, but not destroyed...." [7] Pure religion teaches Apostolic faith.

2) Understand and interpret present history in the light of past history and biblical truth.

Another element in sustaining and strengthening members is to be alert to "revolutions in thought" which alter mores, lifestyles and concepts.

Past revolutions in thought, the Reformation in the sixteenth century, for example, on the heels of the printing press, the discovery of the Americas, and complicated by the Renaissance, encompassed segments of the average person's life. The Industrial Revolution's introduction of power-driven machinery did not reach into every nook of the average person's life.

Not so in this last half century. Every person on this planet has been affected by the discovery of nuclear energy, the probes into space, discoveries in medical research, and electronic communication which has made earthlings neighbors. A lady called an airlines office in Chicago to inquire how long it would take to fly to Los Angeles and heard the airlines employee say "just a minute," and the lady promptly hung up, satisfied with the answer!

Methodist Bishop John H. Vincent was prophetic seventy years ago: "Ideas are the factors that lift civilization. They create revolutions. There is more dynamite in an idea than in many bombs." The church's responsibility is to understand in depth what is happening to our culture in these days of dramatic change.

Every person's life is affected by present-day revolutionary changes. America is different. Life is different. Inadequate housing, lack of health care, unemployment, neglect of ecology, disasters, violence, drugs, overpopulation, homelessness, national debt—all will haunt this nation, and the world, for decades to come.

The moral revolution since World War II prompts lifestyles that shatter long-time principles. Gray is the color of this century's morality. Mainline churches founder in their efforts to forge moral statements on sexuality, abortion, capital punishment, and euthanasia. Meanwhile, the film industry chips away at chastity and decency. In its efforts to be realistic, it is turning actors and actresses into quasi prostitutes. The ten commandments have been reduced to the ten suggestions.

The responsible church in this time between the times helps its members to hear and understand the Word of God: "You must understand this....distressing times will come. For people will be lovers of themselves, lovers of money, boasters, arrogant, abusive, disobedient to their parents, ungrateful, unholy, inhuman, implacable, slanderers, profligates, brutes, haters of good, treacherous, reckless, swollen with conceit, lovers of pleasure rather than lovers of God, holding to the outward form of godliness but denyng its power" (II Timothy 3).

To hold the people we have we must learn to help the people we hold. To do that means becoming students of history as well as students of the Bible so that we present God's Word relevantly. Old Testament prophets were masters of this art.

3) Deepen the Faith.

How can we deepen the faith of "new" church members and long-time members?

a) Emphasize biblical truths.

In Chapter Thirteeen, GETTING SETTLED INTO A NEW CHURCH HOME: SEVEN COMPONENTS FOR THE NEW MEMBER were presented. Examine them again. They are the basics for any Christian life. People who are biblically illiterate and theologically ignorant must be led into biblical faith. Lifting up the basics of life and faith, sets Christ's expectations before the congregation. Healthy churches embrace and teach those basics for growing in the faith.

b) Aim for Christ-likeness.

Words like "assimilation" and "integration" are currently used to describe the church's efforts to hold onto people. The Early Church did not use those terms. It called its members to have the mind of Christ in them. If our goal is to create a homogeneous group of people, we end with "churchism." It is Christ-likeness that holds the people of God together. It is the congregation's task to introduce people to Christ and to lead them into his church where they learn to be in Christ.

The next chapter focuses on the continuing quest of sustaining and strengthening members in special circumstances—those who have lost interest in God or the church or both. They are blotches on our parish registers. What is the cure?

CHAPTER SIXTEEN

SOME CURES FOR THE SLOW LEAK

"You are the salt of the earth; but if salt has lost its taste, how can the saltness be restored?" [1]

"So it is not the will of your Father in heaven that one of these...should be lost." [2]

"Take care that you do not despise one of these...." [3]

There is a leak in the church—the loss of members. It may be a slow leak, but it is draining American churches. Some churches lose more people than they receive in a given year. I am not referring to transfers out, people moving away from the area; that will happen at any church location. I am pinpointing the matter of members who neglect the Word and the Sacraments.

Helping members remain spiritually healthy is a matter of addressing specific remedies.

1) Track worship habits.

Know member worship habits. Computers make this job easy. A church is negligent if it fails to note who did and who did not worship last week. If a person isn't missed, they are likely to say, "I could drop dead and that church wouldn't know the difference." A feeling of not making any difference contributes to collapse. Never give members the satisfaction of saying their church did not keep track of them. Service Clubs make it a monthly ritual to send individual letters to members listing the times he/she attended during the month. It is a good idea for the church, also.

2) Track giving habits.

If a member stops giving, there is a problem. Nip it in the bud. Delay spells disaster. If members are having financial difficulty, suggest they change their pledge downward. Be understanding. Agree on some amount regardless of how little, so that the member(s) feels comfortable and not guilty. Guilt about money causes people to collapse. (Note to the laity: any pastor without access to pledging and giving records is placed at a disadvantage, drastically reducing pastoral care effectiveness. Is there trouble anywhere? The pastor(s) needs to know, too.)

It could be that members who fail to give disagree with how funds are spent and need further explanation, or at least deserve a hearing to express their views. Assure them their views count and will be expressed to the Board. People collapse when they feel nobody listens to them.

3) Communicate crisply, clearly, convincingly.

There are pastors who try to preach via the newsletter. Save it for the pulpit. Use the bulletins and newsletters to communicate what is happening in the church's life and what could happen. Analyze trends. Report facts. There is no room in these communiques for negatives. Inspire! Motivate! Spread a little honey! Save dire financial crises for meetings and informational letters. People tend to collapse when they get this idea: "All they talk about is money!"

4) Find out when people began to hurt and where they are hurting.

A physician asks, "Where does it hurt?" "How long has it hurt?" A physician will not prescribe a remedy without knowing the answers to those questions. It is hard to treat animals because they can't tell us exactly what is wrong. We can't know what is wrong with collapsed members either unless they tell us when they began to hurt and where they hurt. In order for them to tell us, we have to go to them and find out. They are not likely to come to us. This is not easy to do. It takes time. It is tedious. But if you let a disease go on without treatment, death occurs. Members collapse when the church fails to find out what is hurting them. Many churches and pastors are cowardly when it comes to doing this, yearning to protect themselves, unable to take criticism, or are fearful of confrontation. Such attitudes avoid the issue. The church is a healing institution. Go to the hurt and find out why they are hurting, and when it occurred, before a death occurs.

5) Admit mistakes and seek forgiveness.

Collapsed members have a responsibility, too, to tell the leadership when they are hurting. Jesus' advice in Matthew 6 is sound, "...If you remember that your brother or sister has something against you, leave your gift there before the altar and go; first be reconciled to your brother or sister, and then come and offer your gift." Collapsed members are not likely to do that. They are more apt to sound off to people who agree with them, without trying to reach a solution. Although collapsed members can be wrong in their sense of disappointment and criticism, so can the leadership. Both need to admit mistakes and seek forgiveness from one another. Member collapse occurs when forgiveness is not reciprocal. The leadership should be the first to forgive. When forgiveness is not forthcoming from a collapsed member, it is time to shake the dust off and help the collapsed transfer to another congregation. There are times when the hurt is so deep even Christians find it difficult to forgive and forget. This is not right, but that is the way it is. Admit it: there is a time for some people to change church membership. However, make sure that the collapsed is in agreement to a transfer. In the end, it could be the best for the collapsed and the congregation.

6) Seek solutions.

Churches, like individuals, can go their merry way when there is a problem of member collapse. They can react as if the problem will go away on its own. It will not. Delay ingrains hurt feelings. Pastors and church boards need to act when any member shows a sign of collapse. How can a collapsed member be approached? Here is one way that I know works:

"Hello, this is Pastor C at the church. I need your help in solving a possible problem at the church. I need your insight. I know I can trust you. I owe you a visit, anyway. Would it fit into your schedule if I stopped by your home on Monday at 7:00 p.m.?"

(Listen.) The collapsed member will likely be flustered by your approach. Think like the collapsed: "Nobody ever needed my help down there. Nobody ever asked me how I felt. Insight? Trust? What goes on here? The pastor must be up to something. Or, maybe he/she has seen the light. My curiosity is aroused, however. O. K. I'll give it a whirl but act cautious." The collapsed: "No, I can't make it Monday evening." Pastor: "I can understand your busy schedule. Would Tuesday or Wednesday evening be possible. It's a rather urgent matter." The collapsed: "Let's make it Wednesday evening at 7:30. Seven o'clock is too early." Pastor: "Great! I will see you Wednesday evening at 7:30 in your home. Thanks! I look forward to seeing you."

Of course, it will not always work but you have to try. Churches have a habit of giving up on people. Jesus' method was to work through the human mind until a different perspective was planted. We can try, too.

If the collapsed refuses to see you, write a letter communicating concern, love, and hope. You can try again by telephone, after your letter has reached its destination. If the collapsed still refuses to see you, it might be time to shake the dust off your shoes. You will feel as good as you can about the situation when you have forgiven a dozen times and made these efforts to communicate. You will feel worse about a collapsed member if you allow the situation to fester. Doing nothing about the collapsed is a sin of omission. The true shepherd always goes after a lost sheep.

If the pastor is in the picture of disgruntlement or disappointment, the pastor would be wise to take another person with him/her (See Matthew 18:15-20). It may be better if the pastor not go and two people from the EVANGELISM INREACH COMMITTEE go. Talk over the situation and then decide who might best be able to communicate with a particular collapsed member. This process involves hunks of time. It is worth it. There is great joy when a lost sheep or lost coin or lost person is found! Some collapsed people, after they are "found," make the best evangelists for inreach. They have insight. They know how it feels to become collapsed.

*

You arrive at the home of the collapsed person(s) at the appointed time on Wednesday evening. Before you go up to the door, pray about your attitude. "I know these people have fallen away, Lord. Prevent me from being judgmental. Help me to express genuine interest in them, for their sake and not mine. You have sent me here to communicate. I am in your hands. In Jesus' Name. Amen."

So your attitude is not to try to jerk them back into a pew. Your attitude is to try to nurture understanding of the situation. Your goal is to help a person(s) come closer to God. It may be the person will not respond. That is not your responsibility. Your responsibility is simply to go and listen and encourage. An argumentative attitude will only increase tension. A defensive attitude will only muddle the pond. Be Christlike.

How do you begin? The following conversation is only an illustration. Somehow try to put yourself into their shoes. Smile. Listen carefully. Ask questions which garner information. Look people in the eye. Be genuine, open, kind, patient.

Pastor: "I want to thank you for the privilege of being in your home. I feel guilty about not being here sooner. Thanks for seeing me." Collapsed: "That's all right, pastor. We probably should have invited you over some time ago. What is this possible problem at the church that you mentioned?" Pastor: "As you know, we receive new members rather regularly. It is one thing to receive new people; it is another matter to hold onto them. Even people who have been members for some time fall away now and then. It is this slow but dangerous leak in the church's life that I wanted to talk with you about. Why do people fall away? Is it the church's program? Are we not doing enough in keeping in touch with our people? Is it I? I thought maybe you might have some suggestions for me or the church board. I assure you what you say will be held in the strictest confidence. Your name will not be mentioned. I need your help." (Listen.)

Take it from there! You may have opened that can of worms! A crucifixion may take place! You have made yourself vulnerable. So what?! You have nothing to lose since you are coming from a position of confidence in Christ. You are endeavoring to reach a person for whom Christ gave His life. Give yours!

These specific thoughts are helpful:
1) Be alert.
2) Search for the problem.
3) Ask for their help.
4) Seek solutions.
5) Be humble.
6) Never argue or be judgmental.
7) Be winsome.
8) Try to get them to laugh.
9) Plant seeds of truth.
10) Invite them to pray with you.

What is done after the person-to-person talk can make a difference. If there is hope in the situation, plan to do at least four things:

1) Present suggestions and/or recommendations of the collapsed member in writing to the proper committee or board and send a copy to the collapsed member (with a note of thanks for the privilege of conversation together in his/her home), regardless of how insignificant or petty the suggestion or recommendation. Indicate to the committee and/or board the information came from a concerned member, that you would appreciate an answer in writing, and that you would give their answer to the concerned member. This will let the collapsed member know you listened and that you are doing something constructive about it. It may strike the collapsed member that his/her suggestion or recommendation, once seen in writing, was not all that important. Before you present the material, you may need to gain the approval of the collapsed member in regard to wording of the information. Make sure that the information represents the position of the collapsed member. Take no chances of any further misunderstanding.

2) Deliver the answer of the committee and/or board to the collapsed member in person. This gives you a second opportunity to communicate with the person(s) and will give you something specific to talk about. Try to reach an agreement or at least agree that progress is being made.

3) In the event the collapsed starts to appear in church, try

to see that others welcome them naturally. The EVANGELISM INREACH COMMITTEE could do this. Warn people about a put-down as: "Wow! We haven't seen you in a long time. Where have you been?!" It is embarrassing to the collapsed. Try to make their coming back a natural re-entrance into the church's life.

4) See that the collapsed make a connection. This is the responsibility of the EVANGELISM INREACH COMMITTEE. One of the best ways is for the Committee to appoint "unannounced sponsors" for the collapsed. Teach these "sponsors" to approach the collapsed as they would a new member going through the SEVEN COMPONENTS. Tell them that people on their way out can be brought back in.

Reclaiming people involves energy and time. "Backdoor evangelism" is more difficult than other phases of evangelism. It is likely the pastor cannot do it all. Instruct a small group of people how to do this. Reclamation, although more difficult than any other kind of member visit, can be so joyful that you will have all of heaven cheering for the outcome!

Here are a few pointers in instructing such a group of people:

1) No going out to visit with a sense of superiority.
2) No going out to visit with intent to confront.
3) No going out to visit with a "something must be wrong" attitude.
4) Listen with a "sensor" attitude, able to root out what the situation is.
5) Invite suggestions.
6) Give thanks for the privilege of visiting in their home.

Preventive measures for the human body are advised, stressed, encouraged. Unfortunately, poorer people in America are shortchanged healthwise and are more likely to experience unnecessary health problems and premature death. Are the collapsed like poorer people? Have they been shortchanged, neglected, cut-off, forgotten?

Remember in attempting to reclaim the collapsed:
1) They may just want attention. Give it to them!

2) They may be misinformed or uninformed. Communicate what the real situation is.

3) They may have lost faith. Articulate what the faith is.

4) Every person is infinitely precious to God and should be to us, too.

5) Nobody is beyond the reach of God. You could be part of the answer.

6) Reasoning is not always the answer. Paul found this out at Athens. Hangups from the past may be part of the problem. Go beyond reason to the heart of the matter — tell what Christ and his church mean to you.

7) They may be too far out of our reach, but not God's. When you have exhausted all possibilities, be quick to refer them to another church and urge them to try again.

8) Leave some things in the hands of God. We are limited.

9) Be enthusiastic. It is the gift of the Spirit.

10) Be patient about getting people involved.

11) The Collapsed may need a change of pace or be weary in well-doing.

12) Remember that Saul never became Paul until God pointed him in a different direction. That's our job, too.

13) Love them even when they do not love back. Read Matthew 5:43-48.

14) Ask God's forgiveness when you fail. Receive his mercy.

15) Visit members you suspect may collapse before they collapse.

*

What do we do about the "unreachables," the people who at one time said "yes" to Christ and his church and have allowed their spiritual lives to collapse? What do we do about people who are deliberately making a mockery of church membership? What do we do about members who move to another community and fail to transfer? I will be bold to suggest a nationwide transfer system.

Nationwide Transfer System

The churches of America spend untold amounts of money,

energy and time re-converting the converted. Twenty-five percent change denominations. When one of our households moves to another community, that household has to go through the process of finding another church home. Most often we give little or no help to them in making a transfer. We are unaware of what happens to countless people.

Furthermore, the churches of this country allow huge numbers of the collapsed to remain collapsed. In many congregations one-third of the households are inactive. Let's face it, and we seldom do—there are people who have been turned off, unlikely to be retrieved by "their" congregation. In addition, churches in the U.S.A. have a habit of deleting households from the parish register without doing anything about helping the inactive (collapsed) take another step. The backdoor of our churches remain open, and we are doing little about it.

Is there anything that can be done about this? Yes, but what? I offer the suggestions below as one possibility. (Footnote: Roman Catholics have always done a better job of backdoor evangelism because of their member policies. Their members belong to a church according to geographical areas, although members have options. These policies are a spin-off of their style.)

1) Every church body in America adopt this policy: Members who stay within a community but do not respond to efforts made by their congregation to re-enter the life of that church, after a two-year period of inactivity in reference to receiving The Lord's Supper and giving of record, be notified of their options: a) Re-enter the life of their congregation by receiving The Lord's Supper and giving to the cause of Christ and his church; b) Be automatically transferred to the nearest church of the same denomination in the hope that they can respond to that congregation's ministry, or c) Notify their church in writing that they no longer believe in God as expressed in the Christian faith and wish to be dropped. (If a person does this, go evangelize or ask another church to try.)

Such a policy would cause a stirring within congregations! "We shouldn't have such a policy — it might hurt somebody's feelings." "What right does a congregation have to do that?" "That's legalism!" Yet, it might just help the Collapsed to understand that the church is serious about the meaning of church membership. What is expected of members? Do we just let this collapsed business go on unnoticed?

There would be other problems: Would the people go to the church to which they are transferred? Would such churches receive them? Would these people be thought of as outcasts? But, shouldn't we work through such problems? Yes! Because therein are specific opportunities to reclaim people.

This policy would necessarily change constitutions of congregations. It would have to be an announced policy within the congregation and shared with new members. Furthermore, it would need to be announced prior to the close of each church year. Members who fall into this category could be forewarned of their options. Uppermost, members in this category need to know their congregation is reaching out to them with an uplifted meaning of what it means to be a Christian in God's church. In all cases, personal contact with the Collapsed, as referred to above, is obligatory.

Some policy, whether it be the above or not, needs to be adopted by churches so that members know their church is serious about the meaning and purpose of church membership in the Christian faith.

2) Every church body in America adopt this policy: whenever member(s) move to another community, transfer those members to another church of the same denomination in the community where they relocate. The relocated member(s) would be invited to attend their new church home with the option of either staying or transferring to another church in the community. This automatic transfer system, highly publicized throughout the nation, could help close the back door. Of course, some relocated members will not do it. Of course, some congregations do not know when or where members move. But, the post office does! We can educate our congregations to do a better job of tracking members and assuming this rightful responsibility. We can educate our people that moving to a new community means continuing commitment to Christ and his church. It may take decades to

make this work smoothly but it is better than what we are not doing now.

3) The church bodies of America agree on another policy: To "transfer" or refer member(s) who are relocating to a church in a community where their own denomination is not represented. Of course, some denominations will not do this. But, if their people were in an overseas mission field where they were not represented, they might! Why not in our own backyard?!

I challenge the churches of America to come up with policies that address this matter of backdoor evangelism. We are in desperate need of closing the back door.

The next chapter engulfs preventive measures, There is a certain rhythm to be found in church life which helps individual members discover and experience spiritual strength, and helps the whole congregation stay spiritually alive. A healthy church finds the rhythm!

CHAPTER SEVENTEEN

RHYTHM IN THE CONGREGATION'S LIFE

"Rhythm might be described as, to the world of sound, what light is to the world of sight. It shapes and gives new meaning. Rhythm was described by Schopenhauer as melody deprived of its pitch."[1]

"What if you've got it, you don't need a definition, and if you don't got it, no definition is any good."[2]

Rhythm is harmony in motion, whether it be humming a tune, hitting a ball, jumping rope, walking or running, even in crocheting! There is a rhythm to life. Ecclesiastes 3 reflected upon it when the royal philosopher wrote, "For everything there is a season and a time for every matter under heaven...."
There is a rhythm to a congregation's life as in all of life. Finding that rhythm causes a congregation to remain alert and exciting. I am referring to rhythm in a congregation's year around program. Congregational calendars have a habit of becoming clogged with the products of committees and organizations, without much thought of the overall impact, competing against one another for calendar space, personnel, and budget items. The church board doesn't always devote time to such matters as coordinating the entire program of a congregation, with an overall view. A group needs to stand back and take a look at what is happening or not happening in the life of a congregation. It could be called THE RHYTHM COMMITTEE. Its job would be to work with boards,

committees and organizations in answering the following seven questions, before any program is implemented.
  1) What is this program supposed to accomplish?
  2) Is this program consistent with our mission statement?
  3) What ages will this program benefit?
  4) Do we have the personnel to do it?
  5) Do we have the money to do it?
  6) Do we have enough time to do it right?
  7) Will this program fit into the timetable of the congregation?

The RHYTHM COMMITTEE coordinates the congregation's program. It assists the church board, committees and organizations in mapping out a balanced year around congregational program that meets the needs of people in the church and in the community. It is difficult for a committee or organization to look down the lens of its narrow responsibility and determine what is best for the entire congregation. The RHYTHM COMMITTEE can serve as the wide lens of the church's life.

It is best when the RHYTHM committee is made up of individuals who do nothing else but monitor the faith and life of the congregation, appraising the effectiveness of the church's program calendar, and making recommendations to the church board.

There are two specific responsibilities which the RHYTHM COMMITTEE oversees, on an annual basis: 1) A Force Field Analysis Day, and 2) A Calendar Day.

A Force Field Analysis Day

This event can best be held between Easter and Pentecost, possibly on a Saturday a.m., concluding with a cost luncheon. A minimum of three hours is required. Force Field Analysis is simply a time when members gather to express their thoughts and feelings about the program life of the congregation. In a sense, it is an annual assessment of the church's life.

The RHYTHM COMMITTEE makes prior arrangements which include:

1) Explaining in a letter to the congregation the purpose and procedure of the Day, encouraging participation in what promises to be a fun Day, capped off with a cost luncheon.

2) Telephoning all board members, committees, school(s), and organizations, stressing that the success of the Day depends upon their presence.

3) Listing of the board, committees, school(s) and organizations on two separate sheets of newsprint style paper, in length of six to eight feet and two to three feet in width, hung on the wall around a large room. For example: list on one sheet for the church board the following: "Strengths of the Church Board" and on the second sheet next to it "Weaknesses of the Church Board." Do this for all boards, committees, schools, and organizations. Attendees will be writing on these sheets of paper what they think are the strengths and weaknesses of each phase of the congregation's life. The number of sheets will be determined by how many boards, committees, school(s), and organizations in the congregation.

4) Overseeing the arrangements for the cost luncheon.

5) Appointing a Bible study leader and a prayer leader.

The Day's beginning offers opportunity for Bible study and prayer, consonant with how the Apostolic Church functioned. Then commences the Force Field Analysis, as follows:

1) Organize attendees according to groups of five to seven people by simply counting off.

2) Explain that each group will work together as a unit, and will select their own recorder (the person who is to do the printing on the sheets of paper provided). Emphasize that individuals in the group make their own observations, which are recorded on the sheets. Discussion is to be limited. Statements on the sheets are to reflect the thinking of the entire group, not necessarily a consensus. Give the groups five minutes at each station. Blow a whistle at the end of five minutes and shout "SHIFT!" Attendees shift to the next sheet and continue on that pattern until all sheets are completed by every group. For example, if you have a church board, 10 committees, 1 school, and 5 organizations (remember the choirs), it will take an hour and twenty-five minutes plus time it takes for groups to shift. If the RHYTHM COMMITTEE notes any lag in attention during the process, blow the whistle at shorter intervals. Keep it moving! Keep it exciting!

3) Lunchtime! Attendees will be a little fatigued. Some

will have needed to sit while at a station. Just before lunch, encourage everyone to walk around to see the listings. During lunch encourage people to talk with one another about this body of information, listing the strengths and weaknesses of every facet of the congregation's life.

4) Conclude lunch with an explanation of how the information will be utilized. The RHYTHM COMMITTEE is to print out the strengths and weaknesss and mail the information to all attendees. Display the station sheets in the narthex for the entire congregation to see. The church board, committees, school(s), organizations, are made responsible for digesting the information pertaining to them, adopting what seems feasible. and preparing for the next phase of putting together a church calendar. Force Field Analysis Day is only half the job. All attendees on that Day will be expected on CALENDAR DAY, too.

CALENDAR DAY

Another Saturday morning, for example, after Pentecost and before the fall, Calendar Day can occur. The church board, committees, school(s), and organizations by now have written out what they plan for the coming year. They are to come prepared with the following, in writing:

1) What programs they plan.
2) When the programs are projected (dates, times, places).
3) The personnel required to do it, including who will do it.
4) The number of person hours required.
5) What it will cost.

Again, the RHYTHM COMMITTEE will make preparations for CALENDAR DAY. They will:

1) Alert all people who attended Force Field Analysis Day to attend CALENDAR DAY and encourage all members to attend.

2) Hang newspaper print on the walls similar in size as Force Field Analysis Day, with each month of the year listed. For example:

JANUARY

Date   Name of event   Where?   Who will do it?   Cost?

3) Make arrangements for the cost luncheon.

4) Select Bible study and prayer leaders.

After the Bible study and prayer, the church board, committees, school(s), and organizations are invited to put their information on the sheets provided.

Then, take each month at a time beginning with September. Place the newspaper print so the month displayed can be seen by everybody in the room. Note any conflicts in scheduling. Negotiate. Invite questions. How many peaks in the month? How many valleys? Are there any breathers? Is there a rhythm? Are we going forward at a pace we can keep up? Are we serving all age groups? Is there anything we have left out? Do we need to change any traditions?

Marching through each month will be hard work, tedious, but effective. When you have completed the Day you will have accomplished these things:

1) A Church Calendar for the year, for example, September to September, with designation of programs along with dates and pinpointing responsibility.

2) A church budget outlined, ready for the church board to make recommendations to the congregation (whether the budget is for the fiscal year or another plan).

3) An overall view of what the congregation can expect during the coming year.

4) A screening of programs to meet the needs of the congregation and the community.

5) A dovetailing of the church's activity.

6) Program work to be implemented.

In brief, you have set the congregation's program to a rhythm, a harmonizing of the talents, energy, and money available. The year's goals have been outlined and the congregation has a sense of commitment and purpose.

No congregation can afford to be without rhythm. Rhythm does several things:

1) Minimizes overlapping and underlapping of program.

2) Utilizes the time and energy of members in the best possible way.
3) Helps prevent burnout in member participation.
4) Emphasizes the full use of facilities available.
5) Stirs imagination about what could be done.
6) Serves as a think tank.
7) Creates harmony.
8) Analyzes strengths and weaknesses, with emphasis on strengths.
9) Raises the percentage of member involvement.
10) Generates a feeling of progress.
11) Enables members to express viewpoints about their church.
12) Minimizes frustration in doing parish work.

Find the rhythm in your parish's life. Each year make room for a Force Field Analysis Day and a Calendar Day. These two days can make the difference between a church fulfilling the Lord's mission and a church that is caught up in its own tradition.

Know Your Constituency

Another part of rhythm in a congregation is in knowing your constituency. There are volumes written on this subject. CHURCH GROWTH and GEORGE BARNA (THE FROG IN THE KETTLE) are good examples. There are, however, a few simple questions which can help congregations become aware of the profile of their congregation. Forming the answers to these questions can help a congregation prepare programs that meet the needs of their membership.

1) Number of adults?____. Number of children?____.
2) Total number of households in the congregation?____
3) Number of households with children?____
4) Number of households with fathers?____ mothers?____ stepfather?____ stepmother?____
5) Number of households with single parents?____ Fathers?____ Mothers?__
6) Average annual household income? $_____ Lowest? $_____ Highest? $_____

7) Number of households unemployed?____ On welfare?____

8) Members according to age? (list according to categories. e.g. children, youth, adults, senior adults). Number married?____ Single?____

9) Medium age of congregation? ____

10) Households according to length of membership?

11) Make-up of church background? List according to date of baptism and whether baptized as a child or adult; date became an adult member of some Christian church; date became member of this church.

12) Languages spoken? English?____ Spanish?____ Korean?____ etc.

The profile of a community can aid a congregation in reference to providing programs that meet the needs of people. City Hall, County, Farm Bureau — all can give needful information. Maps will reveal where the growth is occurring. Building permits will reveal new housing projects. Keeping track of the number of new residents in a year and who they are in reference to age, language, etc. can help your church be a "planning commission" in itself. How many of our churches have failed to analyze what is happening right around them and suddenly awakened to the fact that the city or township had changed and they had not? Whether a congregation can adapt to change is a matter of spirit, study, prayer, and hard work.

Rhythm does not remain constant. Finding the rhythm is a matter of keeping beat with change.

A final point is not only finding the rhythm but keeping the rhythm in a congregation. One way is by providing GROWTH GROUPS. (Some churches call them "Care Groups" or "Shepherding Groups" etc.)

Growth Groups

A GROWTH GROUP is a small number of people (usually about six to a dozen) meeting weekly in a home for Bible study, prayer, and discussion. Growth Group leaders, specially trained members, meet with the pastor weekly to review Bible studies and possible subjects the Growth Groups might use that week.

They may decide to listen to the tape of the message (sermon) preached the previous Sunday and use it as the basis for discussion. They may pore over a portion of scripture making sure they understand the background and meaning of the scripture chosen so that they are intelligently prepared to lead the discussion. They may select a social concern or a program concern of the congregation, making sure they are equipped to lead a positive discussion.

Growth Groups have limitations: it is difficult to include children and youth; a tendency to become ingrown; a danger in becoming third-rate "pop" psychology trysts; hard for some people to commit themselves to spending a specific time (e.g. an evening a week) to attend.

Regardless, there are these overiding benefits:
1) Provides a support group, especially for people who are hurting.
2) Stirs hunger for biblical knowledge.
3) Enhances prayer life.
4) Increases skills in communication.
5) Deepens spiritual life.
6) Develops a sense of friendship.

GROWTH GROUPS help meet the needs of people in today's world. Lonely singles, frustrated couples, puzzled and frenzied people are in our congregations. GROWTH GROUPS are a kind of anchor that help members keep in touch with God and one another.

IN CONCLUSION

This book has been struggling to be born since the 1950's when I was privileged to serve in the Evangelism Department of the United Lutheran Church in America. During those years, the Church gave me the opportunity to write, teach, and discuss evangelism with lay persons and clergy in the United States, Canada, Puerto Rico, the Virgin Islands, and Argentina. The heartbeat of my ministry has been evangelism. It began with an infant congregation; it matured through participation in a church-wide program in evangelism (The Lutheran Evangelism Mission); and it seasoned as I served a suburban congregation and three central city churches. I have been blessed!

It is my prayer that this book will be helpful to the laity, seminarians, professors of practical theology, Evangelism Committees in congregations, and active pastors as they serve the Master with joy.

I cherish what James A. Michener wrote in THE EAGLE AND THE RAVEN: "In the 1980's, when I was nearly eighty years old, I had some fairly large rusty nails hammered into my trunk (he was referring to how an old tree came to life after such an injection)—a quintuple by-pass heart surgery, a new left hip, a dental rebuilding, an attack of permanent vertigo—and like a sensible apple tree I resolved to resume bearing fruit....Between the years 1986 and 1990 I would write ten books, publish seven of them including two very long ones, and have the other three completed in their third revisions and awaiting publication."

His testimony gave me fresh hope for life in my seventies! Hence, finally, this first full-length book printed during my fiftieth year in the ministry. A second book, INFORMATION TALKS FOR VISITORS (complete manuscripts of the five TALKS shared with visitors), is about ready for publication. A third book, SERMON SERIES, is on the hot plate. I am still striving to bear fruit!

Grace and peace to you, evangelists all!

APPENDIX 1

FORMS THAT HELP

Form A: INFORMATION FOR BAPTISM

Name of church _____ Date of Baptism _____
Address _____ Time _____
Telephone _____ Officiating _____
                                 Child ( ) Adult ( )

Name_____
      (last)   (first)   (middle)
Address_____City_____State_____Zip_____
Date of birth _____ Where? _____
   Telephone ( ) _____

Parents:
Father _____
      (last)   (first)   (middle)
   Year father baptized _____
Member of_____Where?_____
   Telephone ( ) _____
Mother _____
      (last)   (first)   (middle)
   Maiden name of mother _____
   Year mother baptized _____
Member of _____ Where?_____
   Telephone ( ) _____

Sponsors:
  Name _____
    Address_____
    Adult member of _____ Where? _____
    Telephone ( ) _____
  Name _____
    Address_____
    Adult member of _____ Where? _____
    Telephone ( ) _____

Appointment with the Pastor:
Date(s) _____ Where? _____
   Instruction sheet given? Parents ( ) Sponsors ( )
   Date information given to Cradle Roll _____
   Baptismal Certificate given ( )
Date recorded in Parish Register _____
by _____
Remarks:
_____
_____

Form B: INDIVIDUAL INFORMATION FOR CHURCH FILES
(For those who have decided to become a member)

Return to: Name of church and address   Date completed _____
           Telephone of church
                    Please Print. Thank you!
    Please note: All information requested is considered confidential and necessary. Be sure to provide information for all items requested. Your prompt return of this form (both sides) will facilitate record procedure. Thank you! If you have any questions, please telephone ( ) _____.

Name _____
        (last)   (first)   (middle)
Address _____ _____ _____
        (street)   (city)   (zip)
Home telephone ( ) _____
Print in Church Directory? Yes ___ No ___
Business telephone ( ) _____
Permission to telephone? Yes ___ No ___
Male ( ) Female ( )
Date of birth: _____ Birthplace _____
       (month, day, year)
Year of baptism _____ Year of Affirmation _____
Previous church membership (if any) _____
_____
  (full name of former church, street address, city, state, zip)
Name of employer _____
Where?_____
Your present or former occupation_____
Retired? Yes ( ) No ( )
Military status: Active ( ) Veteran ( ) Not current ( )
Education:
High School ( ) College ( ) Degrees_____
Single ( ) Married ( ) Widowed ( ) Divorced ( )
   Separated ( ) Single Parent ( )
Date of marriage: _____ To: _____

Name of church in which spouse is a member?
_____ _____
Where?_____
Child Information (living with you)
1) Name _____
        (last)   (first)   (middle)
Date of birth _____ Date of baptism _____
Date of confirmation_____
2) 3) etc.
Names of children not living with you:
1) Name _____
Address_____
Birth (month, day, year) _____
2) 3) etc.
Relatives in this church _____
Check Areas of Interest and Experience:
( ) Church Council ( ) Choir ( ) Growth Group
( ) Committee _____ ( ) Teaching ( ) Evangelism
( ) Telephone ( ) Instrumental ( ) Youth Ministry
( ) Transportation ( ) Other_____
Hobbies:_____
Print here your church's mission statement._____
_____

   As one of God's chosen people, believing in Jesus Christ as my Savior, I wish to unite with (name of church) and serve our Lord with my time, talents, and gifts of money through this congregation.
                 Write Name _____
                 Date _____
I learned about this church through: ( ) Friends ( ) Relatives
( ) Telephone Directory ( ) Newspaper
( ) Other _____
            _____

For church office use only

Date received into membership _____
How received?

( ) a. Baptism (15 yrs. & younger)   ( ) e. Transfer from other Lutheran

( ) b. Baptism (16 yrs. & older)   ( ) f. From non-Lutheran.

( ) c. Affirmation of faith   ( ) g. Reinstated

( ) d. Transfer from ELCA

Form C: INFORMATION FOR MARRIAGE

Name of church and address   Date of Marriage _____
Telephone of church   Time of wedding _____
                              Officiant _____
Place of wedding _____
Date of rehearsal _____ Time _____
Number of rings ( )
Place of reception _____
Groom_____
         (last)   (first)   (middle)
Home telephone ( ) _____
Business ( ) _____
Address _____
        (street)   (city and state)   (zip)
Date of birth _____ Place of birth _____
Year baptized _____
Adult member of (name of church, city and state)
_____
Occupation_____
Number of previous marriages ( )
Date of death of former spouse _____
Date of divorce _____

Bride _____
        (last)   (first)   (middle)
Home telephone ( ) _____ Business ( ) _____
Address _____
        (street)   (city and state)   (zip)
Date of birth _____ Place of birth _____
Year baptized _____
Adult member of (name of church, city and state)
_____
Occupation_____
Number of previous marriages ( )
Date of death of former spouse _____
Date of divorce _____

Best man: (name, address, telephone, church membership)
_____

Maid/Matron of Honor: (name, address, telephone, church membership_____
_____

Other attendants with same information _____
_____

Address and telephone of Bride and Groom after marriage
_____
_____

Counseling appointments:
Date and time _____
Date and time _____
Date and time _____
Message (sermon) if any, title and text
_____
License Number _____
When mailed to registrar _____
Parish Register record on page _____.
Entered by _____ on (date) _____.

    List other arrangements on form as needed. e.g. Aisle runner, candleabras, number of guests expected, organist, instrumentalists, soloists, bows on pews, guest book, bulletins, names of parents (step-parents), number of pews reserved for family, seating arrangements, etc.

Cost of wedding _____
Payable to (name of church) _____
Payment received on _____ by _____

FORM D: REQUEST FOR LETTER OF TRANSFER

To: (Name of your former church and address including zip code)
_____
_____

From: (Your name and present address including zip code)
_____
_____

    It is our desire to become member(s) of Ascension Lutheran Church, Thousand Oaks, California. Thank you for your ministry to us in the past. We will continue to include all of you in our prayers.

(Your signature(s)_____

Please send transfer to: Ascension Lutheran Church
                            1600 E. Hillcrest
                            Thousand Oaks, California 91362

Form E: INFORMATION FOR FUNERAL

Name, address, telephone of church

                                       Date of Funeral _____
                                       Time_____
                                       Place _____
                                       Officiant _____

Message text and title_____

Name of deceased _____
                      (last)   (first)   (middle)
Date of death _____ Where? _____
Cause of death_____
Date of birth _____ Where? _____
Last Address _____
Telephone _____
Member of _____
                (name of church and address)
Year of baptism ( )   Year of Affirmation ( )
In the life of the church, participated in_____
_____

In the life of the community, participated in _____
_____

Vocation _____ Retired? _____
Survived by:
Wife/husband_____
     Daughter(s)_____
     Son(s)_____
     Grandchildren   (Step-Grandchildren) _____
_____
     Sisters/Brothers _____

Names, addresses, telephones of any unchurched immediate family members, relatives, friends _____
_____

Burial date _____
Time _____ Place _____
       Graveside ( )   Cremation ( )   Inurnment ( )
Information recorded in parish register:
Page _____ by _____
Name of Funeral Home
_____
Name of Director _____Telephone _____

Form F: FRIENDSHIP SLIP

(To be filled out during worship and returned to nearest aisle)
I worshiped today at (name of church) _____
Date_____ Time _____
Print name (please)
_____
Street address_____
City_____ State_____ Zip_____
Telephone (   ) _____
(   ) I am a member.
(   ) I am a visitor and my home church is _____
_____in _____
                             (city and state)
(   ) I am interested in the INFORMATION TALKS FOR VISI-TORS.
(   ) I am interested in becoming a member.
(   ) I will commune today.
(   ) Desire call from pastor.
(   ) I am interested in a GROWTH GROUP.
(   ) Note my new address/telephone.
     (   ) Adult   (   ) College student   (   ) Teen   (   ) Child

Form G: POSSIBLE MEMBER DATA SHEET

Home Telephone ( ) _____
Business Telephone (if usable) ( ) _____
Name(s) _____
Address _____ _____
            (number and street)   (city and zip)
Names and ages of children: _____
_____

Date first attended _____
Record of attendance _____
_____

Checked on FRIENDSHIP SLIP the following:
( ) Interested in the INFORMATION TALKS FOR VISITORS
( ) Interested in uniting. INDIVIDUAL INFORMATION SHEET FOR CHURCH FILES mailed on _____ By _____

( ) Interested in GROWTH GROUP
Date and time of first telephone call _____ By:
_____

Other dates and times of telephone calls and by whom,
1)_____
2)_____ 3)_____
4)_____ 5)_____etc.
Date of Lay Visitor(s) contact _____By
_____

Telephone ( ) Personal visit in home ( )
Comments _____
_____
_____

Date of Pastoral contact _____By
_____

Telephone ( ) Personal visit in home ( ) Office ( )
Comments _____
_____
_____

Data regarding Possible Member(s):
1) Church background, if any_____
_____

2) Name of present church membership_____

Where? _____
_____
(city and state)

3) Is Possible Member baptized? ( ) Yes ( ) No
4) New resident? ( ) Lived how long in area? ( ) years.
Enrolled in INFORMATION TALKS FOR VISITORS ( )
Beginning date of INFO series _____.
Request for Letter of Transfer form received ( ) and mailed
_____
By _____.
Completed form of INDIVIDUAL INFORMATION FOR CHURCH FILES
    Received on _____.
Other data_____
_____
_____
_____

Form H: REPORT FORM FOR EVANGELISTS AFTER MAKING HOME VISITS/TELEPHONE CALLS

Report Form for (date)_____ Time of Report Meeting____
Name of Evangelists _____
_____
_____

Number of cards assigned ____.
Number of households at home____.
Number of people interviewed ____.
Number of households not at home____.
Number of people enrolled for (date) INFORMATION TALKS FOR VISITORS____.
Names of people enrolled
_____Tel.# _____
_____ _____
_____ _____
_____ _____
_____ _____

Names of people who wish to unite
_____ _____
_____ _____
_____ _____

Notes on calls:
#1_____
#2_____
#3_____

DURING REPORT MEETING WITH DESSERT AT 9:15 p.m.
(for example)
1) Teams will be asked to make written reports.
2) Teams will be invited to verbalize reports in this way: refer to call #1, #2, #3, and DO NOT use names!

THANK YOU AND GOD BLESS YOU! SEE YOU TOMORROW NIGHT at 6:20 p.m. sharp, for supper and instruction .

Form I: MEMBER REPORT FORM OF KNOWN PEOPLE WITHOUT A MEANINGFUL CHURCH RELATIONSHIP

Name_____
          (last)   (first)
Children (if any)_____
                 (age)   (age)   (age)
Single ( ) Married ( ) Divorced ( ) Separated ( )
Widowed ( ) Single Parent ( ) Relative ( ) Friend ( )
Neighbor ( ) Acquaintance ( )
Address_____
           (street)   (city and state)   (Zip)
Telephone ( ) _____

O.K. to reveal source of information (circle Yes) (circle No)

Reported by _____
Your Telephone ( ) _____
                         ****

For church office use only: Contacted by _____
                                    Date _____

APPENDIX 2

LETTERS THAT HELP

Letter A: TO FIRST-TIME VISITOR WHO INDICATES NO CHURCH MEMBERSHIP IN THE AREA
(To be mailed on Tuesday following the Sunday the Possible attended.)

Dear Peter Glass:

Thank you for the privilege of worshiping with you! We were honored by your presence. We are hopeful the worship celebration was meaningful and helpful. Please come again!

Always eager to receive impressions and suggestions, we enclose a self-addressed envelope in the event you desire to share something with us. It is our endeavor to reflect Christ and to try to meet the needs of people. Your suggestions can be of help. Thank you!

In the event you are looking for a church home, we hope you will consider First Church. Periodically, we offer what is known as INFORMATION TALKS FOR VISITORS, an update on the world of religion. The next series of TALKS begin Sunday, January 10, 9:30 a.m. in the Library . Please see the enclosed card which explains these TALKS. You will be most welcome!

Thank you for these considerations.

On behalf of the people and pastors,

(signature)

Letter B: TO FIRST-TIME VISITOR WHO DOES INDICATE MEMBERSHIP IN A LOCAL CHURCH

Dear Ann Hastings:

Thank you for the privilege of worshiping with you. You indicated membership in another local church. It is good for us to share the faith and worship together occasionally.

We are always interested in impressions people have when worshiping at First Church, especially those who come from another Christian congregation. If you care to share your insights, please use the enclosed envelope to do this. Thank you!

We pray God's blessing upon you, the people of your church, and your pastor.

On behalf of the people and pastors,

(signature)

Letter C: INVITATION TO THE INFORMATION TALKS FOR VISITORS (sample one)

Dear Mary Hanover:

Remember when Coca Cola endeavored to eliminate classic coke? There was an uproar all over the nation! People were used to the old coke and didn't want to give it up.

Ever try to eliminate God? I have! Yet, there seems to be a nudging in the human heart and a whisper in the inner ear that we still need God. Even people in former communist countries have expressed something of this feeling.

There are those, however, who have eliminated the church and succeeded. Or, put church out of mind for awhile. As one young person exclaimed, "I don't have time for church right now."

Whatever your feelings, what we can do in the church is to share an update on how God communicates with people. It is called INFORMATION TALKS FOR VISITORS and the next series of TALKS begin September 15, 9:30 a.m. Maybe we can't replace the old coke bottle, but we sure can give the contents of a sparkling relationship with God.

You can give it a try without any obligation. If you must miss one of the five TALKS (all on Sundays at 9:30 a.m.), you will receive an outline and audio or video of the missed session and you will have not missed a thing. That sounds fair, doesn't it?!

As we say, why not?! We'll have a coke (classic or diet) or coffee or tea waiting for you!

Thanks for reading this. We hope to see you Sunday, September 15, 9:30 a.m. sharp in the Library .

                        Somebody who cares about you,
                            (signature)

P.S. The enclosed card describes the INFORMATION TALKS FOR VISITORS.

Letter D: INVITATION TO INFO TALKS (sample two)

Dear Betty and Bob:

Why are you receiving a letter from Trinity Church? Because we believe people are the first business of the church.

We also know people are looking for a meaningful relationship with God. Why do we think that? Because you took the time to worship at Trinity. We think you may be looking for something meaningful and purposeful.

What is Trinity doing about this? We offer what is known as INFORMATION TALKS FOR VISITORS—just for you and others like you. The enclosed card describes these TALKS in more detail. The INFO TALKS presented by the pastor(s) are an update on the world of religion. You can get answers to your thoughtful questions. There is no obligation. When you must miss a TALK, we provide you with a tape and outline of the TALK missed so you can keep up. That sounds fair, doesn't it?!

The next series of the INFO TALKS begins on Sunday, March 17, 9;30 a.m. in the Library.

If you have read this far, there is the real possibility that you will attend. That is our hope. Give it a try!

On behalf of the people and pastors,

(signature)

Letter E: INVITATION TO INFO TALKS (sample three)

Dear Sally and Richard:

On this last day of the year, I want to wish you a Happy New Year! I do hope the year ahead will be a year you and I can handle, as I know we can with God's help. I always start out with good intentions and it doesn't seem too long before my resolutions turn to dust. Hope you are more resolute about your resolutions!

There is one resolution that I hope you will make and keep—to attend the INFORMATION TALKS FOR VISITORS.

The INFO TALKS are offered to people who have important questions and who are serious about getting some answers. Questions like these: If there is a God, why is the world always in some kind of mess? Why do bad things happen to good people? Where can I get some straight answers? Why should I believe in God? How can I believe?

Hundreds of people have attended the INFORMATION TALKS FOR VISITORS and received recognizeable answers to such questions. You can, too! And what better time than right now—at the front end of the new year?

The enclosed card explains more about the INFO TALKS. Please take time to skim through it. Talk with God about it. Resolve to do something about it. Since there is no obligation and it is free, you have everything to gain.

There are five TALKS, all on Sundays at 9;30 a.m. in the Library. If you must miss a TALK, we will see that you get an audio or video tape and an outline so you can keep up. You receive a notebook and an outline for every session. You can't find a better bargain than that in this age of uncertainty!

Give it a try, friends! Somebody is reaching out to you. And again, HAPPY NEW YEAR! You and I can handle the new year when we get a handle on our faith.

                        On behalf of the people and pastors,
                                  (signature)

Letter F: INVITATION TO INFO TALKS (sample four)

Dear Henry and Ruth:

There are times in life when we wish we could get some solid answers about who God is and how to get in touch with God. It is this feeling that Ascension Church addresses by providing, periodically, what is known as INFORMATION TALKS FOR VISITORS. Hundreds of people have heard the TALKS and found them helpful.

The next series of the INFO TALKS begins Sunday, May 3, 9:30 a.m. in the Bethlehem Room (building to right of worship center, lower floor.) You can begin this post-Easter series and get answers to your thoughtful questions.

There are five TALKS presented by the pastor(s) and the first one is on BELIEF IN GOD. We begin as if no one in the group believes in God and go on from there. At each TALK, all on Sunday mornings at 9:30 a.m., you will receive an outline to be inserted in a notebook which is provided. If you must miss a TALK, you will receive an outline and tape (audio or video) of the missed TALK. That sounds fair, doesn't it?!

There is no obligation by attending. Come for the information only, if you want. Or, come with the notion of checking us out! This is the way to shop for a church. Find out what a church believes and teaches before you ever decide to unite with a church. This is an intelligent approach.

We will have refreshments waiting for you, plus the notebook and outline. Try to arrive five minutes early. Thanks for reading this letter!

On behalf of the people and pastors,
(signature)

Letter G. INVITATION TO INFO TALKS (sample five)

LAST OPPORTUNITY THIS YEAR
INFORMATION TALKS FOR VISITORS
BEGINNING SUNDAY, NOVEMBER 7, 9:45 A.M.
Offered by Ascension Lutheran Church, Thousand Oaks, Ca.
(1600 East Hillcrest, Telephone (805) 495-0406)

WHAT DO THE TALKS TALK ABOUT? Answer: Beginning as if no one in the group believes in God, the TALKS blanket the basics of the Christian faith. The pastors are the presenters.

WHO ATTENDS? Answer: Visitors from various religious backgrounds and visitors without any religious background. A sizeable group of visitors is already planning to attend.

WHAT DO THE TALKS COST? Answer: Five hours of your time attending five TALKS in a row, all on Sundays at 9:45 a.m. If you must miss a TALK, you are provided with either an audio or video tape. So, you don't have to miss anything. You receive an outline of the TALK, too.

ARE YOU KIDDING?! You will try to hook me into uniting with Ascension church! Answer: No. We are not interested in numbers. We are trying to serve people in the area. After you attend the TALKS, however, you are prepared to take the next step.

AH, HA! Another one of those "HOWEVERS." What is the next step? Answer: It is up to you. If you wish to follow Jesus Christ, then you take the next step. You would make a good Christmas gift for Ascension and Jesus. (Reception of new members is Sunday, December 19.)

WHAT DO I HAVE TO DO TO ENROLL? Answer: Show up. (In the Bethlehem Room, lower floor in building west of worship center. Just follow the signs.)

Letter H. TO THOSE WHO ATTENDED THE FIRST TALK OF THE INFORMATION TALKS FOR VISITORS

Dear Larry and Cheryl LaRusso:

Thank you for making my day by attending the first of the five INFORMATION TALKS FOR VISITORS! I hope it was helpful. I will be telephoning you weekly after each TALK, just to keep in touch and to try to answer any questions you might have.

Here are a few reminders:

1) There is no obligation by attending.

2) If you must miss a TALK, we provide a tape (audio or video) and printed outline of the TALK that was missed. (Please return the tape at the next session.)

3) There are five successive TALKS, all at 9:30 a.m., in the Library.

4) Try to get to the INFO TALKS five minutes ahead of time, sign in, put your name tag on, grab a coke or coffee or tea, and introduce yourself to others who are in the same boat as you!

5) The INFO TALKS prepare you for membership, in the event you so decide. There will be no pressure to do this. There will be a friendly invitation to become a part of the church family at one of the last TALKS.

I look forward to clasping your hand this Sunday, August 30, 9:30 a.m., for the second TALK, "How To Get A Handle On The Bible." This is a most helpful session with suggestions for your home library.

Thank you for being a part of the present INFORMATION TALKS FOR VISITORS!

On behalf of the people and pastors,
(signature)

Letter I. TO THOSE WHO HAVE INDICATED A DESIRE TO UNITE WITH FIRST CHURCH

Dear Philip O'Brien:

There must be rejoicing in heaven about your interest in becoming a part of the First Church family on Sunday, May 26! We sing praises to God! We promise to be faithful in sharing the Good News in Jesus Christ.

Three reminders:

1) Please fill out the enclosed INDIVIDUAL INFORMATION FOR CHURCH FILES and bring it with you to the INFORMATION TALKS FOR VISITORS this Sunday, May 12 at 9:30 a.m. The TALK this Sunday is on WORSHIP.

2) Attend the ORIENTATION SUPPER-MEETING FOR NEW MEMBERS on Sunday, May 19 at 5:00 p.m. This is a free supper, probably the only one you will get around here! Child care is provided. At this SUPPER we will share something about First Church and what we do as believers in Christ. A video will be shown about the spirit of First Church. We will go over the SEVEN COMPONENTS in feeling at home at First (copy enclosed). We will review the RECEPTION OF MEMBER SERVICE so you will feel comfortable in knowing what will occur. At the Supper-Meeting, you will be asked which worship celebration you wish to attend for reception on that great day, 8:00 a.m., 9:30 a.m., or 11:00 a.m.

3) Be ready to have a good time on the day of your RECEPTION, Sunday, May 26. Please arrive fifteen minutes early. Please report to our evangelism chairperson, Bob Wright, in the narthex where your picture will be taken. You will be given a flower. Please wear your new name tag. Your sponsors will be there to escort you to a seat in worship. The congregation will greet you after the Service. What a great day for all of us!

If you have any questions, please call the church office at (805) 529-0351. Thank you! Welcome!

God bless us all as we strive to lift up Christ!

On behalf of the people and pastors,

(signature)

Letter J: TO THOSE WHO BECAME MEMBERS THE PREVIOUS SUNDAY

Dear Evelyn and Jack:

We thank God for you, Evelyn and Jack! What a great privilege to receive you into the family of Saint Andrew's! We trust the worship celebration was meaningful to you. And, we hope your hand became a little tired in shaking hands with everybody!

Your sponsors, Hildy and Warren Appleby, will be guiding you in the days ahead. We hope the SEVEN COMPONENTS will be helpful in feeling at home in your new church home. In ninety days, you will be invited to another Supper-Meeting scheduled for Sunday, September 10, 5:00 p.m. in Fellowship Hall. It will be good to get together and share some thoughts about our common Christian life. Please circle your calendar for that important date. Thank you!

Please contact your sponsor, the church office, or me in the event you have any questions. We stand ready to help. God bless our church life together! Thanks for being a part!

On behalf of the people and pastors,
(signature)

APPENDIX 3

TIPS

A. TELEPHONE CALLS ON POSSIBLE MEMBERS PRIOR TO START OF INFO TALKS (preferably during the week before the start of the series of TALKS)

"Hello, this is _____ from Trinity Church. We are pleased that you took the time to worship at Trinity. Thank you!" (Listen) "We mailed a letter to you about the next series of the INFORMATION TALKS FOR VISITORS. As you recall from reading that letter, the INFO TALKS begin this Sunday, April 21 at 9:30 a.m. We hope you will be able to make time to attend. Do you have any questions?" (Listen)

Thank them! Make pertinent notes on POSSIBLE MEMBER DATA SHEET (see Form G). WARNING: Do not try to get a commitment to attend the INFO TALKS. This is just a reminder call and a welcome.

However, you can report, as follows:
Number of households who spontaneously expressed a desire to attend ___.
Number of households who said nothing in particular ___,
Number of households who refused the invitation to attend ___.

B. TEN TIPS ON MAKING TELEPHONE CALLS ON POSSIBLE MEMBERS

Scripture reference: "I will not accept (any)...bull from your house" (Ps. 50:9)!
1) Place a mirror by the telephone.
2) Put a stopwatch by your telephone.
3) Pray before you pick up the telephone.
4) During the conversation, repeat the person's name several times.
5) Expect a positive response.
6) Never put your hearer on the defense.
7) Never argue.
8) Listen attentively.
9) Be persuasive without being pushy.
10) Learn to be a closer.

C. TEN MORE TIPS!

1) Ask yourself: Why am I making this telephone call and what do I hope to accomplish?
2) Pray for guidance.
3) Your voice will convey sincerity or boredom.
4) The person who answers the telephone (unless a child) is usually the decision-maker.
5) Your first words will be a hit or a strikeout!
6) Know your product (program).
7) Crisp, clear, concise statements encourage positive response.
8) Know when you have a "live one" or a "delayer" on the other end.
9) Know when to quit.
10) Always quit with a smile!

APPENDIX 4

PROGRAM IDEAS

(Ideas for the parish program, not listed in any sequence of importance.)

A) BRING A MEMBER SUNDAY (for example—monthly or quarterly)

The purpose is twofold: a) To personalize membership; b) To help members express interest in one another.

Publicize four weeks in advance. Prepare member cards with name, address, telephone, when became a member, when worshiped last. Arrange cards on tables according to geographical areas. The Sunday prior to BRING A MEMBER SUNDAY, invite members to go to "Friendship Time" and pick up three or more cards. Make it clear that contacts are to be made during the week. Determine which plan to recommend: telephone or personal visit. If personal visit, give material to deliver such as a yearly calendar or Advent or Lenten calendar. Write a few paragraphs of instruction about how to make contact. For example, this telephone call:

"Hello, I am a member as you are of Trinity Church. During this week many of us are contacting our fellow members for BRING A MEMBER SUNDAY on October 31. Have you heard about it?" (Listen) "It is a beautiful idea to help us get to know one another better. I confess I don't know many members. But at least I can start to know a few more beginning with you. I would like to have the privilege of sitting with you in worship this Sunday on BRING A MEMBER SUNDAY. Which worship celebration is best for you, 8:00 a.m., 9:30, or 11:00?" (Listen. You have assumed they will attend!) "Great! I will meet you in the narthex a few minutes before the 9:30 Service. I will have a name tag on. Thank you! By the way, I presume you have transportation?" (Listen. If they do not have a way to get to church, tell them what time you will stop by and what added joy to have a little more time to get acquainted.) Please note: If they cannot attend on the designated Sunday, make an appointment for another Sunday. "I understand it would be inconvenient for you this Sunday. What Sunday would be best for you?" (Listen. Do not press. Note on card nature of refusal, if perchance it should occur. Your responsibility is to invite. Once you have done that, you have done the Lord's bidding!)

B) BRING A FRIEND SUNDAY (for example—monthly or quarterly)

This helps members think of people without a church home. Publicize four weeks in advance. One week prior to BRING A FRIEND SUNDAY, have ready cards with names, addresses, telephones, and place on tables according to geographical areas to be picked up after worship at "Friendship Time." Decide whether contacts are to be made by telephone or visit. Write out an example of visiting, such as the following:

"Hello, we are _____ of Trinity Church. We just stopped by for a few minutes to express our appreciation to you for worshiping at Trinity. We brought along a calendar." (Listen) "The church sent a letter out to many friends of the church telling about BRING A FRIEND SUNDAY which happens to be this coming Sunday, February 8. Have you heard about it?" (Listen) "We hope you will be our friends who will go to worship with us this coming Sunday. Which time of the worship celebration fits best into your schedule, 8:00 a.m., 9:30, or 11:00?" (Listen. You presume they will attend.) Tell them you will stop by and pick them up or meet them at the entrance a few minutes before worship begins. "Terrific! Shall we stop by for you or do you want to meet us at the west entrance to the church?" (Listen) "There is a Pancake Brunch after worship. Will you have time to accompany us? Dutch Treat, of course!" (Laugh and listen) Please note: If they cannot make it on the appointed Sunday, try for another Sunday. If they refuse, thank them for talking with you and go away with a smile. Always leave the door open for another contact. You are responsible for planting the seed only. THANK YOU for being a witness to your faith!

C) REUNION SUPPER MEETINGS

1) Schedule REUNION SUPPER MEETINGS, spotted about three months after each Reception of Members. Ask the new member(s) to telephone and invite their sponsor(s) to the Supper-Meeting. New members are to supply the free meal this time! The agenda could include: A Bible Study and prayer period; an update on the life of the congregation by the president of the con-

gregation; group discussions on how the church can nurture new members; entertainment, such as the church choir or instrumental music. Make it a memorable night!

2) ONCE A YEAR REUNION SUPPER MEETING FOR ALL MEMBERS or call it CELEBRATION OF MEMBERSHIP NIGHT. Review the history of the church; study the Mission Statement of the church in groups; give a progress report on the church's life; challenge the membership with new goals; rejoice together as a family of God; invite a motivational speaker; enlist musical entertainment. Make it a highlight in the congregation's year, apart from an "annual" meeting.

D) SPOT SPECIAL SUNDAYS THROUGHOUT THE YEAR, such as: COMMUNITY SUNDAY (invite mayor and council, police, fire people,etc.); EDUCATION SUNDAY (teachers from schools in the community); SINGLES SUNDAY (recognizing the unmarried, the widow or widower); FAMILY SUNDAY (or Mother's Day, Father's Day, Children's Day); SENIOR CITIZEN SUNDAY (recognizing their input in the life of the church, any anniversaries, etc.); COMMUNITY NEEDS SUNDAY (an outpouring of love to the homeless, the needy, the handicapped, etc.); GOVERNMENT SUNDAY with politicians invited for special prayers. (Warning: adjust the time schedule for worship in order to allow time for such recognitions.)

E) FREE DINNERS AND CLOTHING for the homeless and hungry, especially at Thanksgiving, Christmas, and Easter.

F) PROVIDE OVERNIGHT HOUSING for the homeless (e.g. Saturday night), especially during inclement weather, and provide a breakfast prior to worship. (Yes, invite and take them to worship.)

G) AN EVANGELISM MISSION WEEK (once every year or two).

There are several phases to an EVANGELISM MISSION WEEK:

1) Member households are visited by fellow members the week before the start of the Mission to enlist their attendance at the Mission Services, to encourage them to pray for the Mission, and to urge them to invite and bring unchurched relatives, neighbors, and friends to the Mission Services.

2) Mission Services are held Sunday morning and Sunday through Wednesday/Thursday evenings. The evening worship is an emphasis on preaching, question and answer period, music and singing—in an informal atmosphere.

3) A Missioner is invited, a guest pastor, who preaches and teaches. A nominal honorarium is given.

4) Lay Visits on POSSIBLES are scheduled Sunday through Wednesday/Thursday evenings beginning with a Supper with teaching by the Missioner on how to make calls. For example: 6:00 p.m. Supper, instruction during Supper, visits from 6:30 p.m. to 7:45 p.m., returning for worship (endeavoring to bring POSSIBLES!) at 8:00 p.m. Following worship, a Report Meeting for all lay visitors from 9:10 p.m. to 9:25 p.m.

5) Leadership meetings with the Missioner each evening from 9:30 p.m. to 10:00 p.m. For example: Sunday night the church board; Monday, committees; Tuesday, organizations; Wednesday, Sunday School.

Please note: Congregations in an area can do this simultaneously, with each congregation having its own mission but all congregations coming together at the start of the mission for a Sunday afternoon "Leadership Rally" and an evening "Closing Rally" (Thursday). The local pastors and missioners can also meet Monday through Wednesday/Thursday mornings for Bible study and prayer, and to hear invited lecturers on evangelism (possibly some of the missioners). Congregations can also share the costs.

NOTES

Scripture quotations are from the New Revised Standard Version of the Bible, copyright 1989 by the Division of Christian Education of the National Council of the Churches of Christ in the USA. Used by permission. All rights reserved.

INTRODUCTION

1. EVANGELISM IN A CHANGING AMERICA, Jesse M. Bader, p. 13, The Bethany Press, 1957.
2. MATTHEW 28:18-20 all scripture quotations are from the NEW REVISED STANDARD VERSION OF THE BIBLE, National Council of the Churches of Christ in the USA, Copyright 1990.

CHAPTER ONE

1. EVANGELISM IN THE EARLY CHURCH, Michael Green, p. 7, Wm. B. Eerdmans Publishing Company, 1970, reprinted December 1991.
2. THE WALL STREET JOURNAL, L. A. Winokur, January 6, 1992.
3. THAT THEY MAY HAVE LIFE, Daniel T. Niles, pp. 20,21, Harper & Brothers, copyright, 1951.
4. JOHN 20:31.
5. JOHN 1:39.
6. ACTS 2:2
7. ACTS 4:20
8. GALATIANS 4:4.
9. JOHN 1:14.
10. BEHOLD THE GLORY, Chad Walsh, p. 38, Harper & Brothers, copyright 1955, 1956.
11. HEBREWS 4:15.
12. ACTS 2:37.
13. MAN IN REVOLT, Emil Brunner, p. 494, The Westminster Press. Reprinted from MAN IN REVOLT. Translated by Olove Wyon. ©MCMXLVII by W. L. Jenkins. Used by permission of Westminster John Knox Press.

14. II CORINTHIANS 5:19.
15. I CORINTHIANS 3:17.
16. JOHN 15:8

CHAPTER TWO

1. PROCLAIMING THE PROMISE, Foster R. McCurley, Jr., p. 45, Fortress Press, copyright 1974.
2. ACTS 2:42,43.
3. ACTS 2:47.
4. WHO SPEAKS FOR GOD?, Gerald Kennedy, p. 29, Abingdon Press.
5. GENESIS 12:1,2.
6. EXODUS 3:16,17.
7. I Samuel 16:18.
8. II SAMUEL 7:20-22.
9. PSALM 106:24,25,28.
10. THE PROPHETS AND THE PROMISE, Willis J. Beecher, p. 257, Thomas J. Crowell Co., copyright 1905.
11. JOHN 15:5.
12. PHILIPPIANS 2:5-8.
13. JOHN 1:1-3.
14. MATTHEW 7:29.
15. ROMANS 3:25.
16. PULPIT RESOURCE, Vol. 9, p. 46.
17. JOHN 14:25,26.
18. THE PROPHETS AND THE PROMISE, Willis J. Beecher, p. 417, Thomas J. Crowell Co., copyright 1905.

CHAPTER THREE

1. THE BIBLE IN WORLD EVANGELISM, A. M. Chirgwin, pp. 14 and 64, Friendship Press first published in England by the Student Christian Movement Press, Ltd., 1954.
2. HISTORY OF THE CHRISTIAN CHURCH, Foakes-Jackson, p. 158, quoted in A. M. Chirgwin, THE BIBLE IN WORLD EVANGELISM, p. 22.
3. LUKE 24:45.

4. LUKE 24:46.
5. LUKE 2:46.
6. LUKE 4:18,19.
7. LUKE 4:21.
8. JOHN 4:28.
9. JOHN 4:39.
10. ACTS 8:35.
11. MATTHEW 5:21,22.
12. JOHN 21:25.
13. I CORINTHIANS 3:6.

CHAPTER FOUR

1. I CORINTHIANS 2:9
2. LUKE 11:1.
3. THINGS THAT MATTER, The Best of the Writings of Bishop Brent, p. 55, Harper & Brothers, copyright, 1949.
4. THOUGHTS IN SOLITUDE, Thomas Merton, p. 48, Farrar & Straus & Geroux.
5. MATTHEW 28:20.
6. ACTS 2:42.

CHAPTER FIVE

1. THE INTEGRITY OF PREACHING, John Knox, p. 27, Abingdon Press
2. LUKE 4:14.
3. LUKE 4:18, 19.
4. LUKE 4:21.
5. MATTHEW 7:29.
6. I JOHN 2:5,6.
7. OCCASIONAL SERVICES, A Companion to Lutheran Book of Worship, 1982, p. 193, Augsburg Publishing House and Board of Publication, LCA.
8. I CORINTHIANS 1:21.
9. THE MAKING OF THE SERMON, Robert J. McCracken, p. 17, Harper & Brothers, copyright ,1956.

10. CENTRAL SEMINARY BULLETIN, Marshall Wingfield.
11. HERE I STAND, Roland Bainton, pp. 348,349, Abingdon, copyright, 1950.
12. LUKE 14:3.
13. LUKE 14:6.
14. CREATIVE PREACHING AND ORAL WRITING, Richard Carl Hoefler, p. 45, C.S.S. Publishing

CHAPTER SIX

1. THE LATIN-AMERICA CONFERENCE, Buenos Aires, Argentina, 1949.
2. LEON JOSEPH CARDINAL SUENENS, Archbishop of Mechlin-Brussels, Belgium, Catholic Digest, June, 1964.
3. ACTS 1:8.
4. ACTS 4:12.
5. ACTS 2:43.
6. JOHN 14:12.
7. ACTS 2:42.
8. PSALM 51:11.

CHAPTER SEVEN

1. TWELVE KEYS TO AN EFFECTIVE CHURCH, Kennon L. Callahan, pp. 45,46, Harper, San Francisco, copyright, 1983.
2. ISAIAH 40:3-5.
3. THE OCCASIONAL SERVICES, 1918, The Board of Publication, The United Lutheran Church in America.
4. ROMANS 1:16.
5. LUKE 10:17.
6. ISAIAH 6:8.
7. MATTHEW 28:19.

CHAPTER EIGHT

1. THE APOSTOLIC IMPERATIVE, Carl E. Braaten, p. 61, Augsburg, copyright, 1985.

2. EPHESIANS 4:12.
3. LUKE 10:17.
4. LUKE 10:21.

CHAPTER NINE

1. THE GOSPEL CONNECTION, Michael Marshall, p. 11, copyright 1990 by Michael Marshall, reprinted by permission of Morehouse Publishing, Harrisburg, PA.
2. JOHN 14:12.

CHAPTER TEN

1. THE UNCHURCHED, Who They Are and Why They Stay Away, J. Russell Hale, p. 188, Harper & Row, copyright, 1980.
2. THE LOS ANGELES TIMES, September 21, 1984.

CHAPTER ELEVEN

1. THE PRACTICE OF EVANGELISM, Bryan Green, p. 13. Reprinted with the permission of Scribner, an imprint of Simon & Schuster, copyright 1954, Charles Scribner's Sons; copyright renewed.
2. LUKE 10:17.
3. LUTHERAN BOOK OF WORHSHIP, p. 124, Augsburg.
4. JOHN 3:3.
5. GRIT, GUTS, & GENIUS, John Hillkirk and Gary Jacobson, p. 95, Houghton Mifflin Company, copyright, 1990.
6. ACTS 1:8.
7. MATTHEW 28:20.
8. MATTHEW 28:7.
9. SPORTS ILLUSTRATED, May 11, 1992.
10. DANIEL HUDSON BURNHAM. See Henry M. Saylor, "Make No Little Plans": Daniel Burnham Thought It but Did He Say It? (Journal of the American Institute of Architects, vol. xxvii, p. 3. 1957).
11. MATTHEW 12:30.

CHAPTER TWELVE

1. THE WITNESS OF JESUS, Elmer Ellsworth Flack, pp. 13,14, C.S.S. Publishing.
2. GENESIS 1:1.
3. A MANUAL ON WORSHIP, Paul Strodach, p. xix, Muhlenberg Press.
4. JOHN 4:23,24.

CHAPTER THIRTEEN

1. WHY GO TO CHURCH, Truman B. Douglas, pp. 16,17, Harper & Brothers, copyright, 1957.
2. I TIMOTHY 6:10.
3. MATTHEW 21:22.

CHAPTER FOURTEEN

1. EFFECTIVE EVANGELISM, George Sweazey, p. 17, Harper & Brothers, copyright, 1953.
2. JOHN 10:28.

CHAPTER FIFTEEN

1. II TIMOTHY 1:13,14.
2. PSALM 84:7.
3. ACTS 2:42.
4. JAMES 1:22.
5. EFFECTIVE EVANGELISM, George Sweazey, p. 6, Harper & Brothers, copyright, 1953.
6. THE INVITING CHURCH: A Study of New Member Assimilation, Roy M. Oswald, Speed B. Leas, p. 8, The Alban Institute, copyright, 1987.

CHAPTER SIXTEEN

1. MATTHEW 5:13.

2. MATTHEW 18:14.
3. MATTHEW 18:10.

CHAPTER SEVENTEEN

1. TAKE CARE OF (1965) Dame Edith Sitwell, ch. 14.
2. Louis Armstrong (Saying).

FURTHER READING

Allen, Roland, MISSIONARY METHODS: ST. PAUL'S OR OURS?
Archibald, A. C., NEW TESTAMENT EVANGELISM
Arias, Mortimer, ANNOUNCING THE REIGN OF GOD
Armstrong, Richard Stoll, THE PASTOR AS EVANGELIST
Arn, Charles; McGavran, Donald; Arn, Win; GROWTH, A New Vision For The Sunday School
Barna, George, THE FROG IN THE KETTLE
Bennis, Warren, WHY LEADERS CAN'T LEAD
Berton, Pierre, THE COMFORTABLE PEW
Bonhoeffer, Dietrich, THE COST OF DISCIPLESHIP
Brown, Robert McAfee, UNEXPECTED NEWS
Butt, Howard; Elliott Wright; AT THE EDGE OF HOPE
Chandler, Russell, RACING TOWARD 2001
Coote, Robert B., Editor, MUSTARD-SEED CHURCHES
Costas, Orlando E., THE INTEGRITY OF MISSION
De Dietrich, Suzanne, THE WITNESSING COMMUNITY
de Jong, Pieter, EVANGELISM AND CONTEMPORARY THEOLOGY
Evelan, R. Ray, HOW TO READ THE BIBLE
Fackre, Gabriel, THE WORD IN DEED
Ferris, Theodore Parker, GO TELL THE PEOPLE
Fickett, Harold F., Jr., HOPE FOR YOUR CHURCH
Fisher, Wallace E., BECAUSE WE HAVE GOOD NEWS
                   WHO DARES TO PREACH?
Flack, E. E., THE WITNESS OF JESUS
Gilkey, Langdon, HOW THE CHURCH CAN MINISTER TO THE WORLD WITHOUT LOSING ITSELF
Green, Bryan, THE PRACTICE OF EVANGELISM
Green, Michael, EVANGELISM IN THE EARLY CHURCH
Greenway, Roger S., Edited by, THE PASTOR-EVANGELIST
Hanchey, Howard, CHURCH GROWTH
Hartt, Julian, TOWARD A THEOLOGY OF EVANGELISM

Johnson, Ben Campbell, AN EVANGELISM PRIMER
                       RETHINKING EVANGELISM
Kantonen, T. A., THEOLOGY OF EVANGELISM
Kelley, Dean M., WHY CONSERVATIVE CHURCHES ARE GROWING
Kolb, Robert, SPEAKING THE GOSPEL TODAY
Marty, Martin E., THE SEARCH FOR A USABLE FUTURE
McGavrin, Donald, UNDERSTANDING CHURCH GROWTH
Mott, John R., LIBERATING THE LAY FORCES OF CHRISTIANITY
Murren, Doug, THE BABY BOOMERANG
Mylander, Charles, SECRETS FOR GROWING CHURCHES
Neill, Stephen, SALVATION TOMORROW
Newbigin, Lesslie, THE GOOD SHEPHERD
Niles, D. T., THAT THEY MAY HAVE LIFE
Nygren, Anders, ESSENCE OF CHRISTIANITY
Packer, J. I., EVANGELISM AND THE SOVEREIGNTY OF GOD
Raines, Robert A., NEW LIFE IN THE CHURCH
Sample, Tex, U. S. LIFESTYLES and MAINLINE CHURCHES
Savage, John S., THE APATHETIC AND BORED CHURCH MEMBER
Schweitzer, Eduard, THE HOLY SPIRIT
Schuller, Robert H., YOUR CHURCH HAS REAL POSSIBILITIES
Shoemaker, Samuel M., WITH THE HOLY SPIRIT AND WITH FIRE
                       REVIVE THY CHURCH BEGINNING WITH ME
Spurgeon, Charles H., THE SOUL WINNER
Stott, John R., CHRISTIAN MISSION IN THE MODERN WORLD
                       OUR GUILTY SILENCE
Stuenkel, Omar, CARING ABOUT INACTIVE MEMBERS
Syrdal, Rolf, GO MAKE DISCIPLES
                       WE ARE AMBASSADORS
Sweazey, George, THE CHURCH AS EVANGELIST
Taylor, John R., GOD LOVES LIKE THAT
Thielicke, Helmut, BEING A CHRISTIAN
Trueblood, Elton, THE INCENDIARY FELLOWSHIP

Wagner, C. Peter, YOUR CHURCH CAN GROW
Walker, Alan, THE WHOLE GOSPEL for the WHOLE WORLD
Warren, Max, I BELIEVE IN THE GREAT COMMISSION
Watson, David, I BELIEVE IN EVANGELISM
Webber, George W., THE CONGREGATION IN MISSION
Wietzke, Walter, BELIEVERS INCORPORATED
Wirt, Sherwood, THE SOCIAL CONSCIENCE OF AN EVAN-
   GELIST
Woodson, Leslie, EVANGELISM FOR TODAY'S CHURCH